Face Value

To Diane –

Happy Shopping!

Phyllis Hegner

Face Value

CINCINNATI'S HANDBOOK

to

Discount Shopping

By *Phyllis Hegner*

ORANGE FRAZER PRESS
Wilmington, Ohio

Library of Congress Catalog
Card Number: 95-70159

ISBN 1-882203-06-2

Published by
Orange Frazer Press
37 1/2 West Main Street
Box 214
Wilmington, Ohio 45177

"Veni, vidi, Visa."—
I came, I saw, I shopped.
—Jan Barrett

Contents

Acknowledgments

There were many people who helped make this book. Mike O'Bryant's commitment to this project included many weekdays (often into the wee hours of the morning) and lots of weekends. His involvement clearly overstepped the boundaries of rational thought. He helped compile much of the extensive research, read and commented on each entry, helped organize material, provided maps, and served as my personal chauffeur and flunky. I am grateful to him.

And for: Susan Wingard's enthusiastic support, reading, and comments; Marie Lee's continued encouragement, insights about discounts chains, and retail market advice; Patricia Williams' direction to stores I otherwise might not have considered; Marylynn Kaufman's help with understanding many product lines and enlightening me about the West Side's culture; Ava Koren's support and orientation to the West Side; Ellen Heyob's insight into several businesses; Maria Uhlenbrock's experience as an interior decorator; Jane Geiger's and Joanie Flaig's support and helpful advice; Tim Keeton's and Ed Collier's (two Valley boys) insight into everyday life in the Millcreek Valley (Ed's crash course on electronics was most helpful.); Judi Cettel's aid with new ideas and approaches.

During the year, I counted on Susan Kramer, Kim Anderson, Sherry Zimmerman, Marc Yemiola, and Vicky Valerin to keep me focused and nudge me along. Special thanks to Judy Thompson for her invaluable advice and encouragement; Publisher, Marcy Hawley, for her faith and trust that inspired me to push forward; my parents, brother, and sister, as well as the O'Bryant clan—Shelby, Jackie, Barry, and Margot—for their emotional sustenance

Finally, thanks to the many shoppers, business and store owners, and employees, who put up with my incessant questions, often without knowing what was going on.

Illustrations/Cover Design: Brooke Wenstrup

Cover/Painting of Findlay Market: Christopher O'Leary

Technical support/ Tina Schneider

Introduction

It was a shopping experience that was only to last a summer. Instead, it became a mission lasting over a year. The challenge came in seeking out the real bargains and hidden truths behind the discounting arena in this retail-crazed city. After working in retail advertising for more than 15 years, eight of them as a fashion copywriter for a department store, I already knew how to "reel 'em in and catch 'em". This was an opportunity to go for the bait.

I didn't do it alone. I enlisted help from my good friend Mike O'Bryant, a teacher who was free during the summer months and willing to help tackle the arduous task of nosing around where no consumer had gone before. And so our shopping adventure began—the quest to investigate every discount place we could stumble across in Cincinnati and the surrounding areas to find genuine, bona fide bargains and get the story behind each one. Mike and I popped the top off his Honda Del Sol and drove around the city for a solid month. We hit every major commercial area, every strip mall, and every road that could possibly lead to a discount. We went through back alleys, down dusty, gravel roads (where manufacturers' plants often took us) and to parts of town even the heavily armored wouldn't want to venture. But, this was only our first sweep. Little did we know that we'd be going over and over this trail many more times, until we were absolutely satisfied we had all of the names and places we needed.

It was nice, at times, to have a male perspective. Our interests often took us in different directions. Mine, of course, were geared toward fashions. His were hobbies and books. We both came together on the sporting goods, the goofy novelty shops, and flea markets.

Before venturing out again we went through every single listing (and I mean all of them) in the Cincinnati Bell Area Yellow Pages, the business section of the white pages, and some of the smaller local telephone books. We went through all the local newspapers at the library from the previous and the present year. Anything that remotely looked like it could be a potential bargain opportunity was written down and checked out. This, along with actually driving around the city, gave us plenty of leads. We talked to every expert we could in any related field that could possibly inform us of where they go for the best and most reliable buys—contractors, interior decorators, sales people, manufacturers, seamstresses, retail buyers, and painters, to name a few. Before we knew it, we had over 900 leads. The task of narrowing them down to the best and most legitimate (around 500 in all) felt like pearl diving in an oyster bay with a half a tank of oxygen—lotta work, limited time.

We tracked down and visited all of the places first as inquiring customers. We wanted to get the true picture, not the gimmicks we may have gotten had we first identified ourselves and our mission. The old "redoing my grandmother's house" (which held some truth) was a good way to break into conversation with the home-related discounters. The search for holiday gifts was another easy way to make inquiries about many products. We got some suspicious, sidelong glances because we asked a lot of questions, looked at everything, and bought nothing.

I made over 1,000 phone calls. Shop owners told me everything about their businesses, their lives, their kids' lives. I listened to their views on politics. Others were tight-lipped and suspicious, fearing I was competition or trying to sell advertising. It took time to have them divulge their marketing strategies and their best-kept buying secrets. Few didn't want to talk at all or didn't have the time. There were ways, though, to scope those folks out. In person, most owners or managers were as nice as they could be. Others were nice, but—different. One fellow bragged about having over 30 tattoos on his body *and* a nipple ring. I didn't ask to see them, although he did show me an old picture of his hands when they were adorned with long fingernails that would have made even Howard Hughes envious.

So even after the initial visits and the phone calls, I still found the need to better understand some of the discounting strategies behind these retailers. Thus, I would give Mike a call and drag him out again to a place we had already visited once or twice to learn a little more, and to get a better picture of how the store operated. He didn't seem to mind, though, and after a while it became a ritual. He voluntarily became the navigator, the one I depended on to get us wherever on the landscape we were going. Half the time I didn't know where I was.

The outlet malls, the easiest to find, were the most grueling. We visited every store at each mall within driving distance of the city at least *five times*. It was hard to go to every store in one trip. It took many. And, of course, I was never satisfied. I had to go back and make sure I understood what was going on. Sometimes I hoped for just a simple store, with a simple way of doing business. I even secretly wished some would *close*. The problem is this usually only happened *after* I did the research and wrote about them. That's why I had to develop some type of criteria for choosing the ones that were most likely to remain in business. The listings in this book are solid ones.

We learned early *not* be taken in by the word *discount* or *outlet*. There are too many places that overuse this word. Sometimes the ones that scream the loudest, with huge signs claiming to have the best deals or to be the best outlet, were the worst. Often it was the quiet, little store or the outlet within an out-of-the-way manufacturing facility that offered the most noteworthy selection at the best prices. Several categories like wallpapering and furniture all claim to be outlet stores. In reality there were only a few that offered good buys and trustworthy service. If you think some discount or outlet stores were overlooked in this book, there's a 99.9% chance they were—for good reason. Don't be taken in. The moral of the story goes something like this: *Always* do your homework. It takes some work to really know if you're getting the best or at least *one* of the best buys on whatever you're seeking to purchase. The discounters and retailers chosen in this book, to the best of our knowledge, offer something of substance in the way of value. It's rare that you will just find one that has the exceptional buys. But there are some. These will be featured in this book with symbols. Most, though, are just good sound places to shop for values (often better buys in their specialty or within their overall selection than their competition) and still not get ripped off. Some are in this book simply because they offer quality products at reasonable prices that are a tad better than comparable stores.

Face Value covers a broad range of spending levels. You'll find something for every budget—from flea markets and consignment shops selling recycled goods, to the moderate discounters selling the standard lines, to higher end, off-price stores pushing big ticket items. The biggest requirements are that the stores offer some type of discount and credibility behind the lower prices.

Researching this book only came after spending some bucks. Not only for gasoline and fast-food stops along the way, but for buying the irresistible bargains. They were always tempting us. Lucky for me, I wasn't always the one giving in. There was the time we both bought golf bags. I don't know why I bought mine. I already had a nice one. But the price was just too good. Other great deals we just couldn't pass up included: a 25-lb. box of peanuts; a leather skirt (mine, not Mike's); a couple of push brooms; all kinds of day-old baked goods; used books galore; California Raisin statues; Mr. Pickle pencil toppers (these were supposed to go to my niece and nephew—sorry kids); all kinds of sweatshirts, tee shirts, and sweaters; several pairs of athletic shoes; old Cincinnati Reds railroad posters; two suede jackets; two Budweiser beer mugs; wire cleansing brushes (that will never be used); several bottles of coffee liqueur; an illuminated microscope (you never know when you'll need one of these); two gallons of paint; a basket of fruit; Christmas wreaths and ornaments; a deck of giant playing cards (so Mike doesn't have to wear his glasses); an ice cream scoop; *Life* magazines from our birth dates; two Ohio State pillows and a beach towel (mine); a U.C. blanket (Mike's); 24 pairs of socks all the same style, all the same color (only a guy would do this); a storm door; two wrist watches; a Fun-Mate portable radio; two electric pencil sharpeners; and two larger-than-life thousand dollar bills (to cash in and help pay for the damage). If we were to take a tally of the bargains we bought, who knows how much we spent. The important thing to remember, though, is—it's not how much you *spend*; it's how much you *save*.

—Phyllis Hegner

Warning!

Since the material in this book is time-dated, it's a good idea to phone ahead before planning your shopping trip. It's wise to contact some of the smaller discount stores that are in hard-to-find or out-of-the-way places. You'll want to make sure these stores are still in operation and to find out specific directions on how to get to where you are going.

In today's discount retail market some establishments may open or close before the new season has a chance to begin. Others have been around for many years and will probably be around for many more years. Still others may have moved, opened another facility to expand business, or closed a certain branch of their network of stores to cut costs.

If your schedule is tight you may want to phone ahead to find out how late or early the store remains open or to make sure it has not changed its operating hours. Many stores offer their customers extended shopping hours during the holiday season and special sales events. On the other hand, some smaller discount stores may cut back hours during slack times when business is not as plentiful to reduce costs.

Some stores in today's market are exercising the no frills concept by offering their goods in warehouse-type facilities without fancy displays and only during peak shopping hours. For example, these stores may only be open to the public during the weekends in order to cut costs and take full advantage of the most common shopping times. Stores in this area that have adopted this concept in order to be more competitive are K & G Men's Mart in Sharonville and Azzini Shoe Warehouse in Blue Ash.

Other stores such as Designer Shoe Warehouse are closed for restocking during slower, midweek times. While this concept of limited operating hours has been popular for sometime in larger cities like New York, it is just starting to catch on in the Midwest. *Special Note*: Any references made to prices in this book are purely representational and were valid at the time evaluations were made. These pricing examples are subject to change and were used to give the reader a better understanding of the savings potential.

Of Special Note

Watch for these symbols throughout this book. They are located at the end of entries.

PHYLLIS' FAVORITES: 

FINDLAY MARKET/DOWNTOWN—There is no other place in the city that matches the excitement and thrill of shopping this historic landmark. Squeezing my way through the crowds and hollering to the butcher how thick to cut my pork chops makes me feel like I've gone back to a time when marketing was up close and personal. Overall, the nostalgic experience is one to savor.

JUNGLE JIM'S INTERNATIONAL FARMER'S MARKET/NORTH—Shop here to feel adventurous. Try different varieties of gourmet foods and imported delicacies (some names are unpronouncable). The place has hundreds of choices to drool over, along with the standard grocery fare. The lively surroundings, with a jungle-like atmosphere (watch out for discarded banana peels) and multicultural tempo, boosts the spirits. Get caught up at the international delicatessen by chowing down samples.

MAIN AUCTION GALLERIES, INC./DOWNTOWN—No better place to spend a Tuesday morning. Auctioneer legend J. Louis Karp (Jay to many) is the best floor show in town. Jay's mother Phyllis, who's been running the whole shebang for over 30 years, seats regulars near the front. So, come in like you belong, and maybe she'll seat you up front.

THE PARTY SOURCE/NORTHERN KENTUCKY—Something about the festive atmosphere here makes shoving a shopping cart around the aisles fun. Time passes quickly and one can easily fill a shopping cart, buying more than planned.

TRADERS WORLD FLEA MARKET/NORTH—The market has a gypsy-like feel to it. Eyeballing the overwhelming choices among the clutter is part of the amusement, but so is people watching. There's even a fortune teller that sets up here.

HOT SPOTS FOR BAGGING BARGAINS: 

BEN'S SPORTSWEAR OUTLET/NORTHEAST— It's the best place to bag bargains on "hack-arounds" for the entire family. There are thousands of t-shirts and sweats (especially those with pro and collegiate themes) at stock-up prices. The staff is affable, too.

ELDER-BEERMAN OUTLET/NORTH CENTRAL—A good source for the value-conscious, this clearance center with its vast selection has great buys on family fashions and home furnishings. The electronics department has customers muttering about the good prices, trying to figure out where to put another TV.

FACTORY DIRECT/NORTH CENTRAL— This is the place to pick up inexpensive serving pieces, glassware, and candles. For everyday and holiday needs, the prices are noticeably lower on a wide selection.

FOUR SEASONS GARMENT FACTORY OUTLET STORE/NORTH— Lightweight jackets, tee shirts, golf shirts, and sweats go for the small bucks here. Some may be leftovers from the factory's commercial accounts. These are usually printed with various businesses' logos. So, if anyone asks you why you're wearing a t-shirt that reads Bob's Aluminum Siding or Phil's Carryout, just tell them you work there.

J.C. PENNEY OUTLET/NORTHWEST— Hard not to buy *something*. The clearance center is so well-rounded, there's always a bargain worth buying, even if you don't need it. Departmentalized sections make it effortless to spot values.

SAALFELD PAPER COMPANY/NORTHEAST—The best way to eliminate dish washing is to not cook. Or, you could buy disposable serving supplies and party wares from Saalfeld. The immense selection, which includes storage containers and hard-to-find catering staples, is at better-than-average prices.

VF FACTORY OUTLET/OUTLET MALLS—The huge outlet store has brand-name casuals greatly reduced, more so than most discounters. It's a good source for outfitting the family in spare-time wear. Grab a few pairs of Lee jeans or sweats, a few pairs for a tall, hard-to-fit brother or somebody's kids.

BEST PLACES TO GAWK AT MERCHANDISE:

FERGUSON HILLS/PARIS FLEA MARKET/WEST—It's the best place to spend Sunday morning. Marketers start making their rounds here before the morning dew begins to evaporate. The aisles of this old drive-in are usually filled with hordes of vendors displaying most anything, but by noon they are packing it up to leave.

FRONTGATE RETAIL STORE & OUTLET/NORTH—Filled with uncommon products for the home that pique your curiosity. Push buttons and mess around with gadgets. Take in one of the company's seasonal clearance sales to find prices drastically reduced and get free hot dogs and soft drinks.

MERTACK'S ANTIQUES AND FINE FURNITURE/NORTHERN KENTUCKY—With furniture, antiques, and home accessories tastefully arranged around a historic building, it has lots of decorating ideas. Take a note pad to jot some down. The bistro area in the basement offers a change of pace. Allow plenty of time.

TREASURES, INC./EAST—A unique consigning concept, this vintage house has 15 rooms filled with interesting "stuff" for the home. The prices are reasonable, the staff is knowledgeable, and the atmosphere is relaxed. The owner does a nice job of rearranging displays and varying merchandise. It's never the same.

VALERIE MAKSTELL INTERIORS/DOWNTOWN—If you owned a palace you'd come here to furnish it. It feels like you're shopping in a museum rather than an old warehouse. Though the merchandise is discounted, be prepared to gawk more than spend.

TOP BRAND NAME FASHION DISCOUNTERS:

GENTRY MEN'S CLOTHIER/NORTH CENTRAL—Any man that plays his charge card right will come out of here looking like a million bucks—without dropping a fortune. There just isn't a better place in the city for the businessman to wardrobe himself for the office or after hours. The selection of brand names is voluminous. Prices are good. And service is accommodating. Whether you shop Gentry's regular retail stores, its menswear outlet, or hold out for one of the company's warehouse sales, you can't go wrong. Maybe that's why the major department stores in this area find this discounter such a threat.

K & G MENSWEAR/NORTH CENTRAL—The selection of brand name men's apparel is broad. The savings are inviting with prices than run lean for the budget-conscious.

LOEHMANN'S/NORTH CENTRAL—A good source for uncovering the big fashion names in women's apparel at affordable prices. But, you may have to spend some time on the hunt. Even so, merchandise is well organized and worth checking out. Most people, I know, would never suspect that Adrienne Vittadini blouse I bought here was marked down so much.

SAKS 5TH AVENUE CLEARING HOUSE/OUTLET MALLS—While shopping this clearing house, look around you: Even affluent, overdressed outlet mall patrons rack up the buys here. The selection runs voguish, yet prices are more tolerable for those seeking status looks. So, you can look the part without shelling out the big bucks. I look for the fashions baring price tickets with red slash marks. Don't miss the semi-annual clearance sales.

TALBOTS SURPLUS STORE/DOWNTOWN—The size of the store isn't overwhelming; it's just right. When I worked Downtown, I found it a little too easy to dash in and out of here during my lunch hour. The racks are easy to scan, sizes are easy to pinpoint, and prices are worth checking out.

BEST BARGAINS ON SPORTING GOODS:

ALL ABOUT SPORTS OUTLET CENTER/WEST—The huge clearance center has prices substantially below original retails on one of the largest discounted selections of sporting goods and athletic apparel in the city. I found the store a good source for bagging the bargains, even though they were out of the golf shoes I came to buy.

FINISH LINE OUTLET/WEST—This clearance center is a great place to stock up on athletic apparel. I bagged a nylon windsuit, several t-shirts (with embroidered emblems), and a few sports caps for under $30. The store is small but loaded with good buys.

NIKE OUTLET STORE/OUTLET MALLS—To me, it's worth the trip—even if I don't make it to another store in the outlet mall. The selection of Nike athletic apparel and footwear runs deep. At prices substantially below original retails, it's a good place to save on high performance wear.

OARSMAN RETAIL OUTLET/NORTHERN KENTUCKY—The heavyweight t-shirts and sweats, enriched with embroidered and decorative designs, primarily feature athletic or collegiate team themes. I like them because they look better than the ones imprinted with sticky logos that eventually wash off. Prices are excellent for the quality rendered.

SUPREME GOLF WAREHOUSE TENT SALE/SPECIAL SALES EVENTS—It's a great place to find something else to stuff in my golf bag—like that extra club that will make a difference in my game. Unfortunately, if you're like me (lacking willpower), some will end up at future garage sales. Prices are too good to pass up.

BEST FOOD AND PRODUCE DISCOUNTERS:

FINDLAY MARKET/DOWNTOWN—The first place I head when I come here is to the booth that sells those square baseball cookies. It gives me the energy to fight my way down the long, crowded aisle. Despite the close conditions, the rewards are worthwhile. The market has some of the freshest edibles (mainly meats, cheeses, and produce) at the best prices. The good news is I can buy in as small or large a quantity as I want.

THE DOWNTOWN PRODUCE WHOLESALERS/DOWNTOWN—Head for the Bottoms and buy your produce where your grocer gets it. It's not only fresher, the variety is greater. Though, most only sell to the public in bulk quantities; the prices per item are cheaper. If you want the true picture, hang out for a spell by the loading docks with Joe and the guys at M. Degaro. Mike used to bowl with them and says they're a lot of fun. Besides, their selection of fruits and vegetables is good—and they are friendly.

KLOSTERMAN'S BAKERY OUTLETS/NORTH—Their prices on day-old breads are good, but I like shopping here for different varieties of fresh breads I can't get at the grocery. They're some of the same ones Klosterman's sell to finer restaurants.

SARA LEE THRIFT STORE/OUTLET MALLS—After trekking through all of those stores at the Jeffersonville Outlet Center, I feel

I deserve some reward. So, before I leave, I head for Sara Lee. It's not only a good source for stocking up on frozen desserts and entrees; it's good for grabbing a quick snack. I'm especially fond of the blueberry muffins. A tray of them, among other choices, usually goes home with me.

SHUR-GOOD BISCUIT COMPANY THRIFT STORE/NORTHWEST— Its small store is easy to shop, but don't let size fool you. The variety of packaged snacks and cookies is plentiful. Somehow, the savings make them taste better than they really are.

BEST BUYS ON HOME FURNISHINGS:

ECHO FURNISHINGS/DOWNTOWN—There's no other place around where you'll find as extensive a selection (the Downtown showroom is 2,000 sq. ft. and the one in Milford is 7,000 sq. ft) of quality previously owned furniture and accessories for the home. Antiques and collectibles are also part of the attraction. The owner really knows her "stuff" and keeps prices fair-minded.

FRED SCHMIDT/EAST—The owner is amazing. He can match up any color paint you want—even the most unusual shades. I've heard interior decorators rave over his abilities. Most appreciate his sound advice. Wallpaper is also sold here. Prices are reasonable. Selection is good.

MERTACK'S ANTIQUES AND FINE FURNITURE/NORTHERN KENTUCKY—The selection of quality, brand name furniture and home accessories runs deep here. Prices are always discounted.

WALLCOVERINGS PREFERRED, INC./NORTHWEST—The staff will go out of their way to help you find what you want and direct you to the best prices on wallpaper—so I've found out from several friends and decorators who have recommended their services. I was in the store only minutes before I was approached.

Face Value

Fox's Clothing Co.

Downtown Cincinnati

No one's sure whether the retail tide's going in or out in Downtown Cincinnati. With concentration on building new ball parks and showy department stores, many businesses have a wait-and-see attitude contingent upon the city's projections. Even so, certain value-oriented stores find their niche among the uncertainty. Discounters like Talbots Surplus Store in Convention Place Mall and Fourth Street Men's Outlet cater to business professionals by offering career wear. Others, like longtime favorites Cappel's and Brown's, specialize in offering values on novelty items. Several smaller retailers occupy street-level store fronts in older buildings that date back to the turn of the century. These buildings are like ancient dinosaurs among clusters of modish, state-of-the-art office structures. ¶ Some of the city's historic districts occupying sections of Main, Fourth, and Court streets haven't changed. One commercial district stretches east from the Court House between Main and Vine streets. With the erection of a municipal market in 1829, this area grew as a retail center until the market house was torn down in 1915. Since then an open-air, curb-side market on Court Street has lasted and small businesses have remained. Nearby, the Over-the-Rhine region, reminiscent of the city's German heritage, offers potential for residential and commercial development. The centerpiece of its embryonic progressive effort is Findlay Market. The last remaining public market in Cincinnati with both indoor and outdoor facilities, it brings vitality and excitement to what would otherwise be another decaying urban neighborhood. One other focal point in Downtown's urban renewal is the Union Terminal building. By revitalizing this historic landmark, much of the west end of the Downtown basin has slowly shed its ghetto past and has become a center for developing light industry. ¶ The subject of much of the city's revitalization plans, the riverfront area, which used to be known as the Bottoms, is another region ripe for development. A produce center has been the mainstay of this district since the 1800s. Many of these companies, started by Italian immigrants, are still operated by family members. During the 1920s, the area became a regional produce market and the artery that fed the Tri-State its produce. Today, these produce wholesalers distribute massive quantities of fresh fruits and vegetables that arrive from domestic and foreign growers for local food suppliers. However, while the city's plans for increased development evolve, it's only a matter of time before many of them will be forced to relocate. Take advantage now.

B & B FURNITURE COMPANY/DOWNTOWN—One of the best kept secrets in the city is the 45-year-old family run B & B Furniture Company. While not a major showroom, it has excellent prices on moderate furniture lines such as Bassett. The store is in an old building on Court Street and features furniture for every room in the house on two of its five floors. Partners, David Weitzman and Fred Fiedler, don't exercise high-pressure tactics to sell their goods. One of B & B's best selling points is its *tsatskes,* a Yiddish term Fred uses to describe accent pieces. (There's a good mix of etageres and functional shelving units.) The owners pride themselves on keeping costs down by advertising the old fashioned way—through word-of-mouth. Savings of at least 10%–25% off retail prices are offered daily. Oriental screen dividers and table lamps are priced less than most of the competition. A few hard-to-find objects—roll-away beds, old-fashioned kitchen cabinets—are here, too.
9 E. Court Street; 513/721-3007. Mon–Fri 9am–5pm, Sat 9:15am–2:30pm. VS, MC, DS.

AVOID SHOPPERS' PARALYSIS **Reevaluate your shopping habits. Much of this region is known for tradition. Conservative family values is an area virtue except when it comes to shopping. Don't limit yourself to where your mother always shopped. Open up to new and exciting shopping experiences. The savings may surprise you.**

BROWN NOVELTY COMPANY/DOWNTOWN—In operation since 1923, Brown Novelties has a lighthearted approach to retailing. Watch out for the unexpected, like a raccoon trapped inside a bag and rolling around on the floor, frantically trying to escape. It's fictitious, of course. Or is it? Colorful commemorative banners and party favors hang from the ceiling as part of the store's decor. Odd-shaped inflatables, helium balloons, spinning wheels, carnival-type toys, and life-size cardboard figures are everywhere. While the store specializes in selling to fund-raisers and festivals, the general public is welcome. There's a conservative marketing philosophy—no charge cards, little advertising, low overhead—so prices tend to run on the moderate to low side.
312 W. Fourth Street; 513/421-0064. Mon–Fri 9am–4:30pm, Sat 9am–noon. Cash or check only.

CAPPEL'S/DOWNTOWN—There's no store around like Cappel's. Originally started as a display company in 1946, this family-owned business concentrates on selling novelty items. The usual party favors and decorations, along with the unusual trinkets and paraphernalia, fill the store. While it's easy to be caught up in the allure of these silly little items—miniature brand name cereal boxes and bottles, bouncing eye balls, key chains, pencil toppers, and finger puppets, to mention a few—there's no cause for concern. Many are priced from 3¢ to $2 each, an uncommon commodity in today's retail market. Crafters also find good buys on a wide assortment of silk flowers and supplies. There's even a Bead Room for those into customized bead working. Rich and Ray Cappel are serious about their business. They try to keep costs down to pass more savings on to their customers. Unlike big craft and novelty chains, they remain flexible by selling loose, unpackaged goods in single to larger quantities. The store stocks backup merchandise so plenty is always on hand.

CAPPEL'S ANNEX—Around the corner from the main store, Cappel's Annex has gained popularity in recent years for its infamous haunt shop. Costumes, masks, and party get-ups for Halloween or masquerade parties are always in stock. The store is crawling with rubbery little pets like slimy snakes, scary spiders, and other creepy species found in the miniature bargain bins lining the walls of the store. Many are only a few cents each, so you can go home with a bag full for under $2–$3. Most of the merchandise, whether found at the annex, the main store, or at one of the more recent suburban branches, is priced within reason.
Main Store, 920 Elm Street; 513/621-0952. Annex—Costumes; 130 W. Court Street, 513/621-9499. 3651 Harrison Avenue, Cheviot; 513/481-9888. Crossings of Blue Ash, 9525 Kenwood Road, Blue Ash; 513/984-9888. 3040 Madison Road, Oakley; 513/531-7880. Store hours vary per season. VS, MC, DS.

CINCINNATI BRUSH MANUFACTURING COMPANY/WEST END—In a neighborhood that's seen better days, this unmarked, out-of-the-way store could be easily bypassed. Founded in 1875, it looks like many of the old brick homes in the area that are surrounded by urban industries. Inside, it's more like a large janitorial closet loaded with quality brushes, brooms, and mops. Owners Charlotte and James Bruns give personalized attention and will sell at a bargain price. Primarily selling cleaning, maintenance, and janitorial supplies and brushes to industrial accounts; anyone can buy. Known for their hand-drawn work, they will even refill antique fireplace or antique hair brushes.
2019 Central Avenue; 513/621-0370. Mon–Fri 8am–4:30pm. Cash or check only.

CINCINNATI COLOR COMPANY, INC./DOWNTOWN—In business for over 65 years, Cincinnati Color Company has the experience, the know-how, and the products to service any painting project from professional contractors to do-it-yourselfers. To ensure quality, the company manufactures its own line of Town & Ranch paint for interior and exterior applications yet prices it below comparable brands. It has the largest variety of Krylon spray paints in the city and carries a full line of the true materials the professionals use—painting supplies, stains, varnishes, and lacquers. A computerized

THE PRODUCE WHOLESALERS/ DOWNTOWN—Most people buy their produce the traditional way, through the grocery stores or local markets. But some are willing to venture Downtown to the distributors. On any day from the early hours of the morning (we're talking 4am) to noon the loading docks of wholesalers are busy placing orders and filling huge refrigerator trucks. Most of these, (which occupy warehouses around Pete Rose Way, Plum Street and Central Avenue) are willing to sell their goods to the public. The catch is many items must be purchased in bulk by the case or bag. But, when you break down the cost per item it's much cheaper than buying it at the grocery stores. Try sharing your produce purchases to divide up the costs.

Many varieties of citrus and apples are the most popular choices with other fruits and vegetables in the running. Seasonal items such as evergreen trees, wreaths, poinsettia and fruits baskets are available during the holidays. Some also offer peanuts in bulk along with spring flowers and autumn varieties such as decorative corn, pumpkins, squash and tree nuts. Here is a summary of the main suppliers in the area to help walk you through this nostalgic marketing experience.

Established in 1914, **Sanzone & Palmisano** is in the old United Auction Building which stands alone on Produce Drive among the open parking lots west of Riverfront Stadium. Erected in the 1920's, this building moved the center of the produce trade from Sixth Street to the riverfront. Further down the road is the **Castellini Company**, founded in 1896, and a forerunner of this trade. Easily identifiable by the tall smoke stack atop one of its two buildings, it covers an entire block on either side of Plum Street. Even though it is the largest warehouse in the area and distributes mainly to commercial food services, the public can buy produce here as well. Back up on Plum Street (near Pete Rose Way) are two smaller wholesalers that are the oldest in the business. **Flatow-Riley**, founded in 1891, has a narrow selection of the basics while **Gentille Brothers**, established in 1862, is limited even further by specializing in just tomatoes and bananas. On the corner of Plum Street and Pete Rose Way is **Caruso-Ciresi** which came later to the industry in 1956. This distributor carries many different varieties of produce including some of the more exotic choices. Across the street is **Crossett**, a sister company of Castellini, selling to commercial food services. Located on Pete Rose Way (across from Flanagan's Landing) are the most accessible vendors to the general public, **Fries Brothers** and **M. Degaro Company**. These two wholesalers are more approachable for the novice and offer a variety of seasonal items.

Caruso-Ciresi, 305 W. Pete Rose Way; 513/721-1073. Mon–Sun 4am–noon. Cash only. Castellini Company, Two Plum Street; 513/762-3600. Mon–Fri 4am–noon, Sun 5am–9:30pm. Cash only. Crossett Company, 205 Central Avenue; 513/421-5511. Mon–Fri 4am–2pm. Cash or check only. M. Degaro Company, 225 W. Pete Rose Way; 513/241-1436. Mon–Fri 4am–noon, Sat & Sun 7am–10am. Cash or check only. Flatow-Riley, 43 Plum Street; 513/241-1277. Mon–Fri 4am–12:30pm, Sat 7am–10pm, Sun 6am–11pm. Cash or check only. Fries Brothers, 211 W. Pete Rose Way; 513/621-6978. Mon–Fri 4am–12:30pm, Sat & Sun 6am–10:30pm. Cash only. Gentille Brothers, 316 Produce Drive; 513/381-4300. In season hours Mon–Fri 8am–5pm, Sat 8am–noon, otherwise Mon–Fri 5am–3pm or 4pm, Sat 5am–10pm. Cash only. Sanzone-Palmisano Company, 67 Produce Drive; 513/241-5988. Mon–Fri 3am–5pm, Sat & Sun hours vary. Cash only.

Castellini

tint-machine system can produce just about any shade of paint. A second store has also opened in the Tri-County area.
1400 Vine Street; 513/241-1090. 11465 Springfield Pike, Springdale; 513/772-1090. Mon–Fri 7:30am–5:30pm, Sat 8am–5pm. VS, MC, DS.

CINCINNATI PLAYHOUSE IN THE PARK/EDEN PARK—Established in 1960 with its Shelterhouse auditorium and later opening the Marx, the Cincinnati Playhouse in the Park has gained considerable recognition and stature. Theatre-goers can try their luck at getting half-price tickets for current productions at this magnificent drama house. The tickets must be purchased in person at the box office on the day of the performance between noon and 2pm. The best seats may go quickly so it's best to arrive early.
962 Mt. Adams Drive, Eden Park; 513/421-3888 or 800/582-3208.

CINCINNATI SYMPHONY ORCHESTRA/OVER-THE-RHINE—One way to see the Cincinnati Symphony Orchestra perform without paying higher prices is to purchase "Zip Tickets." Discounted tickets are available 11am–2pm the day of the performance at half price. (Special discounts are not available for POPS performances.) Tickets must be purchased in person on a first-come, first-serve basis. Sell outs are probable so customers must arrive early.
1229 Elm Street, Music Hall; 513/381-3300.

COURT STREET MARKET/DOWNTOWN—Court Street Market is one of the last remaining open-air markets in the city. Stretching from the south side of Court Street (between Main and Vine) are 68 outdoor stand spaces that, when in full operation (on Tuesday and Thursday), are filled with vendors selling high quality foods and fresh fruits and vegetables. For generations, this market has offered superb buys on produce from local growers and other suppliers.
Court Street (between Main & Vine streets). Tues & Thurs 7am–2:30pm.

DUNSKY'S RESTAURANT & BAR SUPPLY CO./DOWNTOWN—This company sells mostly to commercial accounts, but it also has a walk-in retail store located on Court Street. Started by the Dunsky family, the company is now owned by Mike and Ruth Foertsche who manage to keep the store's "Mom and Pop" image. The staff takes the time to educate customers about the finer points of kitchen gadgetry. Devices, dispensers, cookware, glassware, and trays can be purchased individually at wholesale prices. Kitchen appliances, both commercial and standard models, and some furniture can be purchased from in-stock merchandise.
37 E. Court Street; 513/621-8041. Mon–Fri 8:30am–5pm, Sat 10am–2pm. Cash or check only.

ECHO FURNISHINGS/DOWNTOWN—Chosen by *Cincinnati Magazine* as the area's number one consignment furniture showplace, here's' a quality selection of previously owned furniture and home accessories sold on a consignment basis. After collecting furniture from the '50s and '60s era and storing it in her basement, Lisa Johnson decided to open her own store in 1993. The first one

of its kind in the city, it offers exceptional values with a minimum of 40% off retail when compared to buying new items. The main showroom, downtown, is filled with a mix of antiques and traditional and contemporary furniture. With free appraisals and no pickup charges, the store makes it easy for consignors to sell their goods. Items obtained by the store are reduced 25% after 30 days with an average turnaround time of 90 days. Customers with special requests for certain types of furnishings can request to be on the store's "wish list." The store's success has brought a second store, located in the Milford Shopping Center.
13 Garfield Place; 513/684-0010. Mon–Sat 10am–4pm. Milford Shopping Center, Route 50, Milford; 513/831-0100. Tues–Thurs 11am–7pm, Fri–Sun 11am–5pm. VS, MC.

AVOID SHOPPERS' PARALYSIS **Ask about frequent shoppers plans. Some stores will offer an item free after you've purchased a quota over a certain amount of time. You may be asked to fill out a card that serves as a running receipt indicating each time you made a purchase, but if it saves you money in the end, why not?**

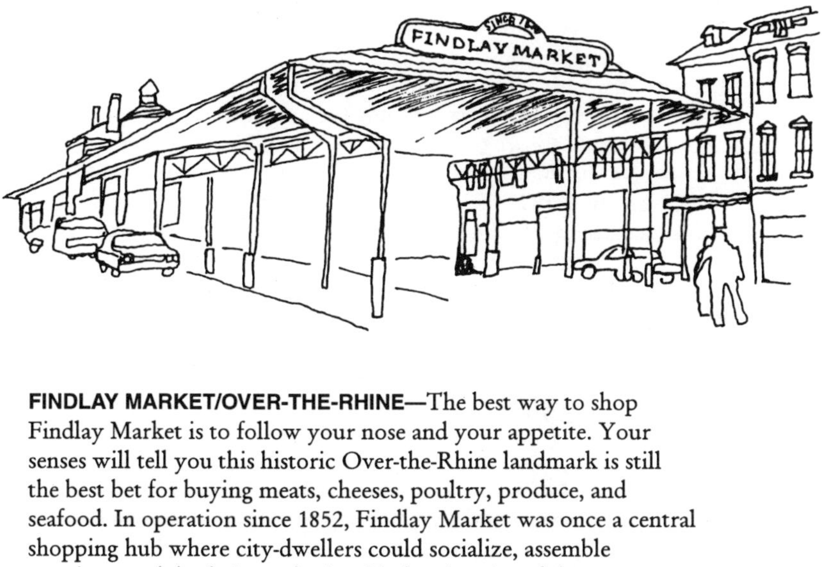

FINDLAY MARKET/OVER-THE-RHINE—The best way to shop Findlay Market is to follow your nose and your appetite. Your senses will tell you this historic Over-the-Rhine landmark is still the best bet for buying meats, cheeses, poultry, produce, and seafood. In operation since 1852, Findlay Market was once a central shopping hub where city-dwellers could socialize, assemble meetings, and do their marketing. Today, in spite of the poor rundown neighborhoods and the limited parking, marketgoers have found that it's still worth the trip to shop here since the foods are not only fresher than the supermarkets—they're cheaper. As you make your way through the crowded, long row of vendor after vendor, you may bump into anyone from an Indian Hill matron to a person making good use of food stamps. The patrons who frequent the market are as varied in backgrounds as the kinds of meats found in the cases, making it much more interesting to shop than Kroger.
117 E. Elder Street (between Elm & Race streets). 513/352-6391. Mon 7am–1:30pm; Wed & Fri 7am–6pm; Sat 6am–6pm. Ask individual merchants for additional hours on Mon, Tues, & Thurs. Cash or check only.

FOURTH STREET MEN'S OUTLET DOWNTOWN—Spencer Hayes, the owner of several clothing manufacturers in New York—Troy Shirt Company, Asher-Weiner, and Hubbard Slacks—recently expanded his operation to include a discount outlet in Downtown Cincinnati. Housed in a building he owns on Fourth Street, its convenient location and daily operating hours from 11am–3pm make this store easily accessible to professional businessmen. One of the store's most unusual retailing strategies relies on a hit-or-miss lucky size system. This is where customers can try their luck at matching a fit from custom-tailored suits, sport coats, and dress slacks that were never retrieved by their original buyers. Personalized name labels are removed from the apparel, brought here, and sold for much less. While greater space is given to these items, along with dress shirts, a random selection of ties and accessories is available. The store also has a small section of women's suits.
8 E. Fourth Street. Mon–Fri 11am–3pm. No phone listing. VS, MC, AE.

FOX CLOTHING COMPANY/DOWNTOWN—At a time when trendy marketing schemes have become the norm in retailing, Dave and Howard Fox are holding onto business the same way their family has for over 56 years. Their neighborly store offers friendly service and clothing priced within reason. They even take the time to mark every item with sales tax included in the ticket price. It's not unusual to see the owners manning the cash register or helping customers. There are bargains on everything from denim jeans and outerwear for adults to playwear and sleepers for infants. Some deals are made right on the spot. While the bulk of the store's merchandise is off-brands bought from low-end importers, there are some notable brand name items among the selection as well as closeouts and irregulars. Originally a jobbing company (an old term for wholesalers) selling to other dealers, the company moved from Pearl Street to its current location in 1955. The old building that embodies the store is tired-looking and worn. Modern-day aesthetics are not a priority with the Foxes. The second and third floors are still set up to service wholesalers. The fourth floor holds the last remaining stash of vintage clothing. Ironically once non-sellers, they've ended up on the fourth floor, but have become clothing relics that customers have bought from as far away as California. The real buys for the average shopper are still found on the first floor.
23 W. Court Street; 513/621-4500. Mon, Tues, Wed 9am–5:30pm, Thurs & Fri 9am–6pm, Sat 9am–5pm. VS, MC.

GENERAL SALES COMPANY/DOWNTOWN—Specializing in selling sales incentives and advertising specialties (including printed items), General Sales Company operates a small store front that displays a hodgepodge of miscellaneous items. This hapless selection varies from electronics and toys to who knows what. Since it's hard to know what will be sold here next, it's best not to make a special trip to this store unless you call first. For those already in the vicinity, it doesn't hurt to check out the store's scant merchandise.
17 E. Court Street; 513/621-2075. Mon–Sat 8:30am–5pm. Cash or check only.

G.I.J. SURPLUS/DOWNTOWN—A fixture on the corner of 12th and Race streets, G.I.J. Surplus Store is easily identifiable by its urban military art work on the building's outside wall. Much of its small selling space is filled with an Army jeep that's not for sale, inflatable rafts, parachutes hanging from the ceiling, and posters of Gen. Douglas MacArthur hawking Ray-Ban sunglasses. Mostly a confusion of clutter with a jumbled assortment of military clothing, the store has everything from jungle fatigues to uniforms and field supplies that look like they've been through the war. The usual trinkets like insignia and ribbons are on display. The best way to get into the patriotic mood is to have your own dog tags personalized while you wait.
Twelfth & Race streets; 513/621-5043. Mon–Sat 9am–6pm. VS, MC.

J.J. NEWBERRY COMPANY/DOWNTOWN—Keeping the feel of a fifties variety store makes Newberry's something of an anachronism. It's even kept its lunch counter where customers can rest, have a soda, or grab a bite to eat. The atmosphere reflects a simpler time. So does its selection and its prices. Displayed in bins throughout the store, trinkets are tempting to buy but hard to justify. Some of the more necessary off-brand basics—health and beauty aids, cosmetics, school supplies, household cleaners, and gift wrap—are better choices. Of course, it wouldn't be Newberry's without the odd-size candies and snacks. The store boasts it has the best caramel corn in Cincy. Go upstairs for off-brand clothing and downstairs for over 3,000 items priced at just 99¢ each. A compact version of Newberry's is in the Swifton Commons Mall.
600 Race Street; 513/621-1833. Mon–Sat 9am–6pm, Sun 10am–6pm. Swifton Commons Mall, Roselawn; 513/351-1115. Mon–Sat 10am–9pm, Sun noon--pm. VS, MC, DS.

MAIN AUCTION GALLERIES/DOWNTOWN—"The most unusual auction in Ohio" is how *Antique Week* described Main Auction Galleries. A Downtown institution since 1871, it still operates every other Tuesday. At its storefront location loyal bidders return week after week, year after year to share in both the bargains and the excitement that come from this type of buying. Items vary. They may range from a box of toys to expensive art. They have set local records for selling art. The last was a painting that attracted worldwide attention and brought a price of $245,000. Auction notices are posted in the paper weekly and inspections are held on Mondays. Occasionally evening auctions are conducted with items that draw higher bids. Many of the items sold later find their way to local flea markets and antique shops with a much higher price tag on them. It's a fast-paced, entertaining way to pick up something at a bargain.
137 W. Fourth Street; 513/621-1280. Call or check Sunday Cincinnati Enquirer *for times. Cash or traveler's checks only.* ☆

MILL END DRAPERIES/DOWNTOWN—Ordinary, run-of-the-mill fabrics are not on hand here—only current, fashionable ones. Specializing in decorative fabrics for draperies, slip covers, and upholstering, this store only buys high-end, first-quality products.

Founded in 1936, Mill End has gained recognition for its superb selection of the unusual and the preferred. After working for the company for over 42 years, Paul Sumner bought the store and is careful to maintain this image by selecting only the exceptional. Even so, by purchasing goods directly from the mills in larger quantities, prices are kept lower than what would otherwise be offered. The store has is its own drapery and upholstery workrooms. Bring in a picture of your fantasy look and the professionals at Mill End will custom design most any pattern.
26 W. Seventh Street; 513/421-1225. Tues–Sat 9:30am–5:30pm, Mon & Thurs 9:30am–8pm. VS, MC, DS.

OHIO BOOK STORE /DOWNTOWN—There are five floors and over 300,000 used books at this downtown store. The old building has rolling library ladders spread throughout the store so that shoppers can make their way up the tall bookcases to choose out-of-reach selections. For collectors this store is a haven. Most of the books are hardbacks from 30–40 years ago with the oldest one dating back to 1620. Several antique wooden cases display many first editions, signed copies, and collectible books like *Little Orphan Annie, Shirley Temple's Fairy Tales, The Wizard of Oz,* and other classics. The store specializes in American history, especially local accounts, and publishes catalogs and books about Ohio and Kentucky that are distributed to libraries and other institutions. More recent editions, local interest books, and maps are highlighted in the front of the store where the cashier will ring up your literary bargains.
726 Main Street; 513/621-5142. Mon–Sat 9am–4:45pm. VS, MC, DS.

The Ohio Bookstore

PETER MINGES & SON/DOWNTOWN—Old-fashioned ambiance reflects a time when real candy was sold in those heavyweight jars that used to be found at the local general store. Some of the same types of candies and confections are at Minges. Unique varieties of bubblegum, jaw breakers, hard candies, and lollipops are sold here. Buying single candies was common in the old days. Today, at Minges, they must be purchased in larger quantities since it's primarily a wholesale supplier (A few individual-size candies are displayed around the counter.) Syrups and confections in industrial-size containers are sold at this little store that looks, we suspect, the same as it did ages ago.
138 W. Court Street; 513/241-7376. Mon–Fri 9am–5pm, Sat 9am–1pm. VS, MC.

PHILLIPS SUPPLY COMPANY/QUEENSGATE—A supplier of industrial and janitorial cleaners and equipment, this store is open to the public. It's just the place to get heavy-duty products that will take care of the tough cleaning jobs and make your house smell like the office laboratory. Yum. A big showroom with numerous quantities of disinfectants, detergents, air fresheners, and deodorizers in industrial-size containers fill the shelves. All the special tools like wet mops, squeegees, dry mops, buckets, and brooms, along with industrial-grade cleaning equipment, are at wholesale prices. Not the place to go if you're chemically sensitive. Or, wear a rubber suit.
1230 Findlay Street; 513/579-1550. Mon–Fri 8am–5pm. Cash or check only.

POLLY FLINDERS FACTORY OUTLET/DOWNTOWN—Back in 1946 Mac and Dick Baylis began an enterprising garment manufacturing company. Baylis Brothers quickly earned a reputation for offering quality and value. Today, this same company distributes woven dresses for girls under the Polly Flinders name to specialty stores nationwide. Its factory store, located downtown on Eighth Street, was one of the first true manufacturers' outlets in the city. The majority of merchandise sold at this store is hand-smocked woven dresses for girls (newborn to size 16) in styles from the current season. The dresses can be purchased at 25%–50% off retail prices and come in assorted prints and fabrics. Socks and hair bows are in stock, as well as some boys' wear.
234 E. Eighth Street; 513/621-3222. Mon–Sat 9:30am–5pm. VS, MC, DS.

REICHERT PAPER COMPANY/QUEENSGATE—Situated in a nondescript warehouse on a dead-end street, this unmarked outlet store has factory-direct savings on the basics. For those who are planning a party or special event, a multitude of paper and plastic partyware—plates, cups, napkins, and table covers—is available in plain colors (no fancy designer prints). When it's time to clean up, the store also sells paper products along with janitorial and miscellaneous cleaning supplies.
1233 Findlay Street (near Union Terminal's Museum Center); 513/621-6866. Mon–Fri 8am–5pm, Sat 8am–12 noon. Cash & carry.

SQUERI'S CASH 'N CARRY/DOWNTOWN—Located in what was once the largest public warehouse east of the Mississippi River, Squeri's wholesale grocery store is on the first floor of this seven-story monstrosity. An abundance of groceries that can be purchased by the public at wholesale prices is positioned around the store in bulk sizes. Large metal racks climb to the ceiling and huge freezer cases display packaged, canned, and ethnic foods, along with a big showing of catering and party supplies. Deserving special mention is Squeri's frozen seafood. Often sold to local restaurants (if that tells you anything), these frozen varieties offer some of the best values and can be purchased in small to larger quantities. Other values are on the many brand name candies and soft drinks sold by the carton or case. A narrow selection of cleaning products and health and beauty aids is also worth checking out. Customers can save an extra 5% when buying items by the case.
49 Central Avenue; 513/579-0044. Mon–Fri 8am–6pm. VS, MC, DS.

ASIDE **Wholesale grocery houses open to the public buy their goods from manufacturers, other wholesalers, or in bulk by the truck load. They sell their products to other grocery stores and restaurants and may also operate a retail store that is open to the public and professional caterers. Since the overhead is much smaller than conventional grocers and the items are bought in such large quantities, they can pass more savings on to their customers. The general rule of thumb to remember when shopping at this type of store is: the more you buy, the more you save. Wholesale grocers offer a wider variety of certain items than what's in the regular groceries. For example, Squeri's on Central Avenue offers a huge selection of frozen fish and canned soups. Many you can't find anywhere else in the city. Quite a few items that can be purchased at wholesale grocers are sold in bulk or in large-size containers. However, some individual portions and sizes can also be purchased. The items sold in these stores include brand names, odd brands, and generic items made by familiar manufacturers. An example of a wholesale grocer in the Cincinnati area is Squeri's.**

TALBOTS SURPLUS STORE /DOWNTOWN—Without exception, Talbots Surplus Store is one of the best places for the frugal career woman to dress herself without spending a fortune. Located in the Convention Plaza Mall, the store caters to Downtown professionals with everything from suits and dresses to fine sportswear in mostly misses' sizes with some petites. Label-conscious shoppers can rack up realistic savings of 50%–70% off original retail prices on catalog overruns, discontinued styles, and previous season merchandise. For those who don't mind doing a few minor repairs, an *as is* rack with damaged goods, clearly marked, brings greater savings. There are a few racks of children's clothing, too. With a constantly changing inventory, the real bargains fly out of here fast, especially since the next closest store is in Lexington, Kentucky.
Convention Place Mall, 435 Elm Street; 513/579-0123. Mon–Sat 10am–6pm, Mon & Fri 10am–7pm; VS, MC, DS, AE, Talbots.

VALERIE MAKSTELL INTERIORS/DOWNTOWN—In a bleak, industrial area of downtown Cincinnati surrounded by overpasses and busy railroad tracks, Valerie Makstell is a precious jewel. Housed in an old warehouse, it features some of the finest furniture and accent pieces in the city. Two floors of this large building are filled with an exquisite selection that is often 25%–35% off retail. Quality brand names and designer labels are easily distinguished among artistically arranged backdrops and painted brick walls that resemble individual rooms. Wind your way through the displays of cozy rooms with skylights and hardwood floors. Don't overlook the small room situated in the building's old safe on the second floor. A treat to visit.
1050 Mehring Way at Freeman; 513/241-1050. Mon–Sat 10am–5pm, Sun noon–4pm. VS, MC, DS.

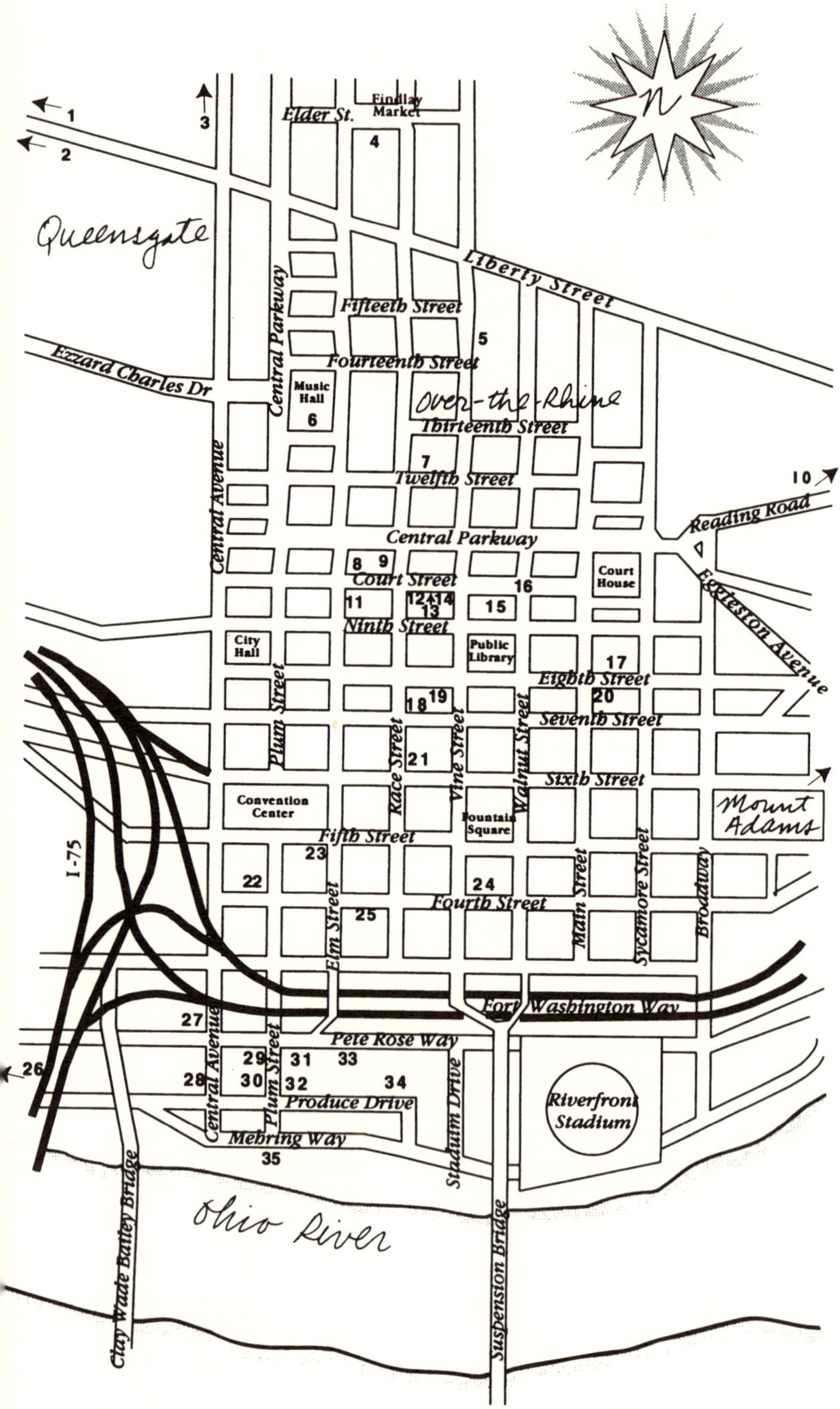
1
2
3
Elder St.
Findlay Market
4
Queensgate
Liberty Street
Fifteeth Street
5
Fourteenth Street
Ezzard Charles Dr
Central Parkway
Music Hall
6
Over-the-Rhine
Thirteenth Street
7
Twelfth Street
10
Reading Road
Central Avenue
Central Parkway
8 9
Court Street
16
Court House
Eggleston Avenue
11
12 14
13
15
Ninth Street
City Hall
Public Library
17
Eighth Street
20
18 19
Seventh Street
Plum Street
Race Street
21
Vine Street
Walnut Street
Sixth Street
Convention Center
Fountain Square
Mount Adams
I-75
Fifth Street
23
22
24
Main Street
Sycamore Street
Broadway
Fourth Street
Elm Street
25
Fort Washington Way
27
Central Avenue
Plum Street
Pete Rose Way
26
29
31
33
28
30
32
34
Produce Drive
Stadium Drive
Riverfront Stadium
Mehring Way
35
Clay Wade Battey Bridge
Ohio River
Suspension Bridge

B & B Furniture - **14**
Brown Novelty Company - **22**
Cappel's - **11**
Cappel's Annex - **9**
Caruso - Ciresi - **29**
Castellini Company - **35**
Cincinnati Brush Manufacturing Company - **3**
Cincinnati Color Company, Inc. - **5**
Cincinnati Playhouse in the Park - **10**
Cincinnati Symphony Orchestra - **6**
Court Street Market - **16**
Crossett Company - **27**
M. Degaro Company - **31**
Dunsky's Restaurant & Bar Supply Company - **15**
Echo Furnishings - **19**
Findlay Market - **4**
Flatow - Riley - **30**
Fourth Street Men's Outlet - **24**
Fox Clothing - **12**
Fries Brothers - **33**
General Sales Company - **13**
Gentille Brothers - **32**
G. I. J. Surplus - **7**
J. J. Newberry Company - **21**
Main Auction Galleries - **25**
Mill End Draperies - **18**
Ohio Book Store - **20**
Peter Minges & Son - **8**
Phillips Supply Company - **1**
Polly Flinders Factory Outlet - **17**
Reichert Paper Company - **2**
Sanzone - Palmisano Company - **34**
Squeri's Cash and Carry - **28**
Talbots Surplus Store - **23**
Valerie Makstell Interiors - **26**

Northern Kentucky

Northern Kentucky is a paradox. Its decaying urban neighborhoods and declining businesses are in sharp contrast to the region's modern growing suburbs. As the I-75 and I-275 expressways were built, the region's outer-lying cities— Florence, Erlanger, and those by the airport—began harvesting major development. Strip malls, sprawling shopping centers, thriving industrial parks, and residential communities are replacing the treed landscape. In comparison, the urban river cities—Ludlow, Covington, Newport, Dayton, and Bellevue—are desperately striving to renew their livelihoods. By recycling rundown neighborhoods and encouraging new development, these cities are slowly being transformed back into prosperity. While the suburbs are promoting new attitudes, these river cities are still flirting with habitudes from the past. ¶ As early as the 1880s, Northern

Kentucky's river region boasted an abundance of industrial factories, breweries and distilleries, bustling hotels, and dozens of cigar and tobacco dealers. As the region grew so did its reputation for offering illicit night-life entertainment. These river cities all had their share of corruption, but it especially thrived during the Prohibition era. As time marched on, Covington concentrated more on building up its traditional business trade. With the operation of several river front beaches, Dayton and Bellevue became the area's recreational center. Newport, which was the most rambunctious of the bunch, was already known as a "Sin City." Illegal gambling, alcohol sales, and prostitution flourished as city officials tolerated these compulsions. The area became the Queen City's "dark side" where Cincinnatians could participate in the pleasures of the night life across the river yet keep these activities out of their own backyards. In the 1970s and 1980s steps were taken through local government to make the region more attractive by encouraging restoration of older houses and commercial buildings, creating historic districts, and cracking down on the vice that still lingered. ¶ Today, nighttime entertainment still predominates in this vicinity—in new dress. Beautiful marinas with open-air bars and eateries are substitutes for beach recreation. Flashy, contemporary night clubs with bright neon lights and fancy restaurants promising grand views of the Cincinnati skyline line the Ohio River's shoreline. Portable eateries and clubs have replaced many of the rundown bars and shifted the emphasis from the shoddy strip joints on Newport's Monmouth Street to the glamorous river front.

COUNTY MARKET TOTAL DISCOUNT FOODS/ALEXANDRIA—This grocery store makes use of bottom line pricing. The store appears to be a regular grocery and even acts like one. But the difference is there's a little more breathing room on the prices. Marketers can buy their foods at the minimum profit margin and save even more on green tag items that are posted all over the store. The selection includes the usual grocery staples with prepriced items from the manufacturers automatically repriced an extra 10% lower.
Alexandria Pike; 606/635-1400. Open 24 hours. VS, MC, DS.

MARIANNE THEATRE/BELLEVUE—Down on the "Avenue" in the heart of Bellevue the Marianne Theatre remains much the same as it has for the last 60 years. Once just your typical neighborhood theatre, it's now one of the few of its kind left in the area. First-run movie titles no longer grace its marquee, only the flicks that are one step away from hitting the video stores. Even so, watching a movie at the Marianne is cheaper than renting one and has more atmosphere.
607 Fairfield Avenue, 606/291-6666. Show times daily 7pm & 9:30pm. Cash only.

MILITARY TREASURES/BELLEVUE—In business for just five years, this army surplus store may not have as colorful a past as some of the others in the area, but it does have some interesting surprises among its military treasures. One of its best is its wide variety of flags. A limited selection of camouflage clothing, camping gear, medals, pins, and the usual provisions make up most of the inventory.
10 Donnermeyer Drive; 606/491-2570. Mon–Sat 10am–6pm. VS, MC.

HOSEA RECYCLED OFFICE FURNITURE/BELLEVUE—Since 1946, when Henry Hosea, Sr. and his two sons packed their first export box in Newport, Kentucky, the company has flourished. Originally export packers and machinery shippers, the company later expanded into hauling and moving office systems and furniture. In recent years, it branched into selling recycled office furniture. Today, their huge 100,000 sq. ft. warehouse facility occupies an entire block in Bellevue's industrial area and is operated by third generation family members. While exploring the contents of this massive building, you can get lost in the vastness of used and new office furniture. Four monstrous floors displaying anything for the home or corporate office—wood and metal desks, chairs, shelving and storage units, room dividers, equipment, and filing cabinets—seem to go on forever in this stark, cold warehouse. Since the company takes some of its services worldwide, look for occasional surprises such as intriguing antique English furniture. The company receives shipments of unusual antique pieces once a month. When buying Hosea's recycled furniture, expect to save as much as 50% off what you would normally pay for newer equivalents. Showroom floor models, which were bought from other furniture suppliers, are also substantially reduced.
241 Grandview Avenue; 606/291-7000. Mon–Fri 9am–5pm, Sat & Sun 9am–3pm. VS.

NORTHERN KENTUCKY WHISKEY ROUTE—It's no secret that Northern Kentucky's liquor stores offer better prices than their conservative neighbor, Cincinnati. As Newport and Covington developed, the selling of alcohol and tobacco products became a prosperous trade. So to attract Ohio customers, many of these liquor stores were built near the bridges stretching across the Ohio River. The latest addition to the region's alcohol trade, **The Party Source,** ☆ is near the 471 bridge on Riviera Drive in Bellevue. This huge superstore, which can be seen from miles away across the river, is the Tri-State's largest. For party planners, it epitomizes one-stop shopping with a heavy emphasis on liquid refreshment. It has a deli with varieties of cheeses, meats, snack dips, and party trays and a customer service center for putting together gift baskets.

Energetic workers use their portable phones to check on items. Well-organized aisles with domestic and imported gourmet snacks and countless bottles of wines, liquors and liqueurs offer endless party possibilities. Rare vintages and premium liquors for connoisseurs are showcased around the store. The best buys on beer, wine, and liquor, though, are at the store's "Case Central" area. There, customers can receive volume discounts when buying by the case. While the prices on alcohol seem quite competitive, the store profits from its total climate by selling the mood. Where the Party Source is just an extension of the river front glitz, a short trip down Route 8 to Newport and Covington offers the *realistic* approach on purchasing discount liquor. One of the older stores is **Bridge Liquor**. As the name indicates it is located by the L & N Bridge on Third and Saratoga streets in a dreary, old gray building with tacky red trim. This is where the "diehards" come to pick up a bottle from behind the counter, sit at the store's three-stool bar, "The Bump I," or enjoy their booze in the parking lot. Across the street is its main competitor, **Holiday House**, easily distinguished by the big whiskey sign atop the building. A block down the road is a cluster of old railroad cars that have been painted red and connected to form the **Cabooze**. This store is combined with a bar that is quiet during the day but wild after the sun goes down. The safest way to buy alcohol at this place is to drive by the pickup window. Down the road from the Cabooze is **Big Daddy's**, a converted old drive-in restaurant. After looking at the store's interior, with its chain link fencing and wire mesh for encasing liquors and cartons of cigarettes, it seems best to just ease up to the drive-through window. All of these places are priced within a nickel or dime of one another. Since their selection is limited primarily to the basic bottle liquors, don't look for the exotic blends. After leaving Newport and venturing down Route 8, your first liquor sighting is **Dick's Wines & Liquors.** Further down, you can't miss **Stadium Liquor**. It's the one with the larger-than-life J.T.S. Brown Whiskey bottle on a pole in the store's parking lot. This liquor store has a better-than-average selection with Ohio price comparisons apparent. Its rowdy neighbor, the (Bridge Discount Liquor) **Bump II**, which used to beconnected to **Bump I** in Newport, has since defected to another owner. Like the Bump I, the identifying element of this store is its long counter that stretches across the floor. Bottles of liquor are lined up almost to the ceiling behind the counter, where rolling ladders commonly found in turn-of- the-century libraries are used to help reach bottles instead of books. Both of these liquor stores are located near the Clay Wade Bailey Bridge on Fourth Street. Cruise further down Route 8, which turns right just past the I-75 bridge. Go past the **Pony Keg Express,** since its prices are out of line, and head for **Liquor Direct,** located in the strip mall right next door. Liquor Direct may not have a broad selection, but what it does have is priced better than any of the other stores. It's a good place to pick up the basics such as a case of Budweiser beer or a fifth of Tanquerey gin. Marking the other end of the route,

you'll drive south on Crescent Avenue to **Cork 'N Bottle**. This liquor store, located within easy access off I-75, is the early version of a super store. It has a huge selection and is especially noted for having unusual gift canisters or special edition bottles issued by the distilleries. The savings vary here. From here you can make your way back to Covington by taking Fifth Street, still Route 8. The next liquor sighting, **Liquor-Kwik**, is marked by the ever-present "Package Liquor" sign atop a fake English Tudor building. Inside, what passes in Covington as a thematic display are carved wood signs indicating a well-organized selection of liquor. On down the road is another attempt at regional architecture. This time it's a New Orleans style balcony with a green and white awning above a typical Northern Kentucky liquor store, the **5th Street Discount Party Shop**. While its selection doesn't seem quite on par with the big guys, its prices match up quite well. A little out of the way as you make your way back toward Newport is **D.E.P. (Discount Everyday Prices) Liquors**. The chain link door and windows may be a little intimidating, but once inside there is a better-than-average selection at the usual competitive prices. Finally, back in Newport, check out **Zakem Brothers** and **Famous Liquor & Wines** package liquor stores. Both are small stores located at the corner of Fifth and York streets and sell the basics. However, Bargain Corner seems to have a slight advantage since it carries that Georgia Moon Corn Liquor in jars.

Big Daddy's Liquor Store & Carryout, West Fourth Street & Central Avenue, Newport; 606/431–1940. Mon–Tues 10am–midnight, Wed–Sat 10am–2:30am, Sun noon–midnight. Cash only. Bridge Liquor "Bump I" East Third & Saratoga streets, Newport; 606/291–8192. Mon–Sun 8am–2:30am. Cash only. Bridge Discount Liquor "Bump II" 407 Main Street, Covington; 606/581–8335. Mon–Sat 8am–1am. Cash only. Cabooze, Third & Monmouth streets, Newport; 606/261–5225. Mon–Sat 11am–2:30am. Cash only. Cork 'N Bottle, 501 Crescent Avenue, Covington; 606/261–8333. Mon–Thurs 8am–10pm, Fri–Sat 8am–11pm. VS, MC, DS. DEP Liquor Outlet, 424 Russell Street, Covington; 606/261–1022. Mon–Thurs 9am–11pm, Fri–Sat 9am–12:30am. VS, MC, DS. Dick's Wines & Liquors, 402 Scott Boulevard, Covington; 606/431–4988. Mon–Sat 8am–10pm. VS, MC, DS. Famous Liquor & Wine, 501 York Street, Newport; 606/581–8650. Mon–Thurs 7am–9pm, Fri–Sat 7am–10pm, Sun noon–6pm. Cash only. 5th Street Liquor Store & Carryout, 433 Johnson Street, Covington; 606/581–4036. Mon–Sat 10am–9:30pm. VS, MC. Holiday House Liquor Store, East Third & Saratoga streets, Newport; 606/261–8875. Mon–Sat 6am–2:30am, Sun noon–9pm. VS, MC. Liquor Direct, 670 W. Third Street, Covington; 606/291–2550. Mon–Thurs 9am–10pm, Fri–Sat 9am–11pm. VS, MC, DS. Liquor Kwik, 430 Bakewell Street, Covington; 606/431–5380. Mon–Sat 6am–1am. Cash only. VS, MC. The Party Source, 95 Riviera Drive, Bellevue; 606/291–4007. Mon–Wed 8am–10pm, Thurs–Sat 8am–11pm. VS, MC, DS. Stadium Liquor, 319 W. Fourth Street, Covington; 606/431–1234. Mon–Sat 8am–1am, Sun 11am–6pm. VS, MC. Zakem Bros. Package Liquor Store, 8 W. Fifth Street, Newport; 606/431–4022. Mon–Sat 9am–10pm. VS, MC.

Bridge Liquor

TOM'S BOOK NOOK/BELLEVUE—Tom Carr, the owner of this store for over 28 years, boasts having the Tri-State's largest selection of used paperback books—over 100,000 copies. In seven small rooms of an old building located in the Bellevue historic district, the books are crammed on the shelves. Even though the store is a bit compact, the books are easily accessible and well organized. Since Tom is the sole worker in his business, he can pinpoint a book almost instantly. While starting with just 500 titles, he was one of the first in the area to sell recycled books and has developed quite a following of regulars (half of whom are from Ohio). Much of his advertising is done by word-of-mouth. His most elaborate broadcast is a handwritten sign in the store window that reads "I must be krazee, but every paperback book in this store is priced at just $1 each."
230 Fairfield Avenue; 606/491-9228. Mon–Sat 9am–6pm. Cash or check only.

AVOID SHOPPERS' PARALYSIS **Take the time to sign your name on mailing lists. It seems like such a hassle to stop and fill out an address card or sign up on a mailing list, but in many cases it's the only way the retailer can notify you of special promotions, warehouse sales, clearance sales, and other sales events. Plus, there's always the added bonus that some retailers may send you discount coupons periodically for buying merchandise at their store.**

GARY'S EVER FRESH PEANUT PRODUCTS/BOONE COUNTY—You would have to be a real peanut lover to buy them in bulk, but every once in a while, when planning a tailgate or Super Bowl party, buying in quantities from this wholesaler makes sense. Peanuts come shelled and are salted or unsalted. A 25-lb. box of loose peanuts, a case of 16 20-oz. bags or 24 10-oz. bags can be purchased at wholesale prices. Tree nuts are available in bulk at certain times of the year, too. If you're willing to make the drive to this out-of-the-way warehouse facility, you'll not only save money, you'll receive fresher products.
1614 Dolwick Drive; 606/525-2442 or 800/332-4279. Mon–Fri 9am–3pm. Cash only.

RICHWOOD FLEA MARKET/BOONE COUNTY—Richwood Flea Market can be spotted off of I-75. It's housed in a cavernous warehouse that has over 300 dealers under one roof. On warmer days there are some outdoor dealers, but most of the action takes place along the "streets" inside. The long aisles in the building are marked with signs displaying Downtown Cincinnati street names. To enter this huge place, marketers must walk through a series of heavy plastic sheets at the doorways that are reminiscent of a science fiction movie or a car wash. Inside, the smells of fast foods, popcorn, and fresh produce infiltrate the senses as patrons scan the subdivided booths. Browsers willing to overlook the tacky and the junky are surprised to find hidden bargains. Don't expect to find what you need, just what you might want.
10915 Dixie Highway; 606/371-5800. Year around. Sat–Sun 9am–5pm.

BILLIES CONSIGNING WOMEN/BURLINGTON—Billies has hundreds of new and gently worn bridal and all-occasion gowns, prom, and pageant dresses at a fraction of the cost of full retail. A beautiful bridal gown that costs as much as $500 might be $100 here. An evening gown originally bought for $100 could sell for $25. There's an impressive collection of after-five dresses, evening bags, and accessories. A small space has been set aside for some women's career suits. For those with more extensive plans, the store specializes in

Billie's Consigning Women

coordinating bridal party attire as well as custom designing. Located in the heart of Burlington's National Register Historic District among a cluster of renovated old brick buildings, this boutique (once the Tousey House of 1822) has special charm and character, as does Billie Burkart, the graceful lady who orchestrates it.

5963 Jefferson Avenue; 606/689-4500. Mon–Fri 10am–5pm, Sat 10am–4pm. (Closed Wed & Sun.) VS, MC, DS.

ARMY STORE GOVERNMENT & FACTORY SURPLUS/ COVINGTON—For 73 years, this surplus army store has welcomed military veterans. You never know who is libel to pull up out front. From a Vietnam vet driving a pickup truck to a former fighter pilot in a custom limousine, they come recounting war stories. Even movie companies shop here while filming in the area. Don't miss the classic Levi's posters hanging on the walls or the miniature doll of Gen. Douglas MacArthur, part of the store's surroundings since World War II. The counter showcases a wide variety of full-size medals, army pins, rank patches, bandanas, and lots of insignia. Shipments ranging from camouflage clothing, fatigues, and footwear to ammo cases, camping equipment, and field gear arrive daily.

508 Madison Avenue; 606/261-0184. Mon–Sat 9am–6pm. VS, MC, DS.

BAKERY-COOKIE OUTLET/COVINGTON—This bakery thrift store is different than most. It sells dated packaged thrift foods yet offers freshly baked gourmet donuts under one roof. The store's generic '50s decor is jazzed up with a black and white tile floor and a Donut Cafe that has a sit-down counter. Customers can order delicious donuts and muffins after saving money on thrift foods such as Shur-Good snacks, Klosterman's breads, Blue Bird Pies, and Frookies Cookies.
512 W. Pike Street; 606/491-6100. Mon–Fri 5am–5pm, Sat–Sun 7am–3pm. Cash or check only.

MERTACK'S ANTIQUES AND FINE FURNITURE/COVINGTON—The large banner hanging on the outside wall reads "Voted Best Furniture Store.", a distinction bestowed upon Mertack's by *Cincinnati Magazine*. The old Commonwealth Building is the home of this fine furniture and antique gallery. Being restored to its original state, the building has had tenants as early as 1874, such as boot and shoe maker W.J. Rouse; a U.S. Post Office; and Victor Rousselat, a children's carriage and toy maker. E.W. Scripps first published the *Kentucky Post* from an office here in 1891. Others included printers, attorneys, and real estate agents. Today, the hardwood floors, long wood-framed staircases, and high ceilings create the perfect setting for Mertack's. An impressive selection of famous, brand name furniture is carefully arranged around the various rooms with fine oak and cherry hardwoods, textured upholstered sofas, rich leather chairs, and matching ottomans interspersed along the corridors. Cubby holes and mantles display unusual knickknacks, while the walls are dressed up with deluxe framed prints, ornate mirrors, and other eye-catching protrusions. The basement, with bunches of plastic grapes dangling from the ceiling trellis, is set up like a bistro with wrought-iron works, accessories, wine racks, gourmet items, and kitchen furniture. You never have to wait for a sale to shop here. Prices average 25%–30% off retail everyday (even on special orders). And, on the third floor, you'll find Mertack's "treasures in the attic" where additional savings on closeouts, floor samples, market specials, and "as is" merchandise can be found. It's a grand store, with quality merchandise and clever decorating ideas. For those who prefer professional assistance, there's an interior decorating service, too.
440 Scott Street; 606/431-3311. Mon–Sat 10am–5pm, Thurs & Fri 10am–8pm. VS, MC, DS.

SHORE TO SHORE/COVINGTON—This modest little store, formerly part of a larger business that made draperies and sold yard goods, still offers its customers a few good buys. While the store no longer makes draperies, it still sells a narrow selection of dress and drapery fabrics. It also carries a limited assortment of sewing notions, bedspreads, comforters, dish towels, and lace trims. If you're in the area it may be worth checking out, but don't make a special trip.
30 W. Pike Street (across from Hills Seed Store); 606/431-0971. Mon–Fri 9:30am–5pm, Sat 9:30am–4pm. Cash or check only.

THE BABY BOUTIQUE/CRESCENT SPRINGS & COLD SPRING—A consignment shop for the quality-minded, this small store has the big names in children's wear—Guess, OshKosh, Buster Brown, and many others. They're sensibly grouped into boys' and girls' sections according to size (0–14). Varying intakes of the most-wanted items such as toys, baby equipment, and children's furniture show up periodically. Maternity wear for mothers-to-be is worth checking out.
2428 High Street; 606/341-2966. 22 Martha L. Collins Boulevard; 606/781-9270. Mon–Sat 10am–6pm, Sun 1pm–4pm. VS, MC, DS, AE.

RAZZA MA TAZZ/CRESCENT SPRINGS—This well-managed consignment shop has the feel of a regular retail store, yet the personal feeling of a neighborhood store. Owner Carol Johnson takes pride in her store and carefully selects the merchandise. The store is uncluttered and well-arranged for shopping convenience. It has an excellent mixture of career and casual wear (even some evening attire) by quality brand names in misses', plus, and teens' sizes. For finishing touches, the store has a nice collection of accessories including new hats and jewelry. The staff is well-versed in offering fashion suggestions. A mini-gallery has crafts and artwork by local artists.
2528 Hazelwood Drive; 606/344-0004. Tues–Fri 10am–6pm, Thurs 10am–8pm, Sat 10am–5pm. Cash or check only.

TRI-CITY HAIR SUPPLY/EDGEWOOD—When buying from this wholesaler, customers will save at least 10%–20% off beauty salon prices. Open to the public, it features Focus 21 hair and skin care products. For those wanting to fine tune their look, hair permanent kits, hair coloring kits, nail polish, and nail care products are in ample supply. Some makeup, tanning products, and hair care appliances are also available. Unlike most beauty supply shops, this one has included a tanning salon in the back room so customers can alter their body color, too.
3095 Dixie Highway; 606/341-2400. Mon–Fri 9am–7pm, Sat 10am–5pm. VS, MC, DS.

GAP STORES DISTRIBUTION CENTER OUTLET/ERLANGER—Be forewarned. Arrive early. Lines have been known to form outside the doors and only a certain number of shoppers will be permitted to enter at a time. Even though there may be a wait to get in, it's worth it. There are only a few outlet stores like this in the entire country. There are exceptional buys on overstocks, end-of-season, and damaged goods. It is a good idea to check merchandise carefully for flaws, which are marked but sometimes hard to find with a quick glance. Newcomers find it a pleasant surprise to discover Banana Republic (a division of the Gap) merchandise among the bargain pickings. The store with its do-nothing interior is at the Gap's Distribution Center, making it easy to replenish supplies (on a daily basis) but not so easy to find. It blends into the surroundings of a busy industrial park. Don't be put off by its out-of-the-way location.
3434 Mineola Pike; 606/525-4713. Mon–Fri 9am–9pm, Sat 10am–6pm, Sun noon–5pm. VS, MC, DS.

ASIDE **What is a *true* manufacturer's outlet? A true factory outlet is a facility that is owned and operated by the manufacturer to eliminate the middleman and pass direct savings on to customers. The store's merchandise comes from a single manufacturer and makes up at least 80% of its inventory. A genuine factory outlet offers an inventory that is primarily comprised of factory closeouts, overstocks, discontinued products, irregulars, seconds, or samples. The brand name products sold through an outlet are normally sold through speciality or department stores. Outlets usually offer a greater selection and size variety than regular retail stores. Examples of true factory outlets in the Cincinnati area are Totes for accessories and rainwear; Whiting Manufacturing Company for linens; Down Lite for down comforters and pillows; and Four Seasons Garment Factory Outlet Store for jackets.**

Oarsman Retail Outlet

OARSMAN RETAIL OUTLET/ ERLANGER—If there is such a thing as finer activewear, Oarsman has it. The selection of heavyweight sweatshirts, sport shirts, and tee shirts has the traditional embroidered emblems sewn on the apparel. This manufacturer's outlet is located at the factory and is the only one of its kind. Much of its stock is sold to small specialty shops in resort areas as far away as Alaska. While some of the items at the outlet are missewn or flawed, many are first quality. The company prides itself on offering original embroidered artwork and decorative designs on its sportswear. One line, the Oarsman 913, features a nautical theme with a rowing oar design. In fact, the store was named after the "Oarsman," a fictitious movie rowing crew the company's president admired. Other items such as sport caps, stadium blankets, throw pillows, and beach towels have embroidered emblems. While the prices on many items are good (a first-quality sweatshirt that normally retails for $50–$60 is here for under $30), check out the half price racks in the back of the store for greater savings. A color-coded system with blue, green, and yellow tags makes it easy to identify perfect, slightly imperfect, and flawed merchandise.
2691 Circleport Drive; 606/283-6710. Mon–Sat 10am–6pm, Sun noon–5pm. VS, MC.

THE SAMPLE SHOP/FORT WRIGHT—First-quality garment samples distinguished by the most current designer labels are constantly arriving at this store via manufacturers' representatives. The selection is often a season or two ahead of what department stores offer. Anyone who wears a misses' size 8–10 will have a good chance of finding high fashion names such as Jones New York, Bushwhacker, and Ceil Bleu (one of the latest lines from France) at exceptional savings. For example, a Marisa Christina sweater, which normally sells for $140 at major department stores, was found here for $82.
Tower Hill Plaza, 1894 Ashwood Circle; 606/331-7728. Mon, Tues, Wed & Fri 9am–5:30pm, Thurs 9am–6pm, Sat 10am–5pm. VS, MC, DS.

ASIDE **What's a sample shop? It's a store that offers clothing items used by manufacturers to represent their products to retail stores. These sample items are usually better made garments and *ahead* of current season merchandise found in the stores. When sales representatives must move on to selling the next season's line, they often sell the older samples to this type of store, which in turn passes the savings on to the customer. Samples of clothing are usually available in certain sizes only depending upon what size the manufacturer likes to use as examples to sell the merchandise. Examples of sample shops in the Cincinnati area are the Sample Shop and the Budget Boutique Sample Outlet for ladies' fashions.**

HATER'S DRY GOODS/LUDLOW—Hater's Dry Goods, which once flourished in Cincinnati with a much larger clientele and several stores, is survived by just one small store in Ludlow, Kentucky. Owner Jim Hater by no coincidence is the son of the company's founder, Milford John Hater. For over 55 years, Milford's main business in Price Hill prospered as his store sold irregular Buster Brown apparel. Ahead of his time, Milford, known as "Milf" by his customers, turned this store into an outlet before many existed in the area. Before long even local department stores like Shillito's began to take a look at his clever merchandising skills. In 1972, with the help of his father, Jim opened his own store in an old rehabbed building in Ludlow's business district. Due to a low overhead, this small variety store is able to keep prices down on basic clothing such as sweatshirts, t-shirts, jackets, sweatpants, athletic shoes, and socks. Some of the other items sold here—thread and needles, cheesecloth by the yard, cotton stockings (like your grandmother used to wear), and cotton socks by Buster Brown—are carryovers from the past. The store also claims to have window shades at the best prices around and will even cut them free of charge.
242 Elm Street; 606/491-8984. Mon–Sat 10am–6pm. Cash or check only.

BLINDS DIRECT/NEWPORT—You can't miss this place. From the outside, its bright blue facade looks like it manufactured one too many blinds in this highly visible shade. Inside, where the company

makes the four or five lines of window treatments that account for 70% of its business, it displays its products against the walls along with a few from other dealers. The most popular product is mini blinds. Made with 8-gauge aluminum (as opposed to the standard 6-gauge), the mini blinds offer better quality at a better price. Other quality products made here include vertical blinds, pleated shades, and cellular shades. These items are well within the main stream of fair market prices.
15 E. Eighth Street, Newport; 606/261-0100. Mon–Fri 9am–5pm. 8309 US Route 42, Florence; 606/525-1311. Mon–Fri 10am–8pm, Sat 10am–5pm, Sun noon–5pm. 671 Ohio Pike, Beechmont Station; 513/752-4555. Mon–Fri 10am–8pm, Sat 10am–6pm. 9696A Colerain Avenue, Marshall's Northgate; 513/741-0700. Mon–Fri 10am–9pm, Sat 10am–6pm, Sun noon–5pm. Loehmann's Plaza, 11974 Lebanon Road; 513/769-0400. Mon–Fri 10am–9pm, Sat 10am–6pm, Sun noon–5pm. VS, MC, DS.

PALM BEACH OUTLET/NEWPORT—When the Mill Outlet at Watertower Square closed, Cincinnati lost one of its long-time discounters. Since then it has reemerged under its original ownership as the Palm Beach Outlet. Located in the old Hyde Park Clothing Manufacturing Plant, it's ironic that it is located down the street from where the clothing was once made. Though the Palm Beach Plant and its on-site factory store are no longer there, the company has reestablished an outlet store similar to the one it began over 40 years ago. While this store occupies only about half the space as the previous tenant, there are plans to expand as the company acquires more lines (including women's wear). Currently the outlet sells only men's wear by Palm Beach and Burberry's. Suits, sport coats, and dress slacks, complemented by dress shirts and accessories, go for at least 40% off department store prices. "Suited for You" separates, a new fitting concept, allows customers to buy coats and slacks separately in different sizes.
Sixth & Washington streets; 606/581-7666. Mon & Thurs 10am–8pm, Tues–Sat 10am–6pm, Sun noon–5pm. VS, MC.

SHOE OUTLET/NEWPORT—Wander through three rooms of a building resembling the framework of an old-time general store. Primarily catering to the businessman, this discounter is partial to certain traditional lines of famous name dress shoes such as Johnston & Murphy, Rockport, and Bostonian. Stacks and stacks of boxed footwear fill the tall shelving units. The outlet has one of the deepest selections around of these well-known brands. Other famous make casual shoes like Sebago, Sperry, and New Balance run a close second. The store has also managed to make room for a small selection of women's walking shoes by New Balance, Rockport, and Sebago. All of the merchandise is first-quality with varying savings from 20%–40% off retail. Sales clerks with shoe horns are eager to assist you. A wide size range from 6–18 AA–EEE makes it easy to be fitted.
Sixth Street & Washington Avenue; 606/291-7444 or 800/473-7444. Mon–Sat 9am–7pm, Sun noon–5pm. VS, MC, DS.

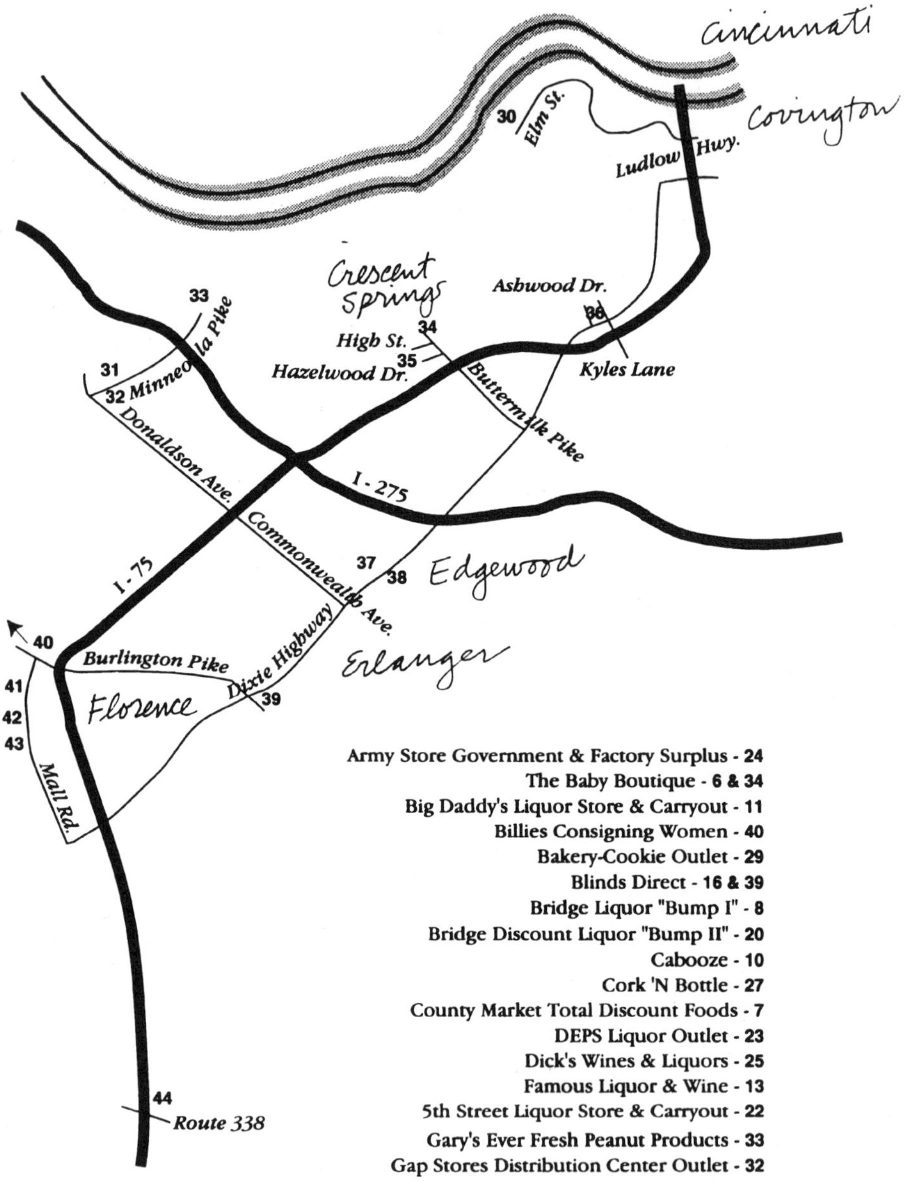

Army Store Government & Factory Surplus - **24**
The Baby Boutique - **6 & 34**
Big Daddy's Liquor Store & Carryout - **11**
Billies Consigning Women - **40**
Bakery-Cookie Outlet - **29**
Blinds Direct - **16 & 39**
Bridge Liquor "Bump I" - **8**
Bridge Discount Liquor "Bump II" - **20**
Cabooze - **10**
Cork 'N Bottle - **27**
County Market Total Discount Foods - **7**
DEPS Liquor Outlet - **23**
Dick's Wines & Liquors - **25**
Famous Liquor & Wine - **13**
5th Street Liquor Store & Carryout - **22**
Gary's Ever Fresh Peanut Products - **33**
Gap Stores Distribution Center Outlet - **32**
Gentry Men's Clothier - **41**
Hater's Dry Goods - **30**
Holiday House Liquor Store - **9**
Hosea Recycled Office Furniture - **4**
Liquor Direct - **18**
Liquor Kwik - **19**

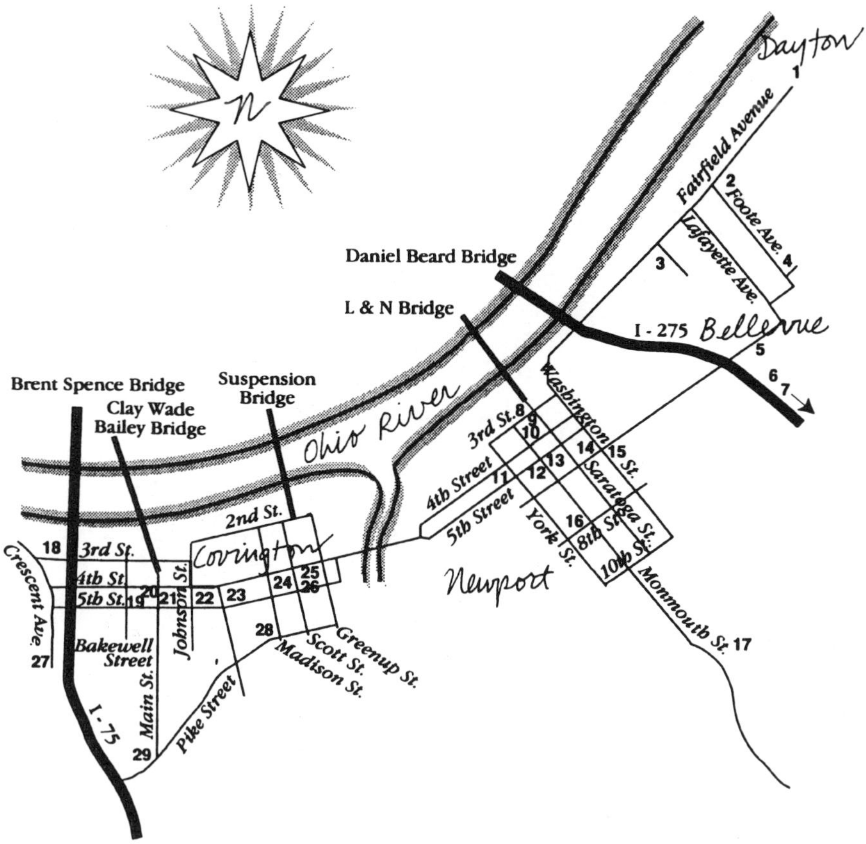

Marianne Theatre - 1
Mertack's Antiques & Fine Furniture - 26
Military Treasures - 5
Oarsman Retail Outlet - 31
Once Upon a Child - 43
Original Mattress Outlet Store - 42
Palm Beach Outlet - 15
The Party Source - 3
Razza Ma Tazz - 35
Richwood Flea Market - 44
The Sample Shop - 36
Shoe Outlet - 14
Shore to Shore - 28
Snooty Fox - 37
Stadium Liquor - 21
Tom's Book Nook - 2
Tri-City Hair Supply - 38
Whiting Mfr. Linen Outlet - 17
Zakem Bros. Package Liquor Store - 12

The West Side

Family, with a capital "F," is the password into Cincinnati's West Side. Reluctance toward change and pride about conservative attitudes keep the natives cautious about frivolous spending, except when it comes to *food*. A slew of butcher shops, small markets, and bakeries flourish with loyal clientele. Many of these small, long-established businesses make the residents the focal point of their trade, while the churches dominate the neighborhoods. Thick with Catholic German and Irish ancestry, much of the area's characteristics were influenced by religion. ¶ One of the earliest areas to develop was Price Hill, due, in part, to the Price Hill Incline built in 1874. A few years later the Price Hill House, a recreation complex housing a dance pavilion, music hall, and observation deck, was included on the hilltop. Even with the coming of streetcar lines and the construction of the Eighth Street Viaduct in 1928, Price Hill was still considered an isolated community. Residents remained in or around the area, built community loyalty, and reinforced a sense of seclusion. As time went on, even though its middle class residents started to move further out, they still remained on the west side. Business districts along Harrison and Glenway avenues began to expand westward, following the spread of home building. As the area became known collectively as Western Hills, old loyalists remained devoted to the neighborhood businesses, which faced increased competition with the coming of the new shopping centers in the 1950s and 1960s. In 1954, the first planned regional shopping center in Cincinnati opened—Western Hills Shopping Plaza. The area quickly became a major commercial center in Western Hills secured by the building of a second major mall next door—Western Woods Shopping Center—in 1963. Together these malls have remained vibrant and have attracted a large number of shoppers and businesses to the area.

RADIO SHACK OUTLET/BRIDGETOWN—For those who don't mind buying discontinued, refurbished (with 90-day warranties), or overstock items, there are good buys. They might include: a rechargeable lantern (in perfect condition) normally selling for $21.99, here, $13.88; a refurbished portable compact disc digital audio player, normally $150, here, $75. The only Radio Shack in Cincinnati like this, it has several aisles set aside for selling surplus items at bargain prices. One day a shipment of clock radios and portable televisions may arrive, the next it may be headphones or something as small as blank cassette tapes. Whatever shows up is worth checking out.
6611 Glenway Avenue; 513/574-0400. Mon–Fri 10am–8pm, Sat 10am–6pm, Sun 11am–4pm. VS, MC, DS.

BROOKVILLE FLEA MARKET/BROOKVILLE, INDIANA—This small flea market has operated in Brookville since the 1940s. For the most part it's a Wednesday market but some of the vendors, such as the one which sells concrete animals, may be open anytime. Parking is lacking and the choices are limited, with only about 40 mini-barns for the vendors to stash their goods. However, when combined with White's Farm Flea Market just down the road, it offers a singular midweek shopping experience.
US Route 52; 317/647-5116. Open year round on Wed.

CAROLINA FURNITURE OUTLET/BROOKVILLE, INDIANA—Located in Brookville's historic district, this small, inconspicuous furniture store has a limited selection in house, but it has access to much more. Owner Luther Noble does business through the usual local furniture suppliers and also makes a trip once or twice a month to North Carolina and Tennessee to fill customers' orders or replenish stock. By hauling his own furniture and eliminating manufacturers' shipping costs, the store's prices run about 15%–30% less than many major showrooms. Customers may choose from in-stock selections or order factory-direct from the catalog (the average wait time is four weeks). For those looking for more furniture bargains, Luther also has an outlet at White's Farm Flea Market, just south of town.
740 Main Street; 317/647-4875. Mon–Sat 10am–6pm. Cash only.

WHITE'S FARM FLEA MARKET/BROOKVILLE, INDIANA—White's Farm Flea Market was forced to move out of Brookville years ago when its slaughterhouse proved to be too much for the city's sewage system. Now, just south in Mound Haven, the market winds around several barns and pole-barn buildings where vendors sell their "stuff" indoors or outdoors. "Honest Ruth" specializes in selling "ole tyme bluegrass and country music" with hundreds of cassette tapes highlighting local talents. It's not uncommon to see some musicians show up at her booth with fiddles and banjos to jam. At the day's end, after slogging through the rubble, there's an auction on the grounds. Bids are made on items, including livestock, from Pygmy goats and puppies to Polish chickens and roosters. Try the Frugal Fashions shop for apparel.
US Route 52; 317/647-3574. Wed only 5am–1pm. Frugal Fashions; 317/647-2717. Open daily. VS, MC, DS.

LAND OF OZ BRIDAL & WEDDING INVITATION OUTLET/CHEVIOT—Since the store hours are limited and appointments are the main way of doing business around here, your first impression of Land of Oz comes via phone. A recorded voice-message that's as mystical as the Wizard from Oz, yet as deeply guttural as a radio talk show host, greets you with an overview of this unusual bridal shop's offerings. Owner Michael Dennis has made it one of his trademarks. That, and several other anomalous ways of employing his services. Perhaps ahead of its time, the shop discounts its commodities differently than what's typical of the industry. With access to goods from almost every bridal fashion manufacturer in the market, it places many orders on merchandise through sample

books. This way, customers can choose from thousands of styles of wedding gowns, bridesmaid dresses, flower girl dresses, mother-of-the-bride gowns, and, of course, wedding invitations. With a low overhead, no excess employees, and no big fancy store to operate, the shop keeps all of its prices at the low wholesale rates. Although the prices are low on merchandise, this one-stop bridal service also offers services at similar discounts. Dress alterations, tuxedo rentals, photography, wedding cakes, and limousine services all have to meet this shop's strict quality standards and still be offered at the wholesale price—even booking a disc jockey for a reception. For four hours of play, a big light show, two disc jockeys, and a video tape of the whole shebang, the fee is $260.
3706 Harrison Avenue; 513/481-2300. Tues & Thurs 6–10pm. By appointment only.

wilson paint company

WILSON PAINT COMPANY OUTLET/FAIRMOUNT—It only makes sense to buy paint for your home where contractors buy their supplies. The Wilson Paint Company outlet store, located at the company's pigment warehouse and factory, is spotted by the bold sign painted on the outside of the building. Once the home of the Adler Underwear & Hosiery Company's woolen mills, the building is also on the former site of the Lick Run Lunatic Asylum. Inside, they may not be crazy, but they do sell everything at the wholesalers' rates.
1616 Harrison Avenue; 513/251-5300. Mon–Fri 8:30am–5pm, Sat 8am–noon.

COST PLUS LIQUOR OUTLET/LAWRENCEBURG, INDIANA—This small store is located next to Whisky's Family Restaurant. Inside, the claustrophobic rooms are piled high with towering cases of beer and wine that form aisle ways leading through the store. Trying to navigate this maze-like interior makes it a chore to find a specific brand. However, like most of Indiana's liquor stores, this one has

good prices on beer. It also has a limited selection of liquor and wine that's sold at Lawrenceburg prices.
Front Street & Eads Parkway; 812/537-3932. Mon–Fri 9:30am–11pm, Sat 9:30–noon. VS, MC, DS.

CUT-RATE DISCOUNT LIQUOR/LAWRENCEBURG, INDIANA—A little off the beaten path, Cut-Rate Discount Liquor offers some of the best prices on beer and alcohol. Housed in a building that used to be a grocery store, the well-stocked aisles are amply marked by wooden divider signs. The front of the store displays smaller one-shot bottles, while the rear is loaded with cases of the most popular brews priced to compete in Lawrenceburg's highly competitive beer market.
424 Walnut Street (off of US Route 50); 812/537-5900. Mon–Sat 9am–9pm. VS, MC.

KATIE'S KLOSET/PRICE HILL—In operation for over 19 years, Katie's Kloset is one of the forerunners for selling gently used apparel. Located along Price Hill's main drags at West Eighth and Enright streets, it's the oldest consignment shop in the Queen City. Like much of the architecture in the area, it has been converted from an old brick building. This one, though, was once a thriving corner drugstore. With its hand-painted wooden sign out front and wrought-iron works along the foundation, the store reflects a bygone era of neighborhood business. Owner Helena Roden has stocked the store with a well-pruned selection of apparel for the entire family. Something different for most consignment shops, it also includes men's wear and some new manufacturers' samples. The store is mercifully uncluttered, and it's easy to maneuver through the organized racks of recognizable brand names.
3647 W. Eighth Street; 513/251-7315. Mon–Fri 11am–4pm, Sat 9am–2pm. Cash or check.

ASIDE **There are just two seasons in the consignment business: fall/winter from August to January and spring/summer from February to July. As in regular retail, your best buys are toward the end of the season. If the merchandise is still not sold it's either returned to the seller or donated to charity.**

MIAMITOWN TRADERS MARKET/MIAMITOWN—Look for the large Traders Market sign painted on the side of a semitrailer (which doubles as a concession stand) off of I-74. This small, open-air market is in a field where the only access to it is through a BP gasoline station. Once there, the vendors' wares are displayed in typical flea market fashion—on the ground, out of the back of a truck or a van, and on portable tables. Some vendors even bring their campers and stay overnight. Looking like leftovers from a yard sale, vendors push the recycling concept to the max. Used clothing, old golf clubs, sporting goods, previously owned housewares, and new or used tools and auto parts reappear here. The ones in higher demand—the antiques, collectibles, and craft items—are harder to spot among the furniture, toys, and appliances.

Though the market is not as large as others in the Tri-State, it's worth a stop if you're in the area. And, when combined with shopping the 20 antique and specialty shops in Miamitown, it proves to be a promising afternoon for exploring used trinkets, gadgets, and timeworn collectibles.
State Route 128 (Exit 7) at I-74/I-275; 513/353-3838. Seasonal market open every Sat & Sun 8am–5pm from April–November.

ALL ABOUT SPORTS OUTLET CENTER/MONFORT HEIGHTS—If you're athletic, or at least like to think you are, one hundred situps with a charge card in each hand will put you in shape for shopping here. The outlet is a regional clearance center for All About Sports stores where everything is priced way below original retails. Loaded with mostly end-of-season and discontinued recreational merchandise, the store is like a giant playground for big kids. Try out the exercise machines. The Pro-Form Cross Walker treadmills and the Pro-Form Steppers are at generously reduced prices. Here, muscular men and shapely girlfriends try out the free weights. Kids are found "hooping it up" at the Double Shot basketball game (it's for sale) or hiding out in one of the fully assembled Camel brand tents displayed on the floor. Guys wearing Pro Bass sports caps are at the showcase where Zebco fishing reels and high powered binoculars are discounted. Golf clubs priced from $5–$29.99 fill the slotted racks. Pull one out and practice your swing. Browse through the racks and racks of workout apparel and windwear topped by labeled signs—Columbia, Nike, Reebok, Woolrich, Speedo, and Russell. Thousands of pairs of footwear for men, women, and children are stacked in boxes along the shelves and the floor. Some of the great wearable buys are a ladies' Head windsuit, normally $159.99, here, $80, and a pair of men's Nike Ultra Force athletic shoes, normally $47.99, here, $29.99. All kinds of odds and ends are found at this outlet (even a Kettler table tennis game), so you may need to pace yourself to get through the store in one full swoop—without breaking your budget or a leg.
5403 North Bend Road; 513/662-7300. Tues–Sat 11am–7pm, Sun noon–5pm. VS, MC, DS, AE.

INDUSTRIAL ROPE SUPPLY COMPANY, INC./SAYLOR PARK—Down by the river and off the beaten path, this rope supplier doesn't see many lassoing cowboys. Instead, there's a captain from one of the barges drifting down river who stops in for the ultra heavy duty ropes. An engineering student from the University of Cincinnati hunts a special strand for a project. A houseboat owner comes looking for new docking hookups. Crafters shop here for twines and smaller ropes. Once in a while, visiting movie companies, in town on a shoot, need some rope for an attractive noose. So if you find yourself at the end of *your* rope trying to locate the right one, this small, nondescript warehouse will have what you need. The place is filled with numerous ropes, cables, chains, wire ropes, and nylon slings—available by the foot or in bulk at wholesale prices.
5250 River Road; 513/941-2443. Mon–Fri 8am–4:30pm. Cash or check only.

FINISH LINE OUTLET STORE/WESTWOOD—Only one of a few in the country, the Finish Line Outlet Store has exceptional stock-up buys on activewear in adult and youth sizes. Activewear averages 40% off regular retails. This includes heavyweight cotton or nylon sweats, tee shirts, gym suits, shorts, and jackets. Many have college or pro team logos or themes. Athletic footwear is 20%–30% off. Marked by quality labels—Nike, Asics, Reebok, and Russell—these bargain prices are hard to pass up. A color-coded discount chart hanging from the ceiling informs you of extra savings (from 10%–70% off the lowest ticket price on the items). Posters highlighting famous sports figures sell way below their original prices ($5.99 each). Team logo sports caps also go for much less.
Western Woods Mall, 6294 Glenway Avenue; 513/481-5875. Mon–Sat 10am–9pm, Sun noon–6pm. VS, MC, DS, AE.

FERGUSON HILLS/PARIS FLEA MARKET/WESTWOOD—Before dawn they begin to arrive. Hurrying to get the best slots between the old speaker poles, the dealers set up with the white face of the Ferguson Hills drive-in screen looming in the background. Soon customers roll in, wandering the vast lot, eyeing merchandise spread out on the ground or roughly displayed on tables. Customers haggle over the worn, the broken, and the unique. As the sun rises, more customers stalk the rows. Surprisingly, many are well dressed, having just come from Sunday services. More deals are sought. More treasures are bought. But as the sun reaches its pinnacle the energy of the market starts to wane. Dealers start to pack up and drift away. While the buying and selling still continues, the market dies a slow death until there's only the debris left from the day's activities. Dormant until next Sunday, dawn will again bring the flock back to pay homage to the remains of others.
2310 Ferguson Road; 513/451-1270. Seasonal market open from April–November. Sun only 7am–4pm.

AVOID SHOPPERS' PARALYSIS **Be leery of an item being sold with no comparative price. If a retailer can sell an item at below the regular or original price you can bet that most of the time they are going to flaunt it. They want their customers to know about the savings they can receive. They'll want to make sure you can see a comparison before purchasing an item, especially if it's substantially reduced below the normal price. If the item is something you need right away and the price is good, you may want to go ahead and purchase it. Whenever an item is marked down from regular retail it means that particular item has been temporarily reduced. It will be marked back up after the sale. However, if you're purchasing an item that has been marked down from the original retail, the price will usually not be marked back up. The item will be sold at the sale price or even lower for the remainder of its shelf time.**

WESTWOOD CINEMAS 1 & 2/WESTWOOD—Easily distinguished by the dark lava rock on the outside of the building, Westwood Cinema is a fixture on Harrison Avenue. Since the late 1930s, this neighborhood theatre has been supplying movie entertainment to the locals. Once a thriving first-run movie house with an art deco interior, it has been remodeled to become more functional. The theatre is now divided into two auditoriums and shows sub-run movies (the ones just leaving the major cinemas) at low prices. The owners, Mick and Jamie Telkamp, cater to the family crowd by offering comedies, classics, old concert films, and more recent movies. Something different for a small theatre, this one has midnight showings every Friday and Saturday. For a change of pace, "cult appeal" movies (ones that have a following) are also shown.

3118 Harrison Avenue; 513/481-3933. Show times vary. Cash only.

Westwood Cinema

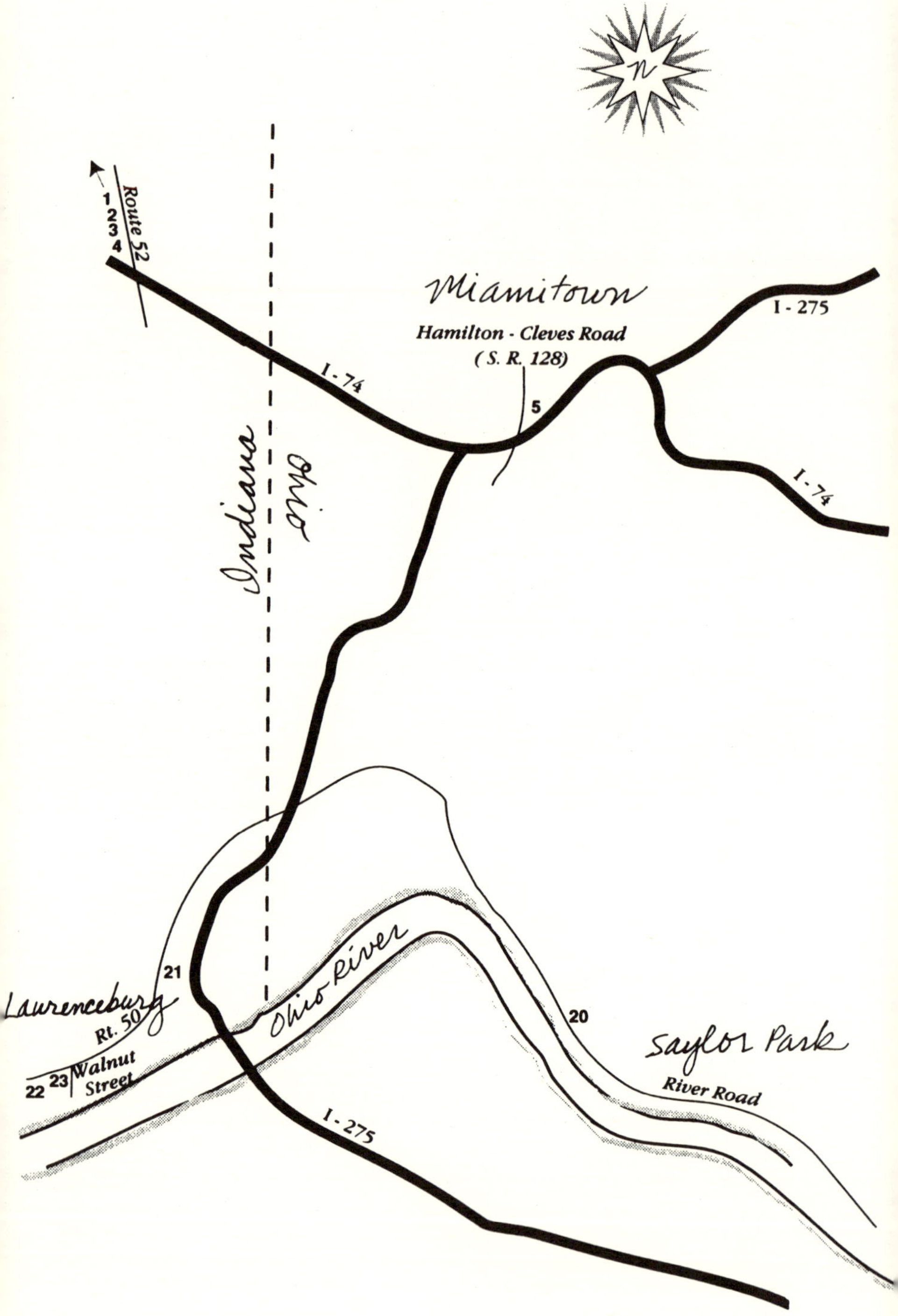
N
Route 52
1
2
3
4
Miamitown
Hamilton - Cleves Road
(S. R. 128)
5
I - 275
I - 74
I - 74
Indiana
Ohio
21
Laurenceburg
Rt. 50
22
23
Walnut Street
Ohio River
20
Saylor Park
River Road
I - 275

All About Sports Outlet Center - 7
Brookville Flea Market - 1
Cappel's - 10
Carolina Furniture Outlet - 2
Cost Plus Liquor Outlet - 22
Cut-Rate Discount Liquor - 23
Discount Produce - 14
Ferguson Hills/Paris Flea Market - 15
Finish Line Outlet Store - 13
Frugal Fashions - 3
Industrial Rope Supply Company - 20
Katie's Kloset - 18
Land of Oz Bridal & Wedding Invitation Outlet - 8
Miamitown Traders Market - 5
Once Upon a Child - 17
Radio Shack Outlet - 12
Velva Sheen Sportswear Outlet - 9
Westwood Cinemas 1 & 2 - 11
White's Farm Flea Market - 4
Whitey's Package Liquor Store - 21
Whiting Mfr. Linen Outlet - 6 & 19
Wilson Paint Company Outlet - 16

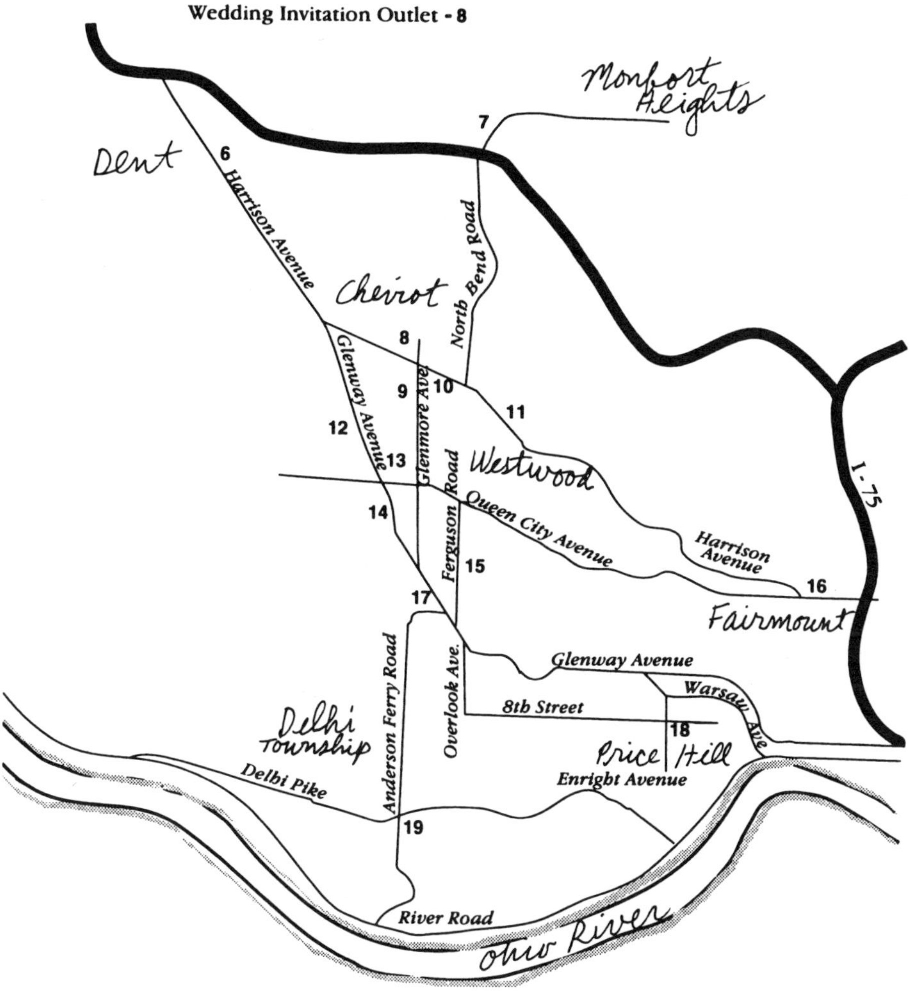

Northwest

Two words are enough to strike fear in even the most dedicated bargain hunter—Colerain Avenue. Venturing down this congested strip is like trying to polka through a clogged artery. A sea of jarring neon signs and flashy billboards pushing retailers in every size and specialty are punctuated by fast food drive-ins and auto dealerships feeding mobile worshippers. The constant interruption of stop light after stop light could frustrate a meditation guru. When shopping this strip you have to be single-minded. Never look further than one side of the road at a time. And, unless you want a dent in your car, forget about turning left. Few outsiders desire to face it, but there always comes a time when the right bargain drives you to it. Throughout the rest of the Tri-State, residents stuck in the traffic of retail strips in their own areas are heard to mutter "I just hope it doesn't become another Colerain Avenue." ¶ Bypassed by canals and railroads throughout most of its history, it was a virtual backwater of Hamilton County. Only after World War II and the subsequent flight to the country did the area became transformed into housing tracks and a vast commercial district. Many of the local communities lost their identities as they were absorbed into this huge conglomerate. The creation of Northgate Mall, after the completion of I-275, added to the out-of-control growth. The mall dominates and has become a point of identification. Many people refer to the area as Northgate rather than Colerain. As the strip reached its saturation point, the township resisted development north of the Circle Freeway. Now, though, new businesses are springing up across the highway, which translates into more mass confusion stretching further out on Colerain. ¶ At the other end of this 10-mile monstrosity is Northside. Once a strong business district, it has been in decline since the 1930s. Today, several unique shops are breathing new life into the business district as it struggles to become another community center like East Side's O'Bryonville. Both North College Hill and Mt. Healthy have seen their business districts shift to specialty shops and service-oriented businesses as they have felt the competition from shopping centers. The Mt. Healthy district has managed to stay healthier. ¶ The twin villages of Greenhills and Forest Park both began as planned communities. Greenhills got its start in the 1930s with a small central shopping area. Forest Park came along later in the mid 1950s. To the north, Forest Park annexed the land around the I-275 exits. Here a strong commercial area has developed centering around the

Forest Fair Mall, which is one of the largest shopping malls in the Tri-State. Even though the mall has struggled with department store anchors coming and going, it has managed to survive by combining retailing with entertainment. It has filled massive vacancies with popular restaurants and trendy nightclubs. A discount movie theatre with multiple auditoriums, a food court that stretches into eternity, putt–putt golf, and an amusement area have transformed the mall into a community recreational center with shopping as part of its pastime. In fact, so many teens have made this their hangout that security has been increased and a curfew enacted.

COCONUTS MUSIC & MOVIES/NORTHGATE—You won't find any coconuts or lemons here. You will find a better-than-average selection of the top picks that cross a broad range of music tastes. Coconuts' prices are held at everyday competitive rates, but this excludes box sets, multiple compact disc sets, special editions, or super high-fidelity compact discs. These stores only carry new selections (no used). They also sell cassette and video tapes. The upbeat stores are spacious, bright, and provide shopping convenience with neatly organized bins and wide aisles. You can't go wrong shopping here.
9674 Colerain Avenue, Northgate; 513/385-7265. Mon–Thurs 10am–9pm, Fri & Sat 10am–10pm, Sun noon–6pm. Rookwood Pavilion, Madison & Edwards roads, Norwood; 513/631-0380. Mon–Sat 10am–9pm, Sun noon–6pm. VS, MC, DS, AE.

MACY'S CLOSE-OUT STORE/ FOREST PARK—Overwhelming choices at Macy's quickly cause fatigue as rack moles spend considerable time digging out fashion bargains. Some racks are a graveyard for the forsaken with clothing that has seen too many storage rooms. And the never-ending rows of ladies' footwear stock everything from trendy platform shoes in ravishing red to low-heel pumps caught somewhere between in-style and on-the-outs. Constant variables of closeouts and overruns from Macy's nationwide department stores are shipped to this mammoth store. Family clothing, along with some bed and bath linens, are featured. Expect to pay 40% off the lowest ticket price (shoes are 20% off). The exception is on the items marked "You Pay."
Cobblewood Plaza, 1139 Smiley Avenue; 513/825-0300. Mon–Sat 10am–9pm, Sun noon–6pm. VS, MC, DS, AE, Macy's.

ASIDE **What's a retail closeout store? They are stores that offer an inventory primarily made up of closeout, discontinued, or canceled merchandise. Examples of retail closeout stores in the Cincinnati area are Big Lots and Odd Lots for general merchandise; Macy's Close-Out Store for fashions; and Tuesday Morning for gifts.**

FASHION WAREHOUSE/GROESBECK—The customer lounge comes in handy when shopping this large warehouse facility. Loaded with juniors', misses', and plus-size casual wear, it's a chore to search through. Look for the sign at the entrance featuring the week's bargain brand names. All the merchandise is first-quality at hefty price reductions (Palmetto's jeans $12 a pair; basic knit tops under $8; a long, wool dress coat $50), but be prepared to rummage through the not-so-famous labels to find the better known ones. Committed shoppers should sign up on the mailing list for notices of sales events.
Groesbeck Plaza, 8255 Colerain Avenue; 513/245-9147. Mon–Sat 10am–9pm, Sun noon–6pm. VS, MC, DS.

GENTRY MENSWEAR OUTLET/GROESBECK—When you hit this store at the right time the buys can be incredible. A generous representation of the big names—Christian Dior, Nautica, Ralph Lauren, London Fog, Polo, Halston, Geoffrey Beene, and on and on—are greatly discounted. The large inventory (even big and tall sizes) from area Gentry Menswear stores is made up of first-quality overstocks and clearance items from previous seasons. Easily accessible (no fighting your way through racks here) sport coats, fine sportswear, dress shirts, and accessories bring good values for your bucks. Particularly impressive is the store's collection of finely tailored suits.
Groesbeck Plaza, 8259 Colerain Avenue; 513/923-9200. Thurs–Sat 10am–9pm, Sun noon–6pm. VS, MC, DS, AE.

J.C. PENNEY CATALOG OUTLET/GROESBECK—Though the store is spread out and takes you all over the place scooping up the buys, it has an appealing lack of confusion. Departmentalized according to lifestyle, category, and size, it's more tolerable to shop than most large clearance centers. The extensive inventory is first-quality overflow, overstock, and discontinued merchandise from JC Penney's catalog service, so anything is liable to show up here. Electronics, sporting goods, housewares, and linens are available, but the main emphasis is on family fashions. The hard-to-find sizes—men's big and tall, women's plus, and petites' sizes—are not neglected. Nor are the specialty fashions. The store even has sizable bridal wear and maternity wear departments. A continuous supply of new arrivals keeps the selection fresh, so scouters can make it a habit to regularly stalk the store. At hard-to-resist savings—an average of 30%–60% off regular retail prices—it's the kind of place you come in looking for one thing and come out with a lot more.
8770 Colerain Avenue; 513/385-9700. Mon–Sat 9am–9pm, Sun 10am–5pm. VS, MC, DS, AE, JC Penney.

SWALLEN'S OUTLET STORE/GROESBECK—It's not until you get inside this nondescript store that you realize it's a warehouse outlet store. The only hint outside is the smaller scratch 'n dent banner next to the Swallen's sign. Inside are major home appliances and electronics ranging from televisions and stereos to cordless phones and answering machines. They bring substantial savings as close-outs, discontinued styles, floor models, and scratch 'n dent items. Some look like they've fallen off a delivery truck, some need a few touch-ups, others look like new. Price reductions match whatever condition you're willing to take. A small selection of ready-to-assemble furniture brings good savings.
8761 Colerain Avenue; 513/385-5866. Mon–Fri 10am–9pm, Sat 10am–6pm. VS, MC, DS, Swallen's.

WESTERN HOME CENTER OUTLET STORE/GROESBECK—If a specific style is no concern, this outlet may have what you need (as much as 50% off or more). Separate from Western Home Center's main showroom (toward the back of the lot), the outlet is filled with counter tops, replacement windows, shutters, sliding doors, lumber, and moldings. While you won't find complete sets, a good selection of custom-made kitchen and storage cabinets can be found here. Many are canceled orders or discontinued styles. Some are damaged, scratch 'n dent, or unfinished products. All sales are final.
7600 Colerain Avenue; 513/931-6300. Mon & Fri 8am–8pm, Tues–Thurs 8am–5pm, Sat 8am–4pm. VS, MC, DS.

FEATHERS AND BIRDS EYE VIEW/MT. HEALTHY—Every room of this turn-of-the-century frame house is dressed up with personality. The first floor, divided by a stained wooden staircase, has previously owned clothing on one side and primitive antiques on the other. An upstairs room has a rustic flavor heavily seasoned with cacti and southwestern spices. Another is stark with a sharp black and white tile floor and sleek furniture displaying contemporary home accessories. Check out the closets, especially the one with 50% off closeouts. Built in 1904 as a residence for the mayor of Mt. Healthy, later a boarding house, and now a consignment shop, the house, itself, is worth the stop.
1545 Compton Road; 513/522-8011. Mon–Fri 9am–5pm, Sat 9am–7:30pm, Sun 10am–5pm. Cash or check only.

RINK'S CRAFTS & FLEA MARKET/MT. HEALTHY—Years ago the old Rink's store was Cincinnati's discount super mart. It was where the early bargain hunters egged on by Willie Thall and the Bargain City Kid would scout out the deals. Now, it's been turned into a charity-bazaar atmosphere with a flea market as the center ring. Carnival and video games are near the front with a boxing school and wholesale furniture store as sidekicks to this 100,000 sq. ft. complex. A bingo parlor is a main attraction, but a sign outside the door boldly states *cheating will not be tolerated.* Vendors push more of the expected flea market items—tools, car stereos, electronics, yard ornaments, antiques. But, some have moved up the ranks to more permanent shed-like structures—a general store, a fabric center, a table shop. Outside, more vendors set up in the parking

lot peddling everything from old junk to new junk.
9651 Hamilton Avenue; 513/521-7465. Indoors Sat–Sun 10am–6pm. Outdoors Tues, Thurs, Sat, & Sun 10am–6pm.

WALLCOVERINGS PREFERRED, INC./NORTH COLLEGE HILL—A good place to buy wallpaper, this independently operated store has more in-stock selection than any place around. And, it's at least 50% off regular retail. Dealing with every major brand, orders from sample books bring 30%–50% off, with a special deal on Waverly (one of the most popular names)—buy 12 rolls and receive 50% off regular retail. Co-owners Kathy Schwegman and Art Stattman have been in the business for over 18 years and place heavy emphasis on offering personalized service. The store has a loyal following and ships to customers that have moved as far away as Washington and Colorado. If you have an unusual request, don't be afraid to ask for it here. The store specializes in filling odd orders.
6829 Hamilton Avenue; 513/931-9500. Mon & Thurs 10am–9pm, Tues–Sat 10am–5pm. VS, MC.

CD WORLD/NORTHGATE—A scaled-down version of the bigger music stores, CD World may not have quantity, but it does have variety. Plug into one of the sound systems to preview a selection from rap, rock and roll, sound tracks, rhythm and blues, country, and jazz. Prices on compact discs hover at the low end (similar deals are on special orders) with greater savings on used labels.
9632 Colerain Avenue; 513/923-1223. Mon–Thurs 10am–9pm, Fri–Sat 10am–10pm, Sun noon–6pm. VS, MC, DS.

BRAZEL NOVELTY COMPANY/NORTHSIDE—On a narrow street in an old building as rugged as the neighborhood, this novelty company hides its bargains well. Many items—plastic dolls, childish trinkets, bright plush animals, smile buttons, and rubbery figurines—remind you of a prize you'd win at a carnival. Still operated by the Brazel family, the store has supplied the works for many a

Brazel Novelty Co.

community fete over its 80-year existence. Varying sizes of roulette and carnival wheels that have seen plenty of action, inexpensive streamers, crepe paper, balloons, and silk flowers are here, too.
4176 Apple Street; 513/541-1318. Mon–Fri 9:30am–4pm, Sat 9:30am–1pm. Cash or check only.

MEES TILE & MARBLE DISTRIBUTORS, INC./NORTHSIDE—The Tri-State's largest distributor of ceramic tile and marble, Mees has the works of a higher order. The showroom displays design with every shade on the palette highlighted in divided sections that delineate the look of a room. Decorative handpainted or textured ceramic tiles form colorful murals for artistic flair. Many imported varieties from Spain, Italy, and Mexico, along with some domestics, are only available around here through this distributor. There's rich-looking marble shaped into table sheets, bird baths, fireplaces, and floor coverings as well. Special orders can be filled by bringing in a picture of what you want. Look for the red tags around the showroom featuring special buys, closeouts, and discontinued ceramic tiles marked for big savings. The company has so much stock that there's a separate warehouse filled with these bargains. Find the case spotlighting an impressive display of marble board games and giftwares from Italy.
1541 W. Fork Road; 513/541-2311. Mon–Fri 7am–5pm, Sat 7am–11pm.

SHUR-GOOD BISCUIT COMPANY THRIFT STORE/ WINTON PLACE—Tucked away on the side of the Shur-Good Distributing Company, this small thrift store is crammed with Delicious and Famous Amos cookies, Snyder's pretzels, and other snack foods at irresistible prices. Although the grocery store may have *fresher* varieties, you'll pay double, even triple the price. Look for the shelf with packs of cookies priced three for $1 or brave some of the trial flavors and test products. Since these packaged foods are designed for a long shelf life, most of the items taste the same. You'll walk out with a bag full for next to nothing.
5035 Winton Road; 513/681-7200. Mon–Fri 10am–6pm. VS, MC, DS.

ASIDE **Baked goods—in fact, most consumables—have a shelf life with specific selling dates showing when they must be sold. The closer these foods come to reaching their expiration dates without being sold, the greater the chance they'll end up in a bakery thrift store. When foods are redistributed from groceries and restaurants to a thrift store they're usually reduced an average of 30%–60% off regular retail prices. The average turnaround time for these foods to be sold at the thrift store is three to four days. If the foods are not purchased, some of the leftovers are sold to area farmers to be used as feed. (Then why doesn't steak ever taste like a cinnamon roll?) Foods may end up at a thrift store that have not met the bakery's or company's quality standards. Some items may have been broken or chipped during distribution or packaged in blemished cartons. Bakery thrift stores in the Cincinnati area include: Nickles, Klosterman's, Butternut, Pepperidge Farm, Shur-Good, Dolly Madison, and Brownberry.**

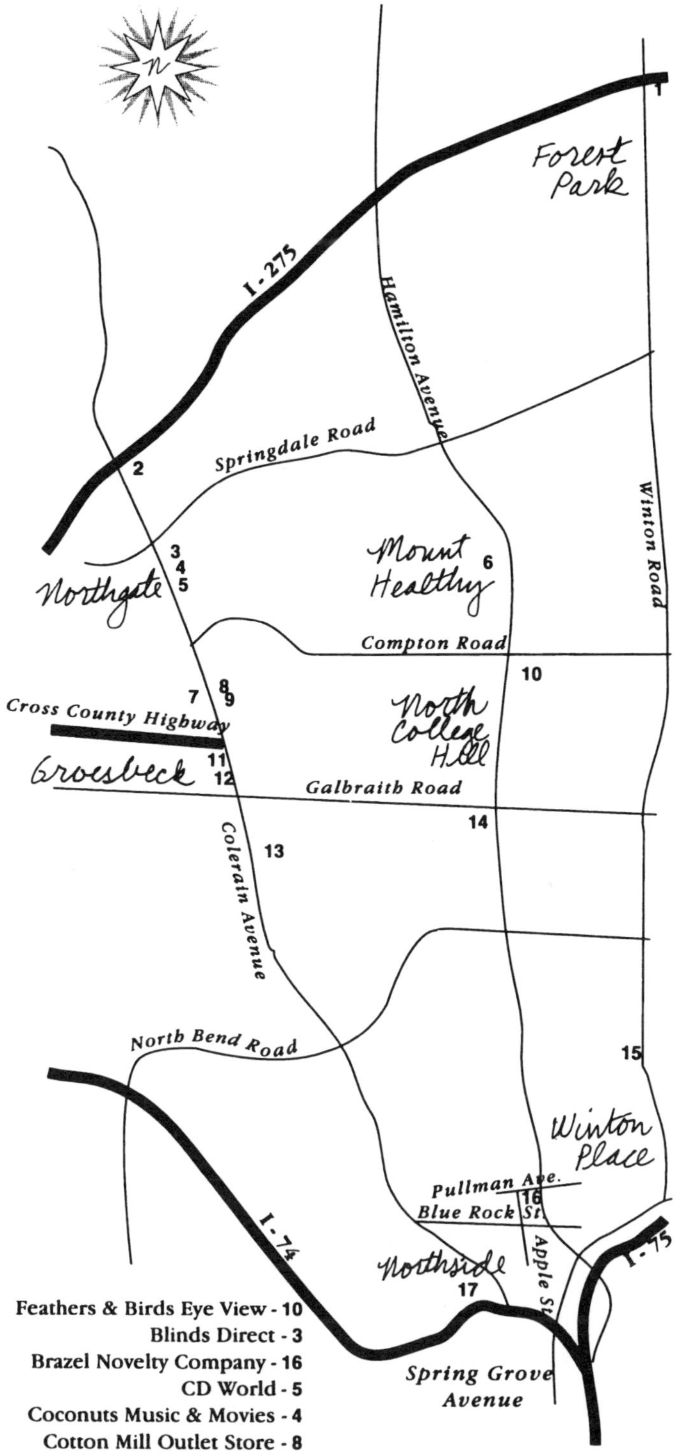

Feathers & Birds Eye View - 10
Blinds Direct - 3
Brazel Novelty Company - 16
CD World - 5
Coconuts Music & Movies - 4
Cotton Mill Outlet Store - 8
Fashion Warehouse - 12
Gentry Menswear Outlet - 11
JC Penney Catalog Outlet - 9
Macy's Close-Out Store - 1
Mees Tile & Marble Distributors, Inc. - 17
Once Upon a Child - 2
Rink's Crafts & Flea Market - 6
Shur-Good Biscuit Company Thrift Store - 15
Swallen's Outlet Store - 7
Wallcoverings Preferred, Inc - 14
Western Home Center Outlet Store - 13

Bridesmaids & More

North Central

The Millcreek Valley

Driving north on I-75 is an olfactory-induced carnival ride. Racing through the Millcreek Valley at breakneck speed, P & G leaves the smell of soap wafting through the air. The rush past other factories is uneventful until the syrupy sweet smell of a distillery elicits some adolescent moment. The mind wanders, wondering whether the workers are allowed to drink on the job. The traffic snaps you back. Another mile of sharp maneuvering and perhaps a little slipstreaming before the odor of tar and paper jiggles the sinuses. You're in Lockland. From there, it's across the bridge, which takes you over the village, past G.E. to I-275, and to the counties that lie beyond. All along this highway that bisects the area between east and west are well-worn industrial communities that are slowly turning into another cog in the rust belt. Populated by families that came north in the '40s and '50s from across the river, the towns are hard working and blue collar. Where a person was once judged by how much they could guzzle and their right cross, they are now measured by how far they can smack a softball. Living in the valley ingrains its people with street sense and teaches them the value of money. Perhaps that's why there has always been an abundance of value shopping skirting the valley.

THE BUNKBED & FURNITURE FACTORY/ARLINGTON HEIGHTS—This small, out-of-the-way store is like a miniature factory. Owner Phil Stephens might be sawing away on handpicked hardwoods or assembling the materials he personally selects. After all, he's the craftsman behind these sturdy, functional bunkbed sets and it does take time to build them right. At least that's what Phil thinks. The words *mass produced* are not in his vocabulary. He began the Bunkbed Factory after buying a set for his children only to have it quickly fall apart. His effort to replace it offered no better quality. Thus, he saw a need to construct durable, yet affordable, bunkbeds. And that's what they are. For the quality and the craftsmanship the prices are exceptional. You'll also find headboards lined up against the walls, children's furniture and futons (complete with cushions), all custom made and reasonably priced.
520 Mill Street; 513/821-1505. Mon–Fri noon–6pm, Sat 10am–2pm. Cash or check only.

BOOKS ON VINE/HARTWELL—Not much sets this store apart from the other used paperback bookstores around the city. The pricing of its well-worn selection is what you'd expect (half off the cover price). It's well organized and easy to shop. Although it runs heavy on romances, there is an adequate selection in most categories.
8376 Vine Street; 513/821-9225. Mon–Sat. 11am–6pm (unofficially open most evenings and Sunday). Cash or check only.

DISCOUNT PRODUCE/HARTWELL—A long row of vegetables line the wall, baskets hang from the ceiling, and fruit is carefully stacked in bins to make the inside of this store look like a farmer's market. Handwritten signs identifing the different varieties and prices are everywhere. A delicatessen featuring hundreds of cheeses and meats has competitive prices. Started by the Kolkmeier family 12 years ago, the company has grown to three stores. Each one is a little different. The largest one, in Hartwell, has a wine section and carries more grocery items such as real Italian pastas and some

gourmet foods. All have a spice rack featuring various seasonings for 98¢ each and offer individually wrapped candies at $1.99/lb. The main emphasis, is on discounted produce. A wide selection of fresh fruits and vegetables run 10%–15% less here than the grocery stores, and it's continuously replenished.
8425 Vine Street, Hartwell; 513/821-5335. 6147 Glenway Avenue, Westwood; 513/481-9284. 8315 Beechmont Avenue, Anderson Township; 513/474-9167. Mon–Fri 9am–8pm, Sat 9am–6pm (Anderson Twp. & Hartwell stores open later on Sat), Sun 10am–5pm. Cash or check only.

Kensington Gallery

KENSINGTON FURNITURE GALLERY/LOCKLAND—The dark interior doesn't mean the store is closed. The owner Joel Schwartz is just saving money. When you enter he'll flip on the lights to his 10,000 sq. ft. showroom. This is for the customers who like to see what they're buying. But, most of his business is through special order catalogs. A former wholesaler now open to the public, the store buys direct from over 200 manufacturers, which translates to "North Carolina prices." Customers often shop the major furniture stores to get ideas on prices and styles. They then come here and buy it for considerably less. Pay cash to avoid a surcharge.
420 W. Wyoming Avenue; 513/761-3350. Mon–Sat 10am–5pm, evenings and Sundays by appointment. VS, MC.

VILLAGE FLEA MARKET, INC./AMBERLEY VILLAGE—From the outside, the rustic barn looks like just another flea market dump.

Inside, it's unlike any other in the area. The first thing you encounter is the jungle—several aisles of overgrown tropical greenery, leafy silk trees, and potted plants. Colorful plush parrots hang on perched pedestals. There are neon signs, mugs, shot glasses, and inflatables. One booth looks like a bar. The fresh smell of soap incense cleansing the air brings you into "Mabel's Boutique." Here, a cozy couch and plush carpeting are overshadowed by glass cases displaying jewelry and statuary, as well as brightly sequined jackets (straight from Los Angeles) hanging along the walls. Find the booth with nothing but movie posters and celebrity press kits. There are antiques, collectibles, even an old-time barber's chair.
2100 Losantiville Avenue; 513/351-3151. Open year round. Sat–Sun 10am–6pm.

GOURMET KITCHEN OUTLET/WINTON PLACE—A place with some of the odds and all of the ends, Gourmet Kitchen Outlet supplies you with the look and the means to be a well equipped chef. The stark warehouse store has prices beneath the mainstream gourmet shops, but the selection is right on par. The usual kitchen appliances—breadmakers, coffeemakers, and mixers—are here. So are the hard-to-find items—ice molds, ice carving equipment, and pasta makers. For quality-seekers, Scanpan bakeware, Henckel knives, and Viking ranges are top choices. Designer chef's *clothing* is available. The store isn't hung up on doing things conventionally. Flatware and glassware can be purchased by the dozen or individually. Haggling over prices is encouraged and customers are free to wander around without being hassled by a sales person.
260 W. Mitchell Avenue; 513/542-5977. Mon–Fri 8:30am–5:30pm, Sat 9:30am–2pm. VS, MC, DS.

RESTAURANT EQUIPMENT OUTLET/WINTON PLACE—It looks like the place where restaurant equipment comes to die. A warehouse full of grease-stained wire and metal fixtures are brought here to await new life. Many are resurrected as customers from around the nation call trying to locate a certain type or part. But, much of what's available, designed for the restaurant business, is perfectly suited for home use. Often it's of superior quality and more affordable. New equipment, bar stools and signs, furniture, chairs, and tables are available, as well as bar mixes and supplies. Generic-looking glassware, trays, and utensils (the kind the restaurants use) are here, cheap. For special occasions, you can rent flatware, glassware, and cooking equipment.
260 W. Mitchell Avenue; 513/542-5900. Mon–Fri 8:30am–5:30pm, Sat 9:30am–2pm. VS, MC, DS.

The Reading Road Bargain District

Shopping has always been a big part of Reading Road. Skirting the industrial areas to the west, its main discount sections run from Swifton Commons Mall north through Roselawn, Reading, and Evendale all the way into Sharonville. The road has seen a number of bargain establishments. Some of the old-timers, such as the Glass Barn and Bargain Barn, remain. Others like Rink's Bargain City, Makro, and Fabric City have fallen victim to the changing times. When Swifton Shopping Center was completed in 1956, it was the model for regional malls, but the rush to the 'burbs left a shadow of its former self. For years, it languished in a retailing twilight zone. Now revitalized as Swifton Commons Mall, it makes its mark as a value-oriented center. ¶ Today, Reading is making a name for itself as a bridal center, but for years the troika of the Glass Barn, Fabric City, and the Bargain Barn attracted the crowds. From as far away as Dayton customers would come, wait in line to get into these stores, then head back home after grabbing a bag of burgers from White Castle across the street. For a while, Cincinnati shoppers were infatuated by Rink's Bargain City. As the store pushed its merchandise during Saturday afternoon's *Big Time Wrestling*, Rink's empire grew from its modest beginnings in Evendale to an area wide chain of discount stores. After the fall of Rink's came the first wave of buying clubs when Makro opened down the road. The store failed after a few years, but it set the stage for purchasing in bulk from warehouse-type stores. While several discount giants have come and gone, a quick survey of what is presently found along Reading Road highlights value-oriented stores found nowhere else in Cincinnati.

BARGAIN BARN/READING—Setting the standard for bare-bones discounting since 1950, the Bargain Barn has scraped away all the fat. Its unpainted cement block building, concrete floors, and utilitarian displays trim overhead. The owner and founder, George Hunt, and son Michael look for closeouts and liquidations on hardware, but most anything is likely to turn up along the aisles. George began the store by borrowing $10,000 worth of hardware

Bargain Barn

from the owner of Dayton's Bargain Barn equivalent and made $700 the first day it opened (which 45 years ago was a pile). Within a year his debt was paid back in full. Down the road, in Mason, a larger store has recently been built. Even though its appearance is upscale by Bargain Barn standards, it has the same great values, just more of them.
9204 Reading Road; 513/733-9770. 826 Reading Road, Mason; 513/398-4224. Mon–Fri 8am–8pm, Sat 8am–5pm, Sun 9am–5pm. VS, MC, DS.

GLASS BARN/READING—From the outside, the Glass Barn looks like one of those tacky, timeworn outfitters you might chance upon while driving the back roads of Tennessee. Lawn ornaments, birdbaths, and outdoor pots in every size and shape dress up the entrance. Inside, it's a free-for-all with a hodgepodge of glassware, stemware, and brassware filling the bins and shelves; wicker and baskets hanging from the ceiling; and bunches of silk flowers lining the walls. Between the concrete floors and warehouse-like building, ambiance takes a back seat. Gone are the days when nothing was ticketed and verbal price quotes were randomly applied to the goods at the counter. Today, this longtime Reading discounter of 65 years still has savings averaging 45%–50% off regular retail prices on closeouts and overruns.
9216 Reading Road; 513/733-4121. Mon–Fri 9am–9pm, Sat 9am–7pm, Sun 9am–5pm. Cash or check only.

STEINBERG'S WAREHOUSE OUTLET/READING—It isn't what it used to be when it was a true warehouse outlet. Much of the store is filled with everything from stereos and audio-visual equipment to clock radios and major home appliances priced the same as they would be at any Steinberg's store. The real values are on scratch 'n dent items, floor samples, discontinued models, and closeouts. The showroom may be crowded, but if you give yourself some room you may come away satisfied.
Sunnybrook Drive & Reading Road; 513/761-9000. Mon–Sat 10am–9pm, Sun noon–7pm. VS, MC, DS.

ELDER-BEERMAN OUTLET STORE/ROSELAWN—Anything found at the Elder-Beerman department store could show up here as clearance or overstock. Marked down at least two major times before they even make it to the outlet store, the items are sold at

hefty price reductions. Electronics and furniture are especially well priced with continuous markdowns until sold. Brand name fashions go quickly from among the large selection of family apparel. Located in the framework of what was once a lavish department store, the merchandise may not be attractively displayed, but its well marked sections include linens, housewares, health and beauty aids, and stationery. The 98¢ endings on prices indicate clearance items at final sales.
Swifton Commons Mall, 7030 Reading Road; 513/731-7400. Mon–Sat 10am–9pm, Sun noon–5pm. VS, MC, Elder Beerman.

ASIDE **What is a clearance store or liquidation center? It's a facility that offers final sales on merchandise brought in from regular retailers (such as department stores, mail order houses, and speciality stores). Inventory sold through these centers usually consists of end-of-season items, returns, broken sizes, damaged goods, and items with final markdowns. Examples of clearance or liquidation stores are Swallen's Outlet Stores, J.C. Penney Outlet Store, and Elder-Beerman Outlet Store. (Although *outlet* is mentioned in the name of these stores, they are really not considered true manufacturers' outlets.)**

ARTFORDABLE FACTORY OUTLET/EVENDALE—This store is like all the other Artfordable frame shops in Cincinnati with a few exceptions. The posters and prints that end up here are drastically reduced. Many are surplus from the other stores. Displayed in bins by topic, flipping through the discontinued, closeouts, and overstocks is a toss up. Others, out of their packages or with damaged shrink wraps, bring greater savings. These are stacked on a large table. Rolled posters are in cardboard bins. Low discount prices on closeout, overrun, and discontinued moldings sold by the foot make it affordable to frame your selections. Gallery or poster framing is another economical way.
10305 Reading Road; 513/733-9800. Mon–Sat 10am–6pm, Sun noon–5pm. VS, MC, DS, AE.

CERAMIC TILE OUTLET/EVENDALE—Home owners and do-it-yourselfers find this outlet store a source for buying quality ceramic tile at better-than-average prices—35%–40% off regular retail. Greater savings are on discontinued styles and closeouts. Owned by Margie Kennedy and Randy Stertmeyer, it's the sole outlet for their national tile distributorship, Oxford Trading Company. This outlet store doesn't dazzle you with elaborate displays. Its functional showroom features several hundred varieties of ceramic floor and wall tile, as well as marble, granite, and natural stone at prices that reflect the no-frills environment. Many are imported since the owners prefer the finer craftsmanship and materials the Italians offer, and they're in stock. So what you see is immediately available. However, special requests can be ordered. A staff well versed in the techniques of applying tile will assist you and cut your selections to exacting specifications. Tile cutting equipment is also available for rent.
McSwain Park, 2915 Glendale-Milford Road; 513/563-7122. Mon–Fri 10am–6pm, Mon & Thurs 10am–8pm, Sat 10am–4pm. VS, MC.

FACTORY DIRECT CANDLES, GLASSWARE, ETC./EVENDALE—A box full of fine crystal, a row of car mats, some packages of noodles; throw in a few Coca-Cola glasses and a case or two of candles and you have Factory Direct. Known for its great buys on closeouts from Indiana Glass and Candle-Lite, busloads of seniors, women's clubs, and special tour groups frequently pull up at its doors. Stacks and stacks of glassware and candles in cardboard boxes or on metal racks are all over the place. Holiday and seasonal items show up according to observances. Seemingly out of place displayed around the plain, functional interior, Colony's better glassware, elegant crystal stemware, wine glasses, and flutes from the manufacturer's New York showroom and warehouse are 50% off regular retail prices. Vases, lead crystal candlesticks, and ice buckets make good gifts. Marzetti's salad dressings, breadsticks, frozen pies, and chip dips are here, too. Items range from first quality and irregulars to discontinued styles, colors, and packages.
Northland Center, 10400 Reading Road; 513/733-0800. Mon–Fri 9:30am–8pm, Sat 9am–6pm, Sun/holidays noon–5pm. (Closed only for Easter, Thanksgiving, Christmas, & New Years.) VS, MC, Golden Buckeye.

PENNY PINCHERS WAREHOUSE OUTLET/EVENDALE—The same heavy, quality sheets of paper department stores use to wrap customers' packages are discounted at this factory direct outlet. A local manufacturer that furnishes wrap to these retailers supplies the outlet. Large bins are filled with eight-foot rolls normally selling for up to $3.99 each, here for $1.25. Or, buy it in smaller quantities at 25 ¢ a foot. In addition, an extensive selection of greeting cards is priced at 50% off regular retail. One wall of the store is devoted to party napkins, cutlery, and paper plates all at 50% off regular retail. Bolts of ribbon (100 yards) cost $3 and bows, balloons, and party favors are discounted.
Northland Center, 10400 Reading Road; 513/769-0666. Mon–Sat 10am–7pm, Sun noon–5pm. VS, MC, DS.

ACT 1 CINEMA/SHARONVILLE—Resist the lure of the week's most talked about movies. Avoid being herded like cattle through the multiplex. Act I Cinema gets the movies that are not too old. Most hit this screen about the time attendance at the big cinemas dwindles to a trickle. The price of $1 during the week, and $1.50 on weekends, makes it attractive for those who have the willpower to wait.
11165 Reading Road; 513/733-8214. Nightly show times 7:30pm.

BAG O' GOLD/SHARONVILLE—No department or specialty store in the city has as many unique accessories as this small shop. Loaded wall-to-wall with everything from the classic to the outlandish, your eye may be diverted by the sparkle and glitz of elegant evening bags on one shelf or the lure of rich leather handbags on another. Only the high fashion names like Sandra Roberts, Sharif, Mylinka, and Samir (the ones stores like Neiman-Marcus carry) are found here. For instance, most department stores around Cincinnati rarely stock boutique handbags. Often, owner

Barry Laffer will go directly to the manufacturers and redesign color combinations on handbags for more originality. He may request a metallic shade or tricolors of red, white, and blue instead of the standard colors. Regardless, items take immediate markdowns of 20%–30% off regular retail the minute they arrive from the manufacturer. You'd be hard pressed to find quality goods like these at any type of discount store. To breathe new life into any outfit, a stunning collection of unique belts, waist wrappers, and high-voltage costume jewelry is at this stand-alone boutique. A store that's been around for over 18 years, it has some grand finds for those who want to have the fashion edge with clever, upscale accessorizing. And, the boutique offers a few extraordinary lines of high fashion casual sportswear.
Loehmann's Plaza, 11974 Lebanon Road; 513/563-4224. Mon–Sat 10am–5:30pm. VS, MC, DS.

D & L SILKS/SHARONVILLE—Piece by piece, each tree in this 12,000 sq. ft. warehouse is hand assembled. The owners of this "fake tree factory," Dottie and Louie (D & L), buy raw materials from various suppliers around the country. Giant palm leaves may arrive one day. The makings for several ficus trees, including the woodbase trunks, may come the next. Trees range from 6–12 ft. in oriental, palm, wisteria, ficus, and even ming varieties. All are strictly made with quality silk materials for that lifelike look. The large showroom looks like a conservatory or a greenhouse. Gorgeous florals are carefully arranged in brass and ceramic pots. Hanging wall trees fill the borders of the room. Ledge gardens and hanging baskets catch you looking up. And, among the greenery, ficus roosters or ostriches can be spotted. Much of what's available is on sale. Dottie and Louie will direct you toward these items. And, if you can't find what suits you, they'll design something more to your liking. Offering the Tri-State's largest selection, it can be overwhelming to shop here. Allow plenty of time to browse. Prices are fair-minded for the quality. However, closeouts found throughout the store bring extra savings. One example of the typical savings found at D & L is in a tall, double palm tree, usually $150, priced at $99. Custom orders are no problem and you may bring in your own containers.
11711 Lebanon Road; 513/563-2329. Mon–Fri 10am–6pm, Sat 10am–5pm. (Other hours by appointment.) VS, MC—$20 minimum.

LOEHMANN'S/SHARONVILLE—Those wanting a status look without paying the higher retail markups will find it at Loehmann's. Insiders know to look for the finer, upscale fashions tucked away in the "Back Room." But, on the main floor you'll find a Sara Roberts suit, regularly $220, here, $139.99; a Carry Back French cuff blouse, regularly $64, here, $29.99; a pair of Calvin Klein hip hugger jeans, regularly $64, here, $29.99; and other designer names at 35%–60% off. The savvy shopper can easily decipher some of the items purposely missing their labels. All of the elements for adding surface interest to your outfits are in abundance—unique belts, interesting handbags, and rich-looking scarves. The open, shared dressing room with fluorescent lighting is

Loehmann's

enough to make you forget about trying on clothing. But, since the store has a strict return policy, it's best to anyway. A few men's accessories—boxer shorts, socks, robes, and gloves—are also discounted. And, designer fragrances are showcased near the checkout area. Signs around the store invite shoppers to join the "Insider Club" to receive sales event notices, coupons, and an extra 15% discount near your birthday.
Loehmann's Plaza, 11974 Lebanon Road; 513/563-4111. Mon–Sat 10am–6pm, Wed 10am–9pm, Sun noon–5pm. VS, MC, DS.

NICKLES BAKERY THRIFT STORE/SHARONVILLE—A wide variety of Nickles breads, buns, cookies, and donuts are brought here from a number of groceries, delicatessens, and restaurants to be resold at hefty savings of 30%–60% off regular retail prices. Some of the baked goods are in restaurant-size portions—huge loaves of bread big enough to feed several families, multi packages of buns with enough for now and some for storing in the freezer, and dinner rolls for big gatherings. Most are in regular portions—single loaves, six or eight pack buns, and a dozen rolls. Snack foods from other sources are on the racks, but the real buys are on Nickles own products. Goods closer to or over freshness dates bring greater savings.
3253 E. Kemper Road; 513/772-8535. Mon–Fri 9am–6pm, Sat 9am–5pm. Cash only.

The Bridal Merchants of Historic Reading

Some call it the "Bridal Capital of Ohio." Some say it's "America's Bridal District." Others don't even know it exists. And why should they? Unless planning a wedding, there's not much reason to shop Reading's Benson Street. But, if you are, you'll find everything you need within several blocks. Benson Street is the central core of a square-mile radius within the city highlighting 25 bridal-related specialty shops. Numbering around a dozen on this street, with the others on Reading and Galbraith roads, each has its own niche, complementing one another with differing facets of bridal wear and bridal service. Collectively labeled "The Bridal Merchants of Historic Reading," these individual stores occupy some of the oldest buildings along Benson. Recently given a facelift with brick sidewalks, gaslight replicas, and parking bays, the tree-lined street has a nostalgic feel. Even with the area's revitalization, these stores would not have flourished if not for the success of Bridal & Formal, Inc. This specialty discounter, one of the top five bridal salons in the country in volume and sales, is the cornerstone of activity on Benson Street. Below are some of the more value-oriented specialty shops along the street.

BRIDAL & FORMAL, INC./READING—The place is bustling. Brides-to-be with their mothers in search of that special wedding gown are captivated by the thousands of styles overstuffing the giant, industrial-size racks. All are carefully wrapped in see-through, plastic garment bags and upon first glance look the same. Not until close examination do the intricate details of each of these beautifully embellished gowns become more distinct. Some are unbelievably heavy with the thousands of beads adorning them. The store's sales approach is assembly line retailing. Customers sign in, choose six or so dresses from the racks, then wait to hear their name called over the speaker system to be assigned a sales assistant. In the background, the nonstop ringing of telephones bring constant interruptions to sales assistants filling orders from all over the country or waiting on local clientele. They're attracted by the savings (starting at 20% off regular retail prices) and the extensive selection. The wide staircase leading upstairs is filled with a rush of sales clerks and customers making their way to the racks upon racks of bridesmaids dresses. Up here, sales assistants are scurrying around the heavily mirrored fitting rooms with tape measures in one hand and pin cushions in another, while suggesting the suitable accompaniments—slips, bustiers, shoes, and, of course, the perfect veil. Clearance merchandise is found on the upper level, as well.

The store's outlet next door has nothing but off-the-rack dresses at even greater discounts. Many of these are discontinued styles.
300 W. Benson Street; 513/821-6622. Mon–Thurs noon–9pm, Fri & Sun noon–5pm, Sat 10am–5pm. VS, MC, DS.

BRIDESMAIDS & MORE/READING—Across the street from the Bridal & Formal, Inc., Bridesmaids & More (the one with the purple awning) offers a change of pace and a change in price. All bridesmaids dresses, including beautiful taffetas and sleek satins, are priced at $49 each (plush velvets are $69). Originally priced up to $249, the economical fee reflects buyouts, overstocks, samples, discontinued, and slightly imperfect styles bought directly from manufacturers. Numbering over 1,000, these off-the-rack dresses are sensibly grouped by color around the lobby of an old bank. Owner Tina Gutierrez softens the decor with her collection of framed, old-time wedding photographs hanging on the walls and delicate lace curtains lining the windows. Behind the counter, the bank's timeworn vault, minus the heavy door, safeguards customers' layaways.
307 W. Benson Street; 513/821-6505. Mon–Wed noon–7pm, Thurs–Sun noon–5pm. (Hours may vary per season.) All sales final. VS, MC.

BELLISSIMA BRIDAL ACCESSORIES/READING—Bellissima is reached by going abroad to a small European village in a charming little boutique on a side street just past the cheese shop. It isn't, of course, but it seems like it should be. Atop Bridesmaids & More, shoppers find Bellissima, which means *beautiful* in Italian, by going under a wooden trestle, down a narrow alley, and up a flight of steps. In what was the bank's executive suite, a wide selection of dainty bridal accessories is artistically contrasted among brightly

Bellissima

painted PVC pipe and plexiglass fixtures. Beautifully embellished shoes and handbags in silk shantung, peau de soie, and satin start at $24.99 (includes custom dying). Fine headpieces and veils in Italian silks, duppioni, brocade, and satin, with lace and beadwork, are ready-made or customized to match the dress. Many are under $100. Don't be fooled. For the quality, the prices are surprisingly affordable. Other items include gloves, gifts, goblets, cake servers and toppers, and unique jewelry.
307 W. Benson Street, 2nd floor; 513/821-4840. Mon & Thurs noon–8pm, Tues, Wed, Fri, & Sat 10am–5pm (Sun noon–4pm Jan, Feb, March). Appointments available.

BUDGET TUXEDO RENTAL/READING—This discount tuxedo rental service has reasonable rates ($58–$80). Inside, mannequins display traditional to contemporary styles in classic and long tail versions. Designer names like Pierre Cardin and Perry Ellis are among the top choices. A knowledgeable staff directs customers toward the most flattering fits.
305 W. Benson Street; 513/821-8838. Mon–Fri noon–7pm, Sat noon–6pm. VS, MC, DS.

Budget Tuxedo

SUGAR MAGNOLIA/READING—The small discounter is jam-packed with samples, discontinued styles, and closeouts that are at least 50% off original prices. The main emphasis is on off-the-rack bridesmaids gowns, starting at $49. Flower girl gowns are $45–$65, with custom-made styles (you supply the fabric) $95–$110. A narrow selection of bridal gowns is priced from $99–$350. It's a bit tight to maneuver around the racks, but designer names such as Jessica McClintock, Alfred Angelo, Gunne Sax, Roberta, and others make it easier to find your way. Keep in mind your choices are hit or miss here since the selection, dictated by manufacturers' discards, constantly varies. Some veils and accessories are available, as well as the owner's wearable art creations.
17 W. Benson Street; 513/761-4696. Mon–Fri 3–8pm, Sat 10am–5pm (Sun noon–4pm Jan–May 15).

THE WEDDING SHOPPE/READING—The shop has the accessories to fill a bride's order and offers services to plan the wedding event. But, the best values found at the Wedding Shoppe are on some of the necessary essentials like shoes and invitations—Color Match pumps at $30 a pair (includes dying) with an extra 10% discount for wedding parties and wedding invitations from every major line are priced at 25% off regular prices.
8 W. Benson Street; 513/821-4424. Mon, Tues, Fri, & Sat noon–5pm, Thurs noon–7pm. VS, MC, DS.

TALK OF THE TOWN & CASABLANCA/READING—Vintage shops offer an alternative to paying higher prices on new clothes while creating a nostalgic wedding affair. Talk of the Town has a small collection of vintage wedding gowns and accessories. Casablanca has tuxedos, suits, and accessories from the 1920s through the 1960s, for the groom. Rentals are also available at both places. *Talk of the Town, 9019 Reading Road; 513-563-8844. Tues–Sat 11am–6pm. VS, MC, DS. Casablanca, 9001 Reading Road; 513/733-8811. Mon–Fri 11am–6pm, Sat 11am–5pm. VS, MC, DS.*

Tri-County Shopping District

Drive around here when fully rested, in a good mood, after a light meal, and with a bottle of aspirin. Tri-County is Cincinnati's shopping hub and not a place for the timid. Its centrality and easy accessibility off of I-275 and I-75 make it a prime retailing location. Tri-County Mall is the nucleus of activity. Over the years, the mall has gone through a metamorphosis from its primitive stage as a single-level, open-air facility to one with an enclosure. In its full maturity, recent expansions have transformed it into a sprawling, two-story mall adorned with synchronized fountains, a glass elevator, and cosmetic imagery. As the mall grew so did everything around it. Boasting the highest consumer traffic in the city, the mall has brought an invasion of mass merchandising chains, specialty shops, off-price stores, and cut-rate discounters to the area. And, just when you thought retail had reached its peak in this highly congested area, another discount mall, Tri-County Commons, has added fire to the shopping scene. Along the main thoroughfares, Kemper Road and Princeton Pike, everything is in continuous motion as non-stop shoppers and a surplus of cars make their way to the countless stores. The effect is a bit disorienting since there are so many. However, the advantage of shopping here is that every type of retailer known to mankind is within close proximity to one another. So it's easy to blow your budget. ¶ North on 747 (Princeton Pike), growth spurts have overloaded this area.

With strip malls, convenience stores, and industrial parks shooting up on every corner, the traffic during peak times virtually slows down almost to a halt. To add to the problem, it's inevitable that while venturing up this street a freight train will stop you either coming or going. Though retailing has grown almost beyond capacity within Tri-County's generative shopping grounds, discounters and regular price stores find themselves going through continuous growing pains trying to keep up with the competition.

BURLINGTON COAT FACTORY/LUXURY LINENS/BABY ROOM/ SPRINGDALE—It's not just a place to buy coats. About half of the store's sales are on other apparel, accessories, and shoes. The coats are, however, what brings 'em in. Where the typical department stores might carry no more than 2,000 coats, Burlington claims to have about 15,000 at prices lower than department and specialty stores. Starting as an outerwear wholesaler in 1924, it became a full-fledged retailer in 1972 after buying a Burlington, New Jersey, coat

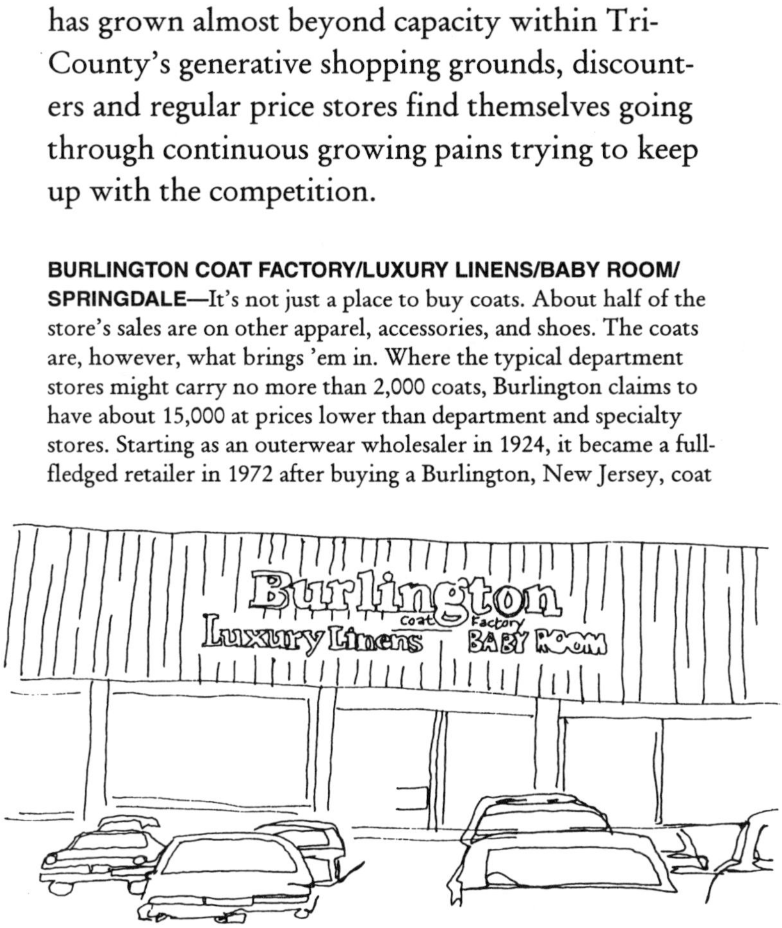

factory and an outlet store. Today, it has over 200 stores, but only one in Cincinnati. Later came Luxury Linens, a separates section of the store devoted to selling brand name bed and bath linens—Martex, Cannon, Springmaid, and Utica—at 20%–50% off department store prices. Another section, Baby Room, features infants' and toddlers' wear, everyday essentials, and larger functional items such as strollers, car seats, and walkers at competitive prices. A complete line of children's furniture is exceptionally well priced. *485 E. Kemper Road; 513/671-3111. Mon–Fri 10am–9:30pm, Sun 11am–6pm. VS, MC, DS, AE.*

BROWNBERRY OVENS BAKERY OUTLET/SPRINGDALE—On the main drag just north of Tri-County Mall, it's hard to drive by this bakery thrift store without stopping. A large bright, green sign—*Brownberry Breads and Buns 50% off*—catches your eye, and before you know it you're in for a bagful. A large variety, more than any grocery store, fills the racks—wheat, rye, bran, 12-grain, raisin, apple honey, cinnamon raisin, orange walnut, and on and on. Other brands on the shelves are Eagle snacks, Mueller's noodles and pastas, and a mix of the lesser knowns. For the health conscious,—Frookies cookies and Health Valley products are available. Individual-size packages of snacks and chips, four for a dollar or 30¢ each, are here, too. Items are taken off the floor before going over freshness due dates.
Crescentville Square, 12179 Princeton Road; 513/671-8520. Mon–Fri 9am–6pm, Sat 9am–4pm. Cash or check only.

CINCINNATI COMPUTER STORE/SPRINGDALE—One of the area's oldest computer dealers, it carries over 35,000 items available from major vendor partners like IBM, Apple, Compaq, NEC, Hewlett Packard, Intel, and others too numerous to list. Most are in stock at the company's 100,000 sq. ft. warehouse and include computer systems, monitors, peripherals, accessories, supplies, network hardware and software, scanners, and printers. The showroom in the main office and Kenwood store highlight many. The advantage of shopping here is in the service. It has one of the best service departments in the city. Experienced computer veterans skillfully guide customers through the complex maze of computer equipment. The staff freely offers sound advice. So, in a sense, you save by receiving solid recommendations. However, if you're looking for *greater* values ask them about their selection of surplus, refurbished, and recycled systems. In a business where equipment changes faster than last season's fashions, much of what is out-of-date for one person's needs may fit well into another's. Money-saving options are available here and the staff is perfectly willing to set you up with a system whether you need the latest state-of-the-art equipment or last year's model. All of it depends on what's in stock at the time, so it doesn't hurt to inquire about the alternatives.
149 Northland Boulevard; 513/772-6000, FAX 513/772-8329. Mon–Fri 9:30am–6pm, Sat 10am–5pm. 7338 Kenwood Road, Kenwood; 513/793-8200. Mon–Fri 10am–6pm, Wed 10am–8pm, Sat 10am–5pm. VS, MC, DS, AE.

DAN HOWARD'S MATERNITY FACTORY OUTLET/SPRINGDALE — First-quality maternity wear (no seconds or damaged goods) is uncovered at this true manufacturer's outlet at greatly discounted prices, many 50% off and more. It's an excellent source for up-to-date fashions, as well as the basics—lingerie, undergarments, nursing bras, and hard-to-find nursing pajamas and nightgowns. In the area for over 18 years, the outlet is one of over 100 in the United States and Canada owned and operated by Dan Howard, one of the the largest family-owned manufacturers in the country.
Burlington Mall, 465 E. Kemper Road; 513/671-2102. Mon–Sat 10am–6pm, Wed & Thurs 10am–8pm, Sun noon–5pm. VS, MC, DS, AE.

Dan Howard's Maternity Factory Outlet

FASHION SHOP/SPRINGDALE—While mother scans the Alfred Dunner rack, daughter tries on Guess jeans. Both will find what suits their tastes here. The store has a broad assortment of misses' and juniors' fashions—anything from classic, famous name career wear to trendy, off-brand casuals. You'll never pay regular retail here. Long clearance racks in the back are jammed full of bargains that will make you drool. Much of the store's merchandise—apparel, accessories, hats, and shoes—is sold at a low margin. The store makes its profit by selling in volume. Discounters for over 60 years, this family-owned company (based in Louisville) has 16 stores in the Midwest, but only one in Cincinnati. Join the Savvy Shopper's Club for advance sales notices, special promotions, and birthday privileges.
Princeton Plaza, 11711 Princeton Pike; 513/671-3456. Mon–Sat 10am–9pm, Sun noon–5:30pm. VS, MC, DS.

Fashion Shop

GENTRY MEN'S CLOTHIER/SPRINGDALE—Its evokes the image of a sophisticated English haberdashery, but it was started here in Cincinnati. For 50 years Gentry has been selling better label men's apparel. The first store was located Downtown, then later moved to Swifton Commons Mall. Now, Gentry has grown to 20 stores across the Midwest, five in Cincinnati. In 1969, the company began its off-price concept where famous name suits, sport coats, sportswear, and accessories average 30%–40% off regular retail prices. With its huge inventory (over 4,000 suits per store) Gentry has more options than most retailers. Sales assistants are not scarce here, either. They'll work with you to match up shirts and ties and see that you're fitted properly. A master tailor is on hand at every store so immediate alterations can be made at a nominal fee. A wide size range, from 36 short to 54 extra long, makes it easy to be fitted. While most would expect this discounter to lack ambiance, the stores are surprisingly appealing and offer a comfortable setting. *Gentry TriCentre, 11489 Princeton Road; 513/772-3000. 6475 E. Galbraith Road, Kenwood; 513/791-9800. Beechmont Mall, 7500 Beechmont Avenue, 513/232-7500. Florence Square, 7701 Mall Road, Florence, Kentucky; 606/282-6000. Mon–Sat 10am–9pm*, Sun noon–6pm. (*Tri-County & Kenwood stores open until 7pm on Sat.) See Northwest District for Gentry Menswear Outlet. VS, MC, DS.*

BLACK & DECKER FACTORY STORE/SHARONVILLE—A Saturday afternoon spent watching *This Old House* or *Yankee Workshop* can inspire even the most hard core couch potato. But no matter what project you take on, the city's only Black & Decker factory store is loaded with a wide variety of power tools and appliances you may need. Generic boxes mean the products inside are reconditioned or discontinued. These go for 15% off regular retail prices. Items in blemished cartons bring some extra savings. In addition, there is a full range of new products, but at no real price advantage. All products have full warranties. So why overpay? Besides, chances are the ones you buy will end up collecting spider webs in the garage. *2310 E. Sharon Road; 513/772-3111. Mon–Thurs 8am–5pm, Fri 9am–5pm, Sat 9am–4pm. VS, MC, DS.*

CD WAREHOUSE/SHARONVILLE—Stocking the best sellers and most current hits, this small shop may not have as deep selection as the superstores, but its prices fair well. Picks from the top ten list, priced at $10.99 each, are excellent buys. A big portion of the store is devoted to over 6,000 used compact discs. All are fully guaranteed and offer greater savings when compared to buying them new. Special requests can be filled within two days.
1657 E. Kemper Road; 513/772-3472. Mon–Fri 11am–8pm, Sat 11am–6pm, Sun noon–5pm. VS, MC.

DISCOUNT CARPET OUTLET/SHARONVILLE—It pays to do your homework before shopping this discounter. If you have a specific style and color of carpet in mind and have researched pricing, you'll be better equipped to know the real deals (some with substantial savings of anywhere from $5–$10 a yard). Others may not be that much better than buying through the regular distributors. This large warehouse facility houses over 1,000 carpets, mostly in full rolls that are stretched across the floor stacked one upon another. It doesn't take a genius to see that this building serves a dual purpose—as a warehouse and retail outlet for one of the well-known distributors in the city. The trucks parked out back will clue you in on which one. However, after figuring it out, don't tell

anyone; it's supposed to be a secret. With its more extensive in-stock collection, one of the workers compared the warehouse to a cash 'n carry pony keg where do-it-yourselfers can instantly pick up carpeting and take it home (all that's needed is the room's measurements). Professional installation services are also available. Overall, the better-known carpeting found here is offered for less simply because it is sold out of a warehouse.
2430 E. Kemper Road; 513/326-4261. Mon–Fri 10am–9pm, Sat 9:30am–5pm. VS, MC.

K & G MEN'S MART/SHARONVILLE—Copying the "weekend warrior" concept popular in New York, K & G sells menswear out of its 20,000 sq. ft. showroom only during peak, weekend shopping times. Half the store is filled with over 8,000 suits and sport coats marked down as much as 60%. The rest is devoted to shirts, sportswear, shoes, and athletic wear. The merchandise is well stocked and easily accessible. It's no-frills merchandising at its finest featuring brands you know like John Henry, Levi's, Ralph Lauren, Adidas, and Rockport.
2430 E. Kemper Road; 513/326-5400. Fri 10am–8pm, Sat 10am–7pm, Sun noon–6pm, VS, MC, DS, AE.

Act 1 Cinema - **16**
Artfordable - **19**
Bag 'O Gold - **3**
Bargain Barn - **34**
Bellissima Bridal Accessories - **26**
Black & Decker - **17**
Blinds Direct - **4**
Books on Vine - **23**
Bridal & Formal, Inc. - **27**
Bridesmaids & More - **28**
Brownberry Ovens Bakery Outlet - **1**
Budget Tuxedo Rental - **29**
The Bunkbed & Furniture Factory - **24**
Burlington Coat Factory - **11**
Casablanca - **32**
CD Warehouse - **12**
Ceramic Tile Outlet - **18**
Cincinnati Color Company - **6**
Cincinnati Computer Store - **7**
Cotton Mill Outlet Store - **37**
D & L Silks - **5**
Dan Howard's Maternity Outlet - **10**
Discount Carpet Outlet - **14**
Discount Produce - **22**
Elder-Beerman Outlet Store - **39**
Factory Direct Candles, Glassware - **20**
Fashion Shop - **8**
Gentry Men's Clothier - **9**
Glass Barn - **35**
Gourmet Kitchen Outlet - **43**
J.J. Newberry's - **40**
K & G Men's Mart - **13**
Kensington Furniture Gallery - **25**
Klosterman's Bakery Outlet - **41**
Loehmann's - **2**
Nickles Bakery Thrift Store - **15**
Penny Pinchers Warehouse - **21**
Restaurant Equipment Outlet - **42**
Steinberg's Warehouse Outlet - **36**
Sugar Magnolia - **30**
Talk of the Town - **33**
Village Flea Market, Inc. - **38**
The Wedding Shoppe - **31**

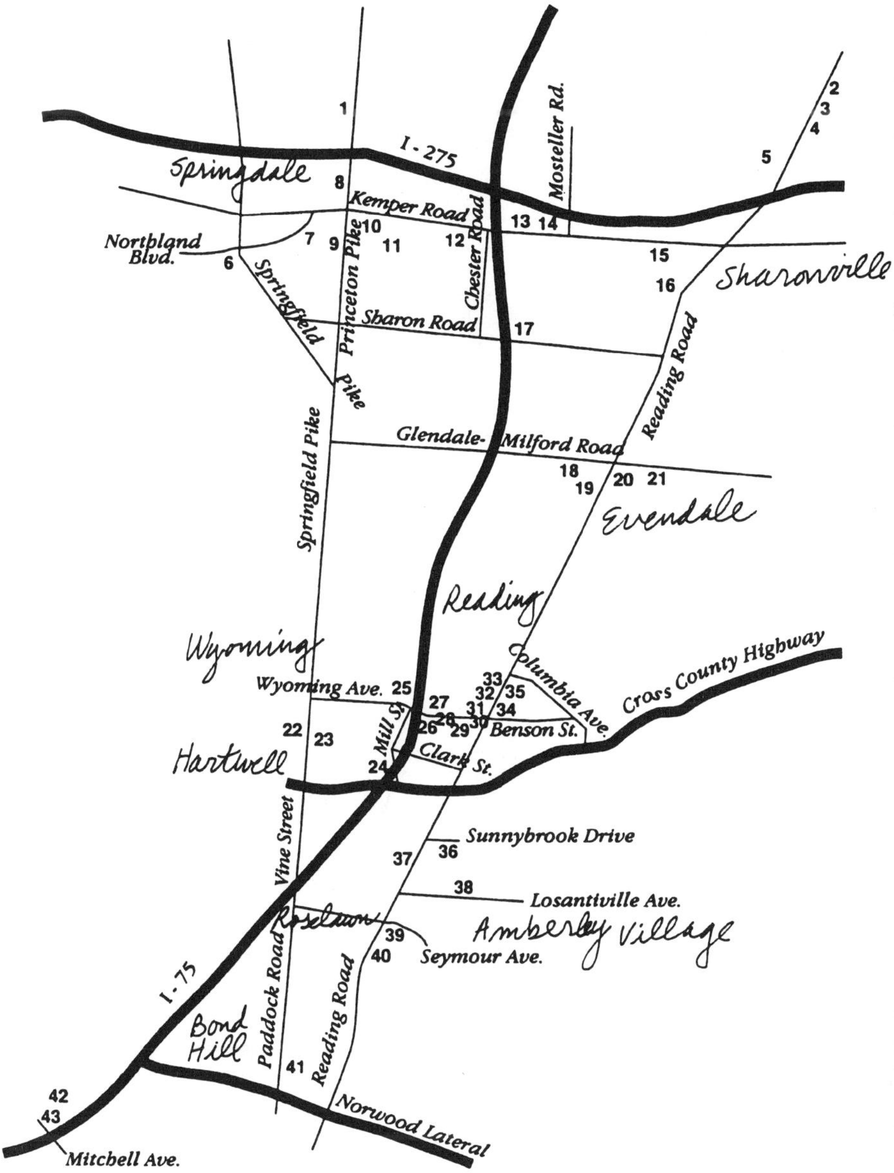
I-275
Springdale
Kemper Road
Mosteller Rd.
Northland Blvd.
Springfield Pike
Princeton Pike
Chester Road
Sharon Road
Sharonville
Reading Road
Glendale-Milford Road
Evendale
Reading
Wyoming
Wyoming Ave.
Columbia Ave.
Cross County Highway
Mill St.
Benson St.
Clark St.
Hartwell
Sunnybrook Drive
Losantiville Ave.
Vine Street
Roselawn
Amberley Village
Seymour Ave.
I-75
Paddock Road
Bond Hill
Norwood Lateral
Mitchell Ave.
1
2
3
4
5
6
7
8
9
10
11
12
13
14
15
16
17
18
19
20
21
22
23
24
25
26
27
28
29
30
31
32
33
34
35
36
37
38
39
40
41
42
43

Jungle Jim's

North

Not long ago, a venture north beyond I-275 was for a ride in the country and to see places where people shucked corn and hurled cow chips. For better or worse, that's changed. Where pastoral barns once stood, now sit back-to-back subdivisions and housing developments. Roads that not long ago saw only tractors, now see a progression of Ford Broncos and Audi sedans. Greater Cincinnati's urban sprawl runs from Downtown Cincinnati right up to Downtown Hamilton. Not much characterizes Hamilton from other midsize Midwestern cities. Located on the Great Miami River it was the site of Fort Hamilton during the Indian campaigns of the late 1700s. The town's growth was stimulated by its proximity to the Miami and Erie Canal. Thus, it became an important commercial and industrial center. At one point, Hamilton was the home of one of the nation's largest paper companies. The Downtown area was a vibrant shopping district that served the needs of this largely blue-collar community. Now many of its retailers and department stores have disappeared. The Downtown is struggling to find its role while this part of the Dixie Highway strip (State Route 4) has become run down. The recent attempt to spark up the city's image by putting an "!" after its name has had little effect. South of Hamilton, Fairfield has a thriving commercial district. Filling most of the area between Hamilton and I-275, it's become a popular bedroom community with easy access to major highways and shopping areas (Tri-County and Northgate). ¶ Nestled in a notch between I-75, I-71, and I-275, Mason has grown out of its sleepy farm town image. No longer considered the "boonies," the farm land is quickly being converted to subdivisions, office complexes, and light industry. Strip malls and fast food establishments crowd the interstate exits surrounding the town. A little further north is Monroe. It's probably no coincidence that midway between Cincinnati and Dayton, in this rural community, are located two of the Tri-State's largest flea markets.

JUNGLE JIM'S INTERNATIONAL FARMER'S MARKET/FAIRFIELD—Jungle Jim's is a safari hunt for food. Pass by the jungle of fake giraffes and apes at the entrance of the Quonset hut. Now you're in a 75,000 sq. ft. facility that takes you grocery shopping by crossing several continents and time zones. Clocks over the cigar store tick away the strokes in international two-steps. The market sells the traditional grocery staples, but offers a much larger variety of specialty foods than most superstores. It boasts Ohio's largest beer and wine department featuring Jungle Jim's reserve cellar wines, and it has a liquor store. There's an inviting cappuccino bar where you can leave your cart and pull up a bar stool to sip one of the tempting selections of gourmet coffees. A huge delicatessen with imported meats and cheeses from around the world (ask for samples), homemade salads, and vegetable trays made up daily is one of the busier spots in the market. Next to it is an imported olive bar and a spice rack with gourmet varieties. By now you are only half way through the store and it's about time for the

mechanical ape dressed like Elvis to belt out a few numbers. He does this in regular 15-minute intervals over by the international foods department. Around here you can also look for the apes floating in small row boats over the smelly, iced-up seafood cases. A butcher will cut fresh chicken and yell for special cuts of meats. But perhaps what Jungle Jim's is best known for is its fresh fruits and vegetables. It's the Tri-State's largest produce market. After all, this is how Jungle Jim himself (James Bonaminio) got his start in the business. He sold fresh tomatoes out of his van years ago after he and his college buddies brought some back from spring break. The police even chased him out of Fairfield. But, that didn't stop him. Later he set up a stand in Hamilton and eventually bought his own lot right in Fairfield. Today, this is where his international market stands, and although the place may carry on with a lot of monkey business, it still has the freshest foods and the widest variety at reasonable rates.
5440 Dixie Highway-State Route 4; 513/829-1919. Mon–Sat 8am–10pm, Sun 9am–9pm. VS, MC, DS. ☆

Army Store Military & Factory Surplus

ARMY STORE GOVERNMENT & FACTORY SURPLUS/FAIRFIELD—The collection of world flags and Desert Storm window graphics identify this army surplus store. But the best things inside aren't for sale. Scattered around the store among the usual surplus trinkets and fatigues are some interesting items you don't want to miss. A test bomb that looks like it's been fired is in the back. A giant boot fills part of the front window. A huge pair of jeans that looks like they could outfit an entire platoon hangs from the ceiling. And, two miniature dolls—one of Gen. Colin Powell, the other of Gen. Norman Schwarzkopf—stand watch over the military treasures in the display case. With new merchandise

constantly arriving, the store is loaded with army surplus goods from the clothing to the gadgets (minus the weapons). It's quirky enough to just come and look around.
4836 Dixie Highway-State Route 4; 513/829-7888. Jan–Mar Mon–Sat 10am–6pm; April–Dec Mon–Fri 10am–8pm, Sat 10am–7pm. VS, MC, DS.

THE ORIGINAL MATTRESS FACTORY/FAIRFIELD—The Original Mattress Factory is original in its marketing concept. Where else could you shop for a mattress and view the one you want being made from an observation deck in a factory showroom? As the former president of Ohio-Sealy Mattress Co. (the world's largest bedding company), Ron Trzcinski brought with him a lot of expertise and brain power when he founded this venture. You might say he has awakened a success story while his competitors still remain asleep on their mattresses doing things the old way. The factory-direct retail operation is based in Cleveland and now has three factories in Ohio including this one. Customers can choose from over 11 different models of mattresses ranging from twin to king sizes and are encouraged to tour this 19,000 sq. ft facility. By eliminating the middleman and selling direct to the customer, prices are kept at least 30%–50% less than comparable brands. The factory makes about 25 mattresses a day. All are hand-crafted with quality materials and Amish-built foundations. Customers can place an order, have it made and delivered within 48 hours. The factory also fills custom orders for odd-size beds including those for campers and antique frames.
Fairfield Business Center, State Route 4; 513/860-9988. Factory Outlet Stores, 700 Eastgate South Drive, Suite 160; 513/752-6600. 7653 Mall Road, Florence; 606/647-7776. Mon–Fri 10am–9pm (Fairfield store opens at 9am), Sat 10am–6pm, Sun noon–6pm. VS, MC, DS, AE.

PARKS ATTIC KIDS' RESALE STORE/FAIRFIELD—The compact shop makes use of its space. Even though the racks and shelves are loaded with children's goods, it's still manageable and easy to shop. The consignment store has a good selection of famous name apparel for kids (newborn to size 14) and much of the necessary equipment—strollers, car seats, carriers—to make life easier for parents. Accessories, tights, and shoes are here to complement the goods. Occasionally decorative items such as wall hangings and drapes will show up on display.
6560-F Dixie Highway-State Route 4; 513/870-9777. Mon–Thurs 11am–5pm, Fri & Sat 11am–4pm. VS, MC.

THE BOOK SHOP/HAMILTON—The writing on this former drugstore window still says "Drug Center" but there's not much else to distinguish this used paperback book store. The selection leans heavily toward romance novels, and books are priced at half off the cover price. The best values are on the few hardback books available. They are former best sellers priced lower than most of the paperbacks.
1018 Main Street; 513/887-2999. Mon, Tues, Thurs, & Sat 10am–6pm, Wed 10am–7pm. Cash only.

C. DATTILO COMPANY/HAMILTON—This produce wholesaler sells largely to schools, nursing homes, and restaurants but also operates a small retail store where the public can buy fresh fruits and vegetables. The good thing about this store is that you can buy quantities as small as a single item to larger amounts at wholesale prices. Fruit baskets can be made up anytime.
207 S. Third Street; 513/863-1991. Mon–Fri 7am–4pm, Sat 7am–1pm. Cash or check only.

ASIDE **It's not uncommon for produce distributors to receive their goods from all over the world. Many types of fresh fruits and vegetables are continuously shipped into these businesses via common carriers or trucking companies. Most of these distributors are concentrated Downtown around Pete Rose Way, Plum Street, and Central Avenue in an area which used to be known as the Bottoms. A good number of them also offer walk-in service to the general public. Customers must arrive during the times trucks are being loaded to buy the produce. This can be as early as 4am and ends around noon. The produce, which is usually much fresher than what's available in the stores, can only be bought in bulk by the case or bag. A much bigger selection of fruits and vegetables is also available at these companies, with different varieties that often cannot be bought anywhere else in the city as part of the normal offerings. While it may be hard to imagine making use of an entire case or bulk quantity of these fruits or vegetables you can save considerably when you take a look at the price you would have to pay per item anywhere else. Customers who buy produce this way will often share the case and the cost with friends or relatives. Wholesale distributors around Cincinnati include: Caruso-Ciresi, Castellini, Crossett, C. Dattilo, Flatlow-Riley, Fries Brothers, M. Degaro, and Gentille Brothers.**

HAMILTON WINDOW AND DOOR MANUFACTURERS, INC/ HAMILTON—The small company, in business since 1955, is buried in the heart of Hamilton and manufactures its own storm doors. With nine styles and three colors (black, white, or bronze) to choose from almost every need can be met. The custom-made, heavy duty doors are fully weather-stripped and feature a full-length piano or continuous hinge. For the quality, the doors are priced reasonably. A Full-Lite glass/screen door can be picked up for $196.50, and for an extra $60 they will deliver and install it. The company also acts as a distributor for replacement windows, offering competitive prices on merchandise and installation.
709 Central Avenue; 513/867-1099. Mon–Fri 8:30am–5pm. Cash or check.

MATHIS FABRIC CENTER/HAMILTON—Charles and Viola Mathis started their business by doing small decorating jobs. First, they did upholstering and made draperies for their own home. Others admired their work and they found themselves doing the same thing for neighbors and friends. After a while they had so many requests they eventually opened their own shop in 1966 and called it Mathis Fabrics. It now has one of the largest in-stock selections of decorator and upholstering fabrics in the Cincinnati area. Viola herself remembers counting up to 5,000 fabric bolts in the store one time, but gave up after that. Lined up along the aisles and walls the bolts fill in much of the selling space. The in stock fabrics, at 50% off the order price, are bought directly from the mills and manufacturers. A remnant room has fabric priced as marked, and a $2 per yard rack offers good buys. Various trims and sewing notions, as well as hard-to-find upholstering and caning supplies, are found here. A section featuring automotive carpeting and seat materials is found near the back. Wallpaper can be ordered from sample books at 10% discounts. Though the store has grown over the years it hasn't lost its small-time "mom and pop" feel. The owners still custom make draperies and hang them for customers without charging decorator fees.
5174 Middletown-Hamilton Road; 513/894-1396. Mon 9:30am–8pm, Tues, Thurs, & Sat 9:30am–5:30pm.

COTTON MILL FACTORY OUTLET/HAMILTON—Leshner's three textile mills in the South produce over 396,000 pounds of towels a week. The company sells these products nationally and internationally. But, it got its humble start in the Cincinnati area when Nathan Leshner emigrated to Hamilton in the early 1900s. He made his living in the new world by gathering waste material via horse and wagon. Later, his company expanded into sorting rags and became a major importer of hair and felt from his homeland—Russia. Eventually, the company grew to be a main supplier of waste paper and rags to industrial mills. During World War II, it grew to be the largest supplier of wiping cloths to the Armed Forces. Today, the company manufactures kitchen and bath towels and operates 15 Cotton Mill Outlet stores in Ohio and Indiana. Converted from one of the company's manufacturing plants, the Cotton Mill store on Hamilton's Central Avenue is the original

outlet. All of the outlets carry a broad mix of Leshner's products—plush towels, wash and dish cloths, bath sheets, pot holders, and oven mitts—at factory-direct prices. Other linens—comforters, bed spreads, pillows, mattress pads, and draperies—are also sold here at reduced prices, as are printed beach towels featuring popular themes (even those with Elvis). Greater savings are on irregulars and seconds.
Central Avenue & Leshner, Hamilton; 513/868-6700. Beechmont Plaza, 540 Ohio Pike, Cherry Grove; 513/528-6065. 7617 Reading Road, Roselawn; 513/948-0264. 673 Loveland-Maderia Road, Loveland; 513/677-8922. 3232 Roosevelt Boulevard, Middletown; 513/241-2524, 8780 Colerain Avenue, Grosbeck; 513/923-3555. Mon–Fri 9:30am–8pm, Sat 9:30am–6pm, Sun 10am–5pm. VS, MC, DS.

PEASE WAREHOUSE OUTLET, INC./HAMILTON—The setting looks like a scene out of a bad detective movie. The warehouse crowds the dead-end street, making parking scarce. Customers enter after climbing up steps leading onto a loading dock. Inside, the three gloomy rooms house various building materials. One room is filled with interior and exterior doors. Solid pine doors up to 36" wide can be purchased for $40–$60, while hollow-core birch or oak veneer doors go for $8–$13. Strewn around another room are kitchen cabinets and vanities of various shapes and styles. A third smaller room is stacked with panel shutters ($12–$15 a pair) and cabinet doors (any size $5 each). Much of what is here is unfinished, surplus, or slightly flawed, but if you pick around you might find what you need. Remember, everything is sold "as is" and all sales are final.
2585 Zimmerman Avenue; 515/867-3195. Tues & Thurs 8am–5pm, Sat 8am–1pm. VS, MC, DS.

CORT FURNITURE RENTAL CLEARANCE CENTER/WEST CHESTER—Under the hanging fluorescent lights at this clearance center showroom you'll find sofas, love seats, end tables, chairs, and office furniture. That's because much of it's the same type of furniture and accent pieces you see in model homes, showrooms, or office lounges. The difference is the pieces that show up here have been previously rented out by Cort Furniture and are now marked down to 30%–70% off original prices (generally averaging 50% off). Surprisingly, much of the merchandise looks like new. Some of the hardwoods like shelving units, dinette sets, and desks need a few minor touch ups, but most are in excellent condition. The type of deals made here are compared to the new prices. A gray salesman desk if bought new would sell for $299.95. Here it's $149. A Lifestyle sofa and love seat would normally sell for $999.95 if bought new. Here they're $549. A signed, double-matted print, usually $139, goes here for $79. A large, metal storage cabinet, if bought new, would run $219.95. Here it's $129. Though this showroom doesn't have as deep a variety as most major furniture suppliers, for those who don't mind purchasing previously rented furniture, it's an excellent source for saving money.
7400 Square Court; 513/777-6104. Mon–Fri 9am–6pm, Sat 10am–5pm. VS, MC.

FOUR SEASONS GARMENT FACTORY OUTLET STORE/MASON—One of the clues this is a true manufacturer's outlet is that the store is actually located at the factory. Items such as jackets are made here, but the company also does commercial embroidering and screen printing on apparel. The small store that now shares its space with its sister company (a billiard supplier) is one of the better places to pick up a custom-sewn nylon jacket (with or without thermal lining) at an exceptional price, often as low as $4–$9. But, the bargains don't stop here. Other items are sold at low factory-direct prices. Sports caps, visors, and short sleeve tee-shirts are normally $1–$2 each but can go for as little as 50¢–75¢. Long sleeve tee-shirts and heavyweight sweatshirts are priced up to $5–$7 each. Lightweight sweatshirts and golf shirts average $2–$4. Several of the items have some type of printing or logo on them. However, plain shirts are also plentiful and, for a little more, can be decorated with your choice of graphics. A bargain section features slightly irregular jackets priced way below their original cost. These can be found in the separate room toward the side. Some are hanging on racks. Others are tossed in cardboard boxes. Some of the best buys are made by rummaging through the deep bargain bins (usually marked by handwritten price signs). It may take some digging, but there's a good chance you'll come up with something. Items range from first-quality overruns and discontinued merchandise to irregulars and misprints. Most garments are sized for adults with some youth sizes as well. Overall, the store is an excellent source for "hack-around" activewear at next-to-nothing prices. In fact, it's not uncommon to come out with an armful for less than $20.
1111 Western Row Road; 513/398-3695. Mon 8:30am–5pm, Tues–Fri 8:30am–6:30pm, Sat 10am–3pm. VS, MC.

KLOSTERMAN BAKERY OUTLET STORES/MASON—A longtime staple in the bakery business, Klosterman's has been supplying the local food industry with breads and related products for over a century. Kim Klosterman recalls stories of her great-great-uncle starting the business by delivering fresh baked French breads and rolls on foot to Downtown restaurants. Today, the business has grown to be the premium supplier of fresh baked breads in the Cincinnati area. It now has eight bakery outlets (four in the Cincinnati area). The outlets carry a wide selection of day-old breads in the popular varieties—from wheat, rye, sour dough, and enriched white to sandwich buns, hot dog buns, and rolls—at hefty savings. An example of the kind of savings found here comes in buying white bread. Normally sold in the grocery for $1.59 a loaf, you can buy four loaves for $1. The best part about the outlet (other than the prices) is the selection. A section with fresh baked breads from Klosterman's restaurant line of products includes French breads, croissants, rice sticks, and other multi-grain varieties not available at the grocery. Assorted snacks, soft drinks, and snack cakes are available. A great place for filling large orders for special events or fund raisers.
1130 Reading Road, Mason; 513/398-2707. 5000 Paddock Road, Bond Hill; 513/242-9551. 934 Main Street, Hamilton; 513/863-3232. 5814 Madison Road, Madisonville; 513/561-8308. Mon–Sat 9am–5pm. Some store hours may vary slightly. Cash or check. Buckeye card.

AVOID SHOPPERS' PARALYSIS **Watch for the misuse of regular pricing. This is where doing your homework really pays. By familiarizing yourself with the regular or original price of the brand name items you're interested in, you'll be better able to determine whether you're receiving the best possible deal. When you see an item marked "regularly $159.99, now $69," the regular price could be what the item has been briefly and legitimately listed at between sales or it could be a false price that is suggested by the manufacturer. Don't be fooled into purchasing the item if you're uncertain about the real savings you'd be receiving. If you have seen the item priced for more at other stores, then this is a tremendous buy. However, if this item is available at a store you're not used to shopping, you may want to compare prices before you make your selections. Most retail establishments that offer straightforward savings on merchandise will encourage their customers to shop around and compare prices. They truly want to satisfy any doubts their customers might have about their purchases.**

FRONTGATE RETAIL STORE & OUTLET—CINMAR, L.P./LEBANON—Frontgate pushes high-caliber products in its catalog (over 20 million are sent out each year) that enhance comfort and lifestyle for the total home environment—indoor, patio, garden, and pool. The company sells everything from Speakman shower heads found in the world's finest hotels to the same type of Ping-Pong tables used by professional associations. Their repertoire includes commercial grade outdoor cooking equipment, Thistletex bath towels from Scotland, handmade mosaic tables, stainless steel kitchen tools and utensils from Bavaria, and a personal-size Aromasteam sauna. Vendors range from prominent worldwide manufacturers to small ones that handmake their own products.

There's even a full-time person on staff to test products and back up manufacturers' claims. The company began in 1991 when John O'Steen and Paul Tarvin started a direct mail-order company. Together they founded Cinmar, L.P., located in a commercial park just north of Kings Island. There, at the company's only retail store and outlet, customers purchase regularly priced merchandise or save on overstocks, closeouts, in-store specials, and out-of-season items. Products carry a money-back guarantee for 395 days and shipping costs on returned merchandise are covered. Batteries are free for any items requiring them. Free assembly is available. For assistance with technical questions and product information a staff of well-versed product specialists is on hand. Look for the company's product displays at local events such as Homearama and the Cincinnati Flower Show. Inquire about extra savings on items from the Frontgate catalog.
2800 Henkle Drive; 513/933-8050 ext. 382. Tues–Sat 10am–6pm, Thurs 10am–9pm. VS, MC, DS, AE. For a catalog and phone orders call 800/626-6488 daily 8am–midnight. Product Specialists 800/537-8484.

RADIO OUTLET/MONROE—While the store doesn't look like much in the converted gas station right off the expressway, it has a powerhouse selection of the top name automobile stereo equipment and electronics. The Radio Outlet buys the reliables factory direct—Alpine, Sony, Pioneer, Kenwood, JVC, and others. When compared to competitors' prices, the store claims it beats them by at least 10%–15%. Products can be installed (by appointment) right on the premises and free of charge with a purchase of $100 or more. For those under $100 there's a $35 charge. Installed products come with a 1-year warranty, while over-the-counter products are guaranteed for up to 30 days. The after-market price of a car stereo (the amount the car dealers charge) can run an average of $600–$800, while the Radio Outlet claims to offer a better quality 4-speaker system, fully installed at an average of $350–$400. Accessories, CBs and antennas, car alarms, and radar detectors are also discounted for extra savings over competition. Discontinued and demo models bring even greater savings. Some home stereo and home electronics are also available. All products sold here are authorized by the factory dealers.
1260 State Route 63, Monroe; 513/539-8944. 1008 State Route 725, Centerville; 513/438-3300. Mon–Sat 9am–8pm, Sun 11am–6pm. VS, MC, DS, AE.

TRADERS WORLD/MONROE—As you enter this 50-acre complex the larger-than-life plastic horse rearing up over the entrance signifies what's in store. Traveling up the tree-lined driveway to the connected pole-barn buildings fancied with deluxe trims and awnings, you'll have your choice of 6,000 parking spaces. Around the perimeter you'll see 120 different flags flapping in the wind. It's all part of Traders World Flea Market. And once inside, you'll find yourself overwhelmed with the numerous shopping choices (over 700 booths) among the cluttered decor. Amidst a nostalgic country setting, the large facility seems like it was built just to house the

relics and collectibles of the owner, Jay Frick, Sr. The rustic, wooden beams crossways over the aisles are topped with make-believe Indian scouts and stuffed wild animals—raccoons, coyotes, foxes, and water fowl—standing watch over the crowds. Every crossway is adorned with a woodcarved sign that proclaims some type of homey, cliched wisdom. Several chained-off booths display the old modes of transportation like Model T and Model A Fords and century-old horse carriages. One booth showcases a 1959 Buick Invicta, an old Wurlitzer juke box, and a stuffed grizzly bear with a sign next to it that reads "Please don't touch Bearsky." Three Tiffany-style lamps with leaded glass domes and numerous lights hang from the ceiling at various points along the way. Each was handmade at the turn of the century. At the end of Building 10 you'll find the gingerbread woodwork that once graced the interior of a 1930 ice cream parlor. Though you'll find yourself distracted with all of these side attractions you'll need to really concentrate when it comes time to do the shopping. You'll find everything from A to Z. A butcher, a travel agency, a watch shop, and a toy tractor shed are a few of the regular booths. The place is also crawling with crafts, baseball cards, comic books, and old magazines. For the kids there are plenty of pogs and slammers, dolls, and toys on every other corner. An antique wing is one of the more popular spots for collectors. But, if you still don't find what you want inside, try your luck outside where there are over 300 spaces for vendors. Or, if you just prefer to pass the time and get a bite to eat, sit yourself down at one of the indoor concession areas. There you can do a little people watching or take in a sports game on one of the big screen televisions.
601 Union Road (I-75 & State Route 63—Exit 29); 513/424-5708. Indoor/outdoor market. Open year-around. Sat & Sun 9am–5pm. ☆

TURTLE CREEK FLEA MARKET/MONROE—Turtle Creek suffers a little when compared to its larger neighbor, Traders World, across the highway. Even so there are a few things that go beyond the typical flea market fare of lawn geese, baseball cards, and video tapes. Cruising along the aisles you'll come across a man pushing the same kitchen knives you see advertised on late night TV. You know, the ones that will cut through anything. In this case he is working on a hammer. Another booth sells goods from Mexico. Serapes right out of a spaghetti western, leather bags, and flannel bajas fill the space. Some of it's even a little surreal. Row after row of Styrofoam heads atop silver shelving peer out from under wigs at passersby. A rest near the main snack bar is unsettling. Behind patrons sitting at tables chomping on hotdogs, a singer belts out a song at the karaoke machine. It's loud, she's bad, and no one seems to pay any attention. If you can stand the singing for five minutes you can also have your portrait drawn here for $5.95 (extra if in color). From the looks of it, Lincoln and John Wayne recently had one done. Further wandering takes you past a magic shop, fake flower peddlers, and the guy pushing photographs on a pony. Outside the garage sale atmosphere prevails. You can root through the tables of tacky trinkets and glasses, rusted tools, and used toys. Pick up something and the owner is likely to shout out a price; put

it down and you'll get another—only lower this time. If you're interested, it's now time to play let's make a deal, which is the real flea market experience.
320 N. Garver Road (1-75 & State Route 63—Exit 29); 513/539-4497. Indoor/outdoor market. Open year-around. Sat & Sun 9am–5pm.

CAESAR CREEK FLEA MARKET/WAYNESVILLE—This indoor flea market is like a mini mall for items that haven't found a place in regular retail stores. Competition is stiff when it comes to standard items sold here like lawn ornaments (especially those silly dressed-up geese), athletic socks, boots, and video tapes. Baseball cards, crafts, wood carvings, and baked goods are sold at every other corner. Among the six long aisles there are several pet shops, furniture booths, a key shop, and even bubbling spas and hot tubs. Outside is the section for the garage sale items that never seem to sell well at home. In the summer, this area sees plenty of action with a circle of dealers completely surrounding the facility. Though many find haggling over the prices exciting, the best part about coming here is watching the people. There's a high concentration of clientele wearing tee-shirts and caps with all sorts of odd sayings and metal chains connecting their jeans pockets. Many bring their dogs which look as well fed as their owners. One lady who frequents here rides around in an electric cart with her two poodles dressed as goofy as the geese lawn ornaments. But, perhaps the greatest thrill is to sink your teeth (if you brought them) into one of those spicy metts, juicy burgers, or strip steaks grilled over an open fire by the outdoor vendors. To top it off you'll want either a creamy ice cream cone or a powdered funnel cake. Yum...?
I-71 & State Route 73 (Exit 45 off I-71); 513/382-1669. Indoor/outdoor market. Open year-round. Sat & Sun 9am–5pm.

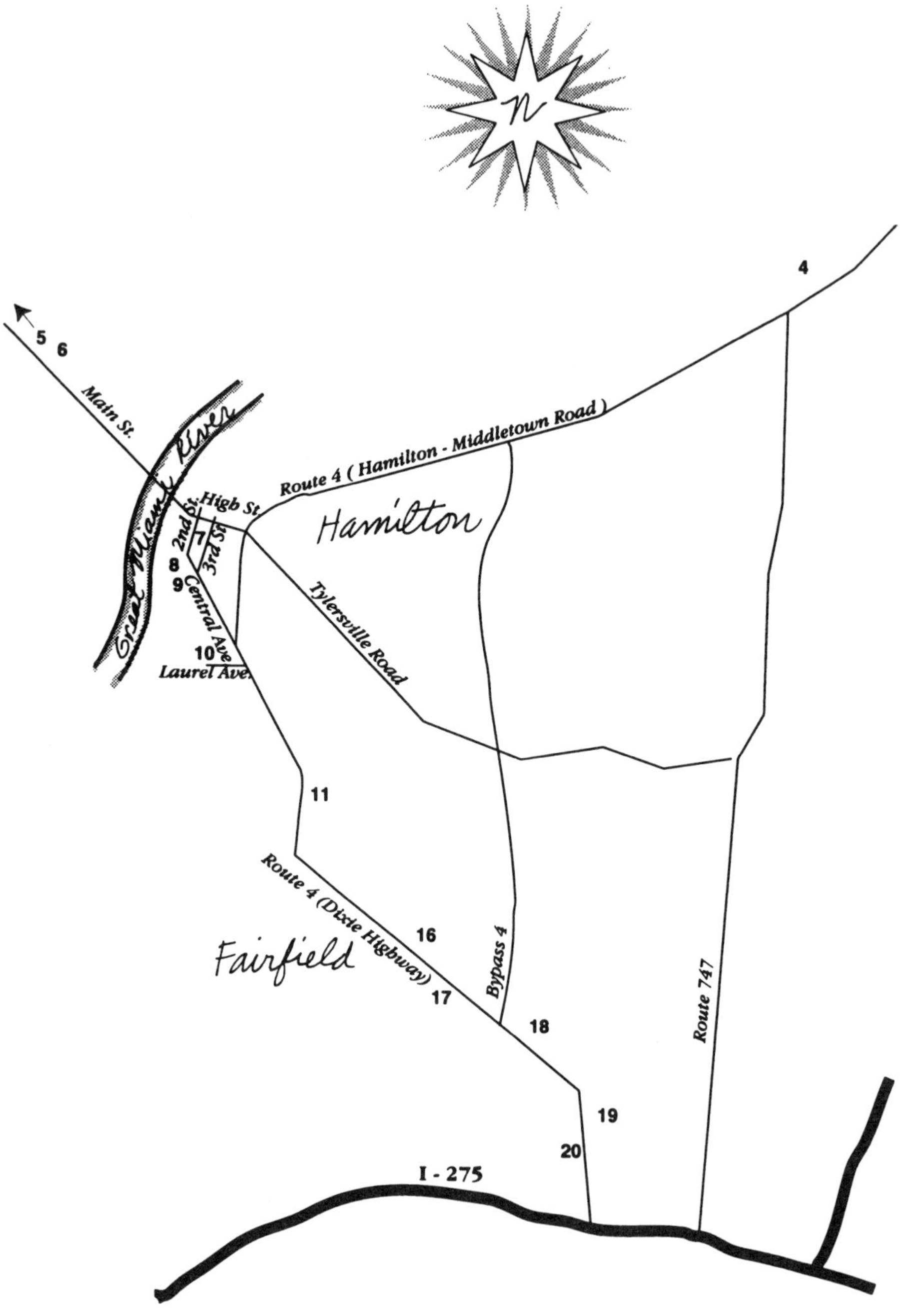

Army Store Factory Surplus - **11**
Bargain Barn - **13**
The Book Shop - **5**
C. Dattilo Co. - **7**
Caesar Creek Flea Market - **22**
Cort Furniture Rental
Clearance Center - **12**
Cotton Mill Factory Outlet - **9**
Four Seasons Garmet Factory Outlet - **15**
Frontgate Retail Store & Outlet - **21**
Hamilton Window and Door Manufacturers - **8**
Jungle Jim's International Farmer's Market - **16**
Klosterman's Bakery Outlet (Mason) - **14**
Klosterman's Bakery Outlet (Hamilton) - **6**
Mathis Fabric Center - **4**
Once Upon a Child - **17**

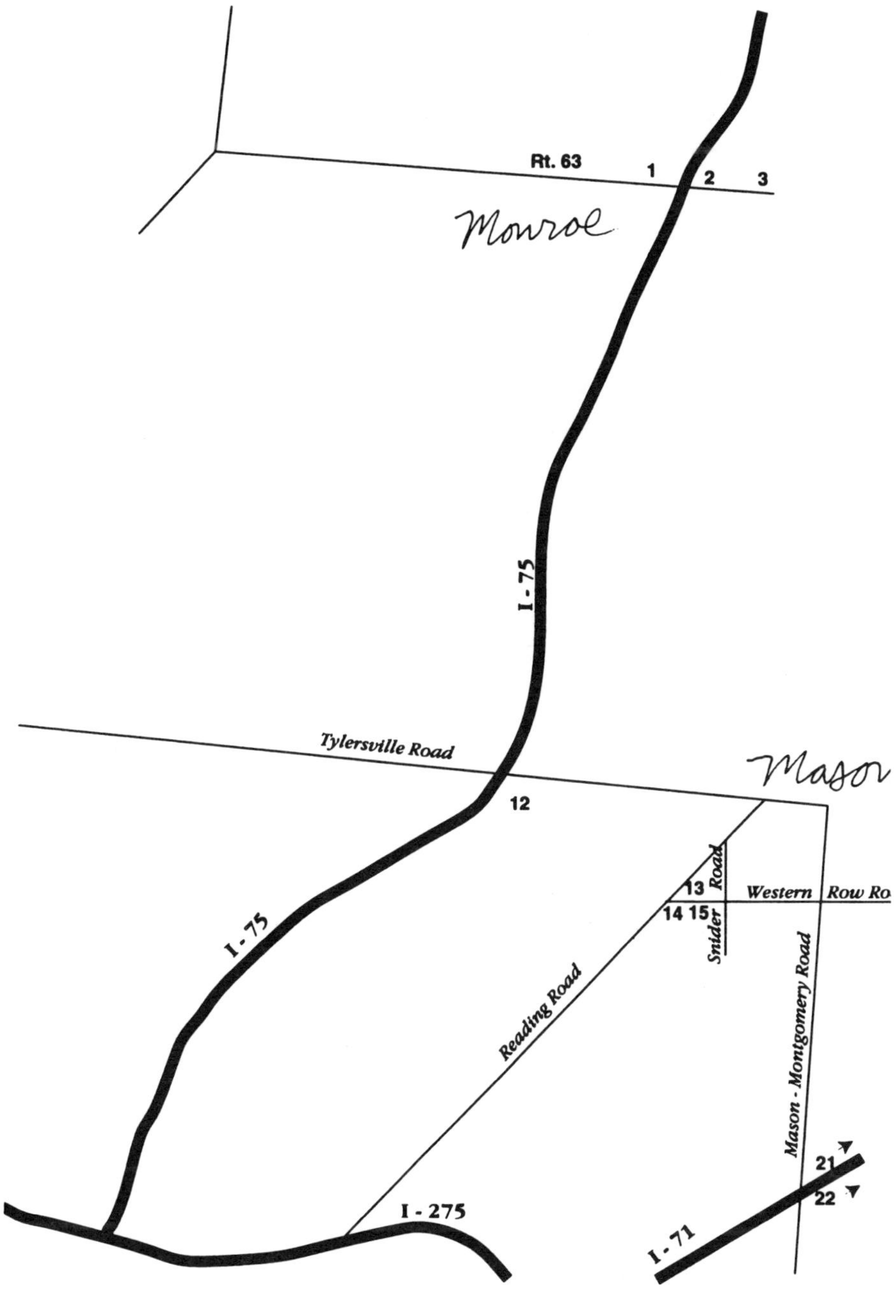

Original Mattress Factory - 19
Parks Attic Kids' Resale Store - 18
Pease Warehouse Outlet, Inc. - 10
Radio Outlet - 2
Traders World - 3
Turtle Creek Flea Market - 1
Whiting Manufacturer Linen Outlet - 20

Office & Industrial Liquidators

Northeast

Montgomery Road is a linear plane that crosses through the passages of time. It's forever been the main thoroughfare connecting the business and residential communities of the Northeast, reflecting the changing lifestyles of city dwellers as they transmogrified into suburbanites. It is, of course, directly related to advancements in transportation. First, it was a stagecoach route (that likely followed an Indian hunting path or animal trail) with stops at 16 Mile and 20 Mile Stands. Later, railroads and streetcars made locating near it more attractive to commuters. Finally, the convenience of I-71 brought more progress, and more relief. And because the road parallels the interstate, it has managed to escape the traffic flow problems that have plagued other commercial areas such as Beechmont and Colerain avenues. The interstate affords quick and easy access to the surrounding neighborhoods. ¶ Both Evanston and Norwood began as bedroom communities along the streetcar lines stretching out from the city on Montgomery Road. By the turn of the century, Evanston sought annexation to the city, while Norwood developed an industrial base and remained independent. As these communities grew commercially, their middle-class residents moved further out and the working-class moved in. The sense of community in Evanston was destroyed when I-71 split the neighborhood. Norwood, however, was aided by its close proximity to the interstate and the Norwood Lateral (which connects Cincinnati's major interstates, I-71 with I-75). The centerpiece of this development has been Surrey Square. It has remained a viable commercial shopping center though its tenants have fluctuated and major industries have folded. Even with the closing of the GM plant, Norwood hasn't been able to shake its Southern rural image and it retains its working-class values. ¶ Further north, along Montgomery Road, Pleasant Ridge, Kennedy Heights, and Silverton grew from subdivisions into villages. The first two eventually linked up with Cincinnati, while Silverton went its own way. ¶ With the anticipated construction of I-71, Kenwood developed as a commercial district. Today, its crossing at Montgomery Road is the site of two major shopping malls. It's a part of town thick with vanity license plates and a high concentration of designer fashions. ¶ Further north Montgomery Road is highly commercial. Montgomery's location made it one of Cincinnati's more desirable residences. The heart of Montgomery was strained by the fast residential development, and historic buildings along the road were threatened. The city has worked hard to preserve its image by encouraging renovation of these old structures and creating an architectural style that reflects a bygone era. The business district, now known as Olde Montgomery, boasts several historic landmarks. Just to the west Blue Ash has made no such attempt. It has aggressively pursued light industry in what was primarily agricultural property. Retailing here has picked up along Kenwood Road in the form of strip malls and the Reed Hartman area where industrial warehouses are used to sell stockpiled goods. The city has also attracted upscale housing that has spilled over from Montgomery. ¶ In recent years, the commercial strip along Montgomery Road has stretched out beyond the I-275 beltway. The Landen development has attracted young professional families residing in suburban bliss as the urban sprawl from which they escaped springs up around them. Today, this area along I-275, I-71, and Fields-Ertel is quickly becoming an example of an "edge city." It was first a rural area, then a home for commuters, and finally a destination in itself, complete with its own set of industrial parks, office complexes, and strip malls. The bottom line is, the area keeps evolving and though it may *look* different than it did when the Indians were here, in the end, Montgomery Road is *still* a hunting path.

OFFICE FURNITURE OUTLET/EVANSTON—It's where previously owned office furniture remains idle until ready to be shipped off again. The one-room display area is like a gallery for those pieces that have endured the rigorous, day-in, day-out use. Many of the items are brought in after they've been shuffled around an office or two, maybe remaining stationary for years, maybe not. Some look like new; some show office battle scars and scratches. A network of wood and steel desks, filing cabinets, and conference and computer tables form a maze around the large space. Bookcases, shelving units, and drawing boards fill in the borders. In the back are special buys on odds and ends, from small one-drawer filing cabinets to

stacked chairs. Cushioned desk chairs, with or without rollers and side arms, are lined up in several rows ready for inspection. Many of the items are priced reasonably, and when compared to buying new, they offer excellent savings. The factory seconds and closeouts that show up here are also good buys.
1601 Dana Avenue; 513/531-0900. Mon–Fri 9am–6pm, Sat 9am–4pm. VS, MC.

ADMIRAL WINDOW WHOLESALE/NORWOOD—The cramped showroom leaves little space for anything but a couple of window displays and a couch to rest on while awaiting service. But, it's still worth checking out. Anyone who has shopped around knows it's easy to drop a bundle when buying windows. At Admiral the choices are simple and the prices are right. Single-hung windows up to 100 united inches (the measurement along two sides of a window opening) are $109 each. Double-hung are $139 each. Single-hung windows don't move on the top half, while double-hung windows tilt in for easier cleaning. The well-engineered windows are vinyl and double-paned and come with a lifetime guarantee. Other products found here include bay windows, insulated windows, patio doors, and aluminum storm doors.
3740 Montgomery Road; 513/531-8393. Mon–Fri 9am–5pm, Sat 9am–1pm. VS, MC, DS.

Mrs. Allison's Cookie Company

MRS. ALLISON'S WHOLESALE COOKIE CO./NORWOOD—Since 1930, this wholesale bakery has been satisfying taste buds in Norwood and around the city with its fresh baked cookies. Walk-ins off the street are drawn in after passing by the window and spotting the different varieties—super chip, oatmeal (the most popular choice), cinnamon, rum, chocolate macaroon, fudge drops, and others. The tasty bite-size tea rings and drops (try the super butter), as well as, the regular-size cookies are offered for a mere $1.65/lb.–$1.70/lb. Peanut butter cookies are $2.50/lb. Mixing flavors is encouraged since it's hard to decide which ones you like

best. It's surprising how many cookies are in a pound—the generous helping fills a small bag. Holiday and seasonal cookies at $2.70/lb. and date bars (during Christmas time only) at $4.95/lb. are available, too.
4357 Montgomery Road; 513/531-0557. Mon–Fri 7am–4:30pm. Cash or check only.

BEN'S SPORTSWEAR OUTLET/NORWOOD—Any old-time bargain hunter worth her charge card will remember Ben's when it was a Downtown department store. Ben's voluminous clothing deals were always worth the drive. Since then Ben's has moved to Norwood with a different focus. The long, one-room store is loaded wall-to-wall with sweatshirts, sweatpants, and tee shirts. Old Ben himself points customers to bargain buyouts and closeouts on endless rows of tables that stretch back to the rear of the store. Well-organized stacks, conveniently arranged in adult and youth sizes, make the buys seem more worthwhile. Sport caps, hats, and brand name athletic shoes are also found here at good prices, as well as a small selection of men's career suits—a carryover from the old days when Ben's was a fuller-size department store.
Norwood Plaza, 3825 Montgomery Road; 513/531-1876. Mon–Sat 10:30am–8pm, Sun 11am–5pm. VS, MC, DS, AE.

AVOID SHOPPERS' PARALYSIS **Make a mental note of the store's return policy. Retailers like you to know in order to avoid misunderstandings and risk losing your business. Therefore, find out if the merchandise you have purchased is a final sale. If not, upon returning it, will you receive cash, a credit, or be able to exchange it? How many days will you have to return your purchases? Most department stores will allow you to return an item anytime (as long as you have the receipt). They'll often allow you a certain time period to receive the sale price if the item went on sale soon after you purchased it. Most outlet and discount stores used to offer *final sales only,* but some have begun to offer better return policies.**

HAIR LUCKY BEAUTY SUPPLY/NORWOOD—A beauty supply shop that meets the needs of the African-American, this one pushes all the necessities at better-than-average prices. Over 50 brands of hair care products including Jheri Redding and Four Phase are neatly arranged on shelves lining the aisles. There's more nail care and cosmetics than most places, too. One wall is covered with hair extensions in varying lengths. Another features handbags, hats, and accessories. Hair colorings and hair appliances are behind the counter, and a collection of fashion jewelry is displayed in showcases. Bargain bins with everything from hair accessories and bows to toothbrushes and pantyhose offer extra savings.
Norwood Plaza, 3861 Ivanhoe Avenue; 513/351-8886. Mon–Sat 9:30am–8pm, Sun 11am–5pm. VS, MC.

OFFICE & INDUSTRIAL LIQUIDATORS/NORWOOD—The warehouse is huge—70,000 sq. ft. to be exact. It has four long floors and occupies more space than a football field. Crowded with used office furniture and industrial fixtures, it's a recycling resting ground

where items sit until ready to be moved on to yet another company or home den. Towering stacks of chairs, filing cabinets along most every wall, and hundreds upon hundreds of desks and chairs occupy most of the space. It makes you wonder where they all came from, who occupied them for eight hours a day, and what happened to *them*. Mazes of partitions and shelving units in various heights are on display as well. Though the surroundings are stark, cold, and uninviting, it's a place that warrants investigating before paying the higher price of brand new merchandise.
4817 Section Avenue; 513/731-7772. Mon–Fri 9am–5:30pm. VS, MC, DS.

Record Theatre music & Video

RECORD THEATRE MUSIC & VIDEO/NORWOOD—For low prices and a great selection, Cincinnati music lovers rely on the Record Theatre. In a market where there is widespread price disparity, it has consistently offered better savings on records, compact discs, and cassette tapes. The large showroom features one of the most extensive selections in the city. All categories of music are well represented among its 100,000 titles. Used selections are also available. There's even a collection of old-time 45s. Additional incentives are offered through the store's stamp saving program. Customers receive a stamp for each dollar spent. When a stamp booklet is filled they can redeem it for $5 credit. Video tapes and storage cases are here, as well.
Surrey Square, 4590 Montgomery Road; 513/531-8877. Mon–Sat 10am–10pm, Sun noon–7pm. VS, MC, DS.

SAALFELD PAPER COMPANY/BOND HILL—While shopping here you'll be among caterers, deli owners, and others connected with the food service industry—mostly because it's the best place in the city to shop for paper serving products and plastic partywares. Wholesale discounts (offered to professionals and the general public alike) are available on a huge selection—paper, Styrofoam, and plastic plates and cups; deli wraps and table covers; and plastic cutlery and storage containers. At the back of the store a "Repack Super Saver Aisle," with items retrieved from damaged boxes, has greater savings. In the front are featured closeouts. There are industrial-size cleaning supplies and storage items, too.
4510 Reading Road; 513/641-5000. Mon–Fri 7:30am–5:30pm, Sat 9am–1pm. VS, MC, DS.

ASIDE **What's a wholesaler? Wholesalers usually sell merchandise to retail stores or other commercial businesses. A wholesaler generally sells merchandise in bulk or larger quantities. Some wholesalers will also offer their goods to individuals at the same prices they sell to the retail stores. The catch is that these individuals have to buy their goods in larger quantities as well. Sometimes the items a wholesaler sells are industrial or commercial grades and more durable. These items may be more expensive than their retail counterparts. Examples of wholesalers in the Cincinnati area include: Dunsky's Restaurant & Bar Supply, M. Degaro Company, and Saalfeld Paper Company.**

SOCK STORE/NORWOOD—The building in Norwood looks more like a place that would sell hub caps than socks. But, don't let that fool you. Inside are plenty of good buys on styles for the entire family. Although you'll find yourself rummaging though the piles of unorganized goods to find what you want, the low prices are worth the trouble. They include: footies, 3 pair for $2; men's sport socks, 3 pair for $2; girls' lace socks, 3 pair for $2.50; kids' socks, 3 pair for $1.50 or 50¢ a pair; and girls' knit tights (sizes 4–6x) just $1 a pair. Similar deals are on a narrow selection of sweatshirts and tee shirts. Owner Lloyd Merida operates the business as a sideline. He points out, "My real job is ministering for my church." A former General Motors worker, he felt a calling to leave the local manufacturing plant just before retirement and has never regretted the move, especially since the factory shut down soon after. Since the early '70s he's been selling socks to supply his needs and those of his ministry. He started by borrowing $1,000 and selling from his house, then out of his car, and later at area flea markets. The first day at the market he took in over $1,200. Most of the merchandise he receives is through a supplier in Tennessee. Styles range from lighter to heavier weights. Since there are some irregulars, check merchandise carefully.
5000 Montgomery Road; 513/351-6657. Mon–Sat 10am–6pm. Cash only.

THE SURPLUS WORK CLOTHES CO./NORWOOD—The place looks as neat and tidy as the uniforms it sells. Shirts and slacks, precisely folded and arranged in orderly stacks, are stockpiled on the shelves. Names like OshKosh, Red Cap, and Dickies are among the choices. Painters' pants (the kind with the extra loop) and those white, generic-looking caps destined to be speckled with dabs of paint are displayed. Plenty is on hand at prices under the big discount chains. Supplying individuals and companies alike (sometimes 20–30 items at a time), the store stocks only new merchandise (some closeouts) bought directly from the manufacturers. There are enough scrubs, lab coats, and smocks to outfit entire teams of medical technicians and nurses. With sizes that run deep and in various lengths, customers are easy to fit. Seasonal, insulated winter wear is also available. Now expanding its lines to include work boots and shoes, the store, owned by John and Bonnie West, has come a long way from the old days when it sold only used apparel.
4553 Montgomery Road; 513/631-2749, FAX 513/631-2812. Mon 9:30am–7pm, Tues–Sat 9:30am–5pm. VS, MC.

LOSHIN'S DANCEWEAR/ COLUMBIA TWP.—Giggling girls fill the store as drill team advisors ponder over the right colors. Primping around the mirrors are future ballerinas and drama students fitting the right costumes. They've all come to Loshin's, which for 50 years has been outfitting performing groups and individuals. Once located Downtown, it was forced to move (like so many businesses) when the convention center was developed. Now on Kennedy Avenue, just off of I-71, the store has lost nothing in its move. Buying goods directly from the manufacturers, owner Charles Mendell keeps prices down on the store's broad selection of dance and recital wear—one of the best in the city. Many types of footwear—ballet, tap, jazz, or toe shoes and boots—are available. Ask about volume discounts.
5141 Kennedy Avenue; 513/531-5800. Mon–Fri 9:30am–5pm, Sat 9:30am–1pm. VS, MC, DS.

VELVA SHEEN SPORTSWEAR OUTLET/COLUMBIA TWP. —The founders of Velva Sheen so admired a silkscreening process they named their company after it. To them, the quality looked like velvet with a sheen. That was over 60 years ago when it was nothing more than a small screen printing shop located downtown. Today, it has grown to be one of the largest sportswear imprinters in the world with its factory headquarters just outside of the city in Fairfax. Specializing in imprinting tee shirts, sweatshirts, jerseys, jackets, and gym suits, the company has a screen library of over 80,000 plates with hundreds of new ones being processed each day. While many of the old-time bargain hunters remember the company's Gilbert Avenue outlet for its famous buys on misprints and irregulars, the company now has five area stores (two are just north of Cincinnati). The misprints and irregulars are still sold there, but the flaws aren't as noticeable. More upgraded and first-quality activewear is now available. Some of the better buys are on apparel featuring themes—Disney, Looney Tunes, and sporting teams. Customers, too, have the option of selecting plain colors or adding a transfer design from the many choices for a low fee. A separate area has youth sizes at reasonable prices. Since team orders and special requests for events like retirements and reunions are commonly filled here, volume discounts are offered.
5245 Ridge Road, Columbia Twp.; 513/731-8358. 3621 Glenmore Avenue, Cheviot, 513/662-5403. 530 Ohio Pike, Cherry Grove; 513/528-5080. Mon–Sat 10am–8pm, Sun noon–5pm. VS, MC, DS.

THE WAREHOUSE OFFICE FURNITURE MART/COLUMBIA TWP.—This office furniture store had been Downtown since 1902 but has recently moved to Columbia Township next to I-71. There's little made for the office that won't eventually show up here. Prices on used furniture will depend on availability and condition of the constantly changing inventory, but you can always expect to save 50% over the cost of a new piece and sometimes as much as 80%. A vast selection of new furniture is priced at least 20% off retail.
5140 Kennedy Avenue; 513/241-1111, FAX 513/241-9145. Mon–Fri 8:30am–5pm. VS, MC.

EVERYBODY'S RECORDS, TAPES & CD'S/PLEASANT RIDGE—The store is a throwback to the '60s. The outside, with its painted black facade, brightly-colored lettering, and neon window signs, looks like a giant psychedelic poster that would glow under a black light. The inside has rock 'n roll tee shirts on hangers swinging from the ceiling and posters spread out over the walls. Owner Marilyn Kirby remembers her store when it had just one aisle of "vinyls." Today, after several expansions, it's not only larger, but it has a separate store next door just for old-time relics—from single '45s to classic record albums. The main store has updated to modern day standards by carrying compact discs and cassette tapes, but still gives oldies and old-time rhythm and blues a priority. Hard-to-find imports are also uncovered along with the usual best sellers—rock 'n roll, jazz, soul, and blues. Metal and punk music are not left out, but classical and new age have been. Even with the coming of the mall stores and the chains, Everybody's has endured simply because the diehards find the selection and the price still worthwhile.
6106 Montgomery Road; 513/531-4500. Mon–Sat 11am–9pm, Sun noon–9pm. VS, MC, no checks.

HAIR PLUS BEAUTY SUPPLY/PLEASANT RIDGE—The everyday staples for do-it-yourself hairdos are substantially less than regular retailers and salons at this beauty supply shop. And, they're offered in greater selection. Hair Plus Specializes in brand name hair care products for African-Americans. You'll find shampoos, permanent kits, relaxers, and hair colorings by the hundreds lining the shelves. Hair beads and barrets to synthetic and human hair, along with hats, handbags, and jewelry, are well-stocked. It's the kind of store to stock up on all the essentials.
6207 Montgomery Road; 513/351-4411. Mon–Sat 9:30am–7pm. VS, MC.

REGARDING BOOKS/PLEASANT RIDGE—With an interior more like a small library than a used bookstore, Regarding Books offers a comfortable, uncluttered setting. Wooden bookshelves and glassed-in cases hold a well chosen selection of quality, used, hardback books at half off their original prices. Also, there are a few new hardbacks priced at 40%–50% off. One enclosed case showcases rare collectible books. Through the store's Internet computer network system, other books can also be ordered.
6095 Montgomery Road; 513/531-4717. Mon–Sat 10am–7pm, Sun noon–5pm. VS, MC, DS, AE.

COVER-UPS, INC./SILVERTON—Every inch of space in this small interior design studio is occupied by display samples and manufacturers' catalogs. Swatches of fabric, carpeting samples, wallpaper cutouts, and upholstery samples are scattered about. The studio also claims to have access to the largest supply of designer fabrics in Cincinnati. In the back, upholstering and other work rooms are busy with designers who never stop. They offer tips on the finer points of decorating, assist customers with their selections, and track down orders. Nothing is in stock. Everything is ordered

factory direct, from wall coverings and drapery fabrics to furniture and carpeting. Savings on merchandise average 10%–25% off regular retails. Customers, too, are encouraged to come in and make use of the shop's services without being charged steep hourly design fees. Some have been known to pack a lunch and stay for hours to search through the many books for decorating ideas. Others bring in pictures or even pillows and cushions to try to match colors. With a 21 year history, the shop is a valuable resource for exploring decorating ideas.
7428 Montgomery Road; 513/984-8111. Mon–Fri 10am–5pm, Sat 10am–2pm. VS, MC.

Lite House annex

LITE-HOUSE ANNEX/SILVERTON—The store is a house of illusion. A mixture of chandeliers and swinging candelabras cascade from the ceiling. Each light is attached to a long string that, when given a yank, switches on the light that is caught by mirrors. Lamps, track lighting, and outdoor lanterns protrude from the walls. Floor and table lamps in various shapes, along with open boxes of hardware and stacked lamp shades, clutter the aisles. Bubble globes (the ones that look like fish bowls) and cone-shaped light covers stand in line on the shelves. Even replacement parts, including light bulbs and glass panels, flicker in the bins. As the annex for area Lite-House stores (one is right across the street), it is regularly stocked with discounted items. Many are refurbished, rewired, and reconditioned. These are marked with drastic price reductions. A small fix-it shop in the back is busy restoring models.
7301 Montgomery Road; 513/791-2001. Mon–Thurs 9:30am–5pm, Fri 9:30am–6pm, Sat 9:30am–6pm. VS, MC, DS.

ALL MY CHILDREN MATERNITY OUTLET/KENWOOD—It began as a consignment shop in her basement. Barbara Schulman saw a need for more desirable choices in maternity career wear after her own quest fell short. But, that was 12 years ago. Today, more options

are available including those within her own outlet stores. Shedding the consignment business and now selling new merchandise, her stores (one in Kenwood, the other in Cherry Grove) offer a wide variety. Prices hover around 20%–60% below retail. Barbara's regular buying trips to New York pay off. Her strategy is to hit the vendors at the end of the merchandising season while prices are lower. Since the vendors operate a season or two ahead, this works well in coordinating the current selection in her stores. When they're available, she also purchases buyouts and closeouts. Most everything she selects is first-quality and runs on the moderate end. For one-of-a-kind looks, though, try the manufacturers' samples. A plaque on the wall that announces "Voted Best Maternity Shop" by *Cincinnati Magazine* is a reward for her efforts.
7876 Montgomery Road, Kenwood; 513/793-0333. 8435 Beechmont Avenue, Cherry Grove; 513/474-5501. Mon 10am–6pm, Tues–Fri 10am–8pm, Sat 10am–6pm, Sun noon–5pm. (Cherry Grove closes at 5pm on Mon & Sat.) VS, MC, DS.

WALL DECOR OUTLET STORE/MADEIRA—This lone store offers several framing options for those wanting to save a few bucks, but its main attraction is in its large selection of pre-framed prints. These go for 40% off. Most of the prints are standard, poster types that are more affordable. A few are limited editions. Customers can buy prints already framed or choose from the in-stock selection and frame their own picks. A do-it-yourself work area with all the framing supplies saves customers 25%–40% with the store's factory-direct buys. Or, for those who prefer custom framing, you'll receive 25% off regular prices. Ready-made wood frames, precut mats, and photo frames in standard sizes are the best buys.
*7336 Kenwood Road; 513/793-0787. Mon–Sat **10am–6pm, Tues & Thurs 10am–8pm** VS, MC, DS.*

JEAN-A-FAYE CONSIGNMENTS, INC./DEER PARK—A consignment shop with a different bent, this one is for the plus-size woman. Career and casual wear, in sizes 14–26, are emphasized here with notables like Pendleton, Liz Claiborne, and Jones New York sprinkled throughout. Everything from dressy looks to activewear fill the racks. A full range of accessories, handbags, jewelry, and shoes make it easy to shop in one stop. Owner, Kathy Feltner, has also expanded her business to include a children's consignment shop next door. It has kids' clothing, toys, furniture, equipment, and a play area for tots.
8314 Plainfield Road; 513/891-2434. Tues & Wed 10am–5pm, Thurs & Fri 11am–7pm, Sat 10am–4pm. VS, MC, DS.

AVOID SHOPPERS' PARALYSIS **Be on guard! Don't fall for bogus marketing scams or traps. A merchant can sometimes make use of some unethical practices to entice shoppers. A crafty retailer may display a big sign in the store that reads "For Sale" or "Special" but there's only one problem; the merchandise isn't actually on sale. It has just been arranged a certain way, with a sign placed over it, to look like it has been marked down. This leads the unsuspecting shopper to assume the goods are priced for a great deal. You may also want to be careful when purchasing merchandise that's been tossed into a certain**

bin. Just because a bin is out in the store doesn't mean it's filled with bargains. Some merchants will even highlight the bin in the back of the store to entice the shopper into thinking there is a terrific deal available on the floor. Another trick of the trade you'll want to avoid is being misled into thinking there is a wide savings range available on lots of merchandise in the store. An unscrupulous merchant may lead you to believe that most of the selection ranges in savings of up to 70%, when there may be just one or two items in the entire store that have been discounted this deeply.

Inch by Inch

INCH BY INCH/MONTGOMERY—With over 1,300 consignors, Inch By Inch has an excellent all-around selection of previously owned apparel. On the main level are women's career and casual looks, maternity wear, and evening attire. Fashions by Liz Claiborne, Albert Nipon, Ellen Tracy, and Ann Taylor are typical rack occupants. Upstairs, children's wear by Gap and Gymboree are common. A good mixture of Fisher-Price and infants' equipment, toys, and books should be checked out. Juniors' wear includes popular Guess and Limited trends. Accessories for both women and children are more of a priority here than in most consignment shops. The store, owned by Terry Kelly, has been in business for over ten years but occupies a building that's been around much longer. As part of Montgomery's historic business district, the old house is a landmark that dates back to 1870.
9429 Montgomery Road; 513/745-0066. Mon–Sat 10am–5pm. VS, MC, DS.

AROUND THE HOUSE CONSIGNMENTS & GIFTS/MONTGOMERY—This place will consign just about anything in home furnishings that isn't fastened down. One of the first in the area to master this recycling concept, Around the House has everything from a genuine pig scraper to elegant Waterford crystal. Everyday and fine china, lamps, linens, cookbooks, art work, and pottery are regularly on display. Occasionally, sterling flatware will also show up. A big seller is the primitive kitchenware. One of the most unusual items sold here was a lifelike, cardboard cutout of Barbra Streisand. It went for $50. Owners Diane Rudolph Sutphin and Linda Miller Dotson, high school friends of 25 years, learned the shop was for sale through a classified ad. Diane said, "We went to view it one day, and bought it the next." They've had a field day ever since by adding personal touches like their bulletin board "promo." Here, consignors push items they can't possibly carry through the doors. A restored 1938 Waco airplane, old collectible automobiles, sofas, and kittens are a few examples. All that's required is a photograph and description. In the heart of Montgomery's historic business district, the store is above Larosa's Pizzeria.
9419 Montgomery Road (2nd floor—above Larosa's); 513/745-9909. Mon–Sat 11am–5pm. VS, MC, DS.

DOWN LITE INTERNATIONAL FACTORY OUTLET/SYCAMORE TWP.—Generations ago, feathers from around the farm were collected to make pillows and bedding. The soft underplumage of water foul (known as down) was found to be the best. As part of a family-run business that traces its roots back years to Europe, brothers Marvin and Larry Werthaiser, cousin Marty, and partner Bob Altbaier began Down Lite International in 1983. The manufacturing company makes down and feather pillows and down comforters—the plump kind, like the old days, stuffed so full you can sink yourself knee deep into them, though the allergy-sensitive should beware. The Werthaiser's parents, both survivors of a German concentration camp, began their feather business back in the old country after World War II. With one factory in Blue Ash and another in Loveland, the majority of feathers for the operation come from China—where natives eat a lot of geese and duck. Specializing in top-quality products, one of Down Lite's first customers was L.L. Bean. Today, the same high-caliber goods it sells to major retailers, like Bloomingdales, Neiman-Marcus, and Eddie Bauer, can be purchased at up to 40% less at the company's local outlet store (seconds and irregulars bring greater savings). The outlet is one of six in the country. One, called Outdoor Adventures, is in Traverse City, Michigan. Another, Three Dog Down, is as far away as Montana. Other items sold at the outlets include down outerwear and winter wear by names like Columbia, The Northface, London Fog, Woolrich, and Fox Run. Warm hats, ski gloves, and accessories are here, too.
7818 Palace Drive; 513/489-DOWN (3696). Sept–April 30 Mon–Sat 10am–6pm, Sun noon–5pm; March 1–Aug 31 Mon–Sat 10am–5pm. VS, MC, DS.

PEPPERIDGE FARM BAKERY OUTLET STORE/SYCAMORE TWP.—Bite-size goldfish crackers; cookies in varying shapes and flavors; frozen layer cakes and desserts; boxed croutons, stuffing, and bread sticks; and numerous whole grain breads and rolls—they're all at the Pepperidge Farm Bakery Outlet. Older, perhaps, than what you would expect to find at the grocery, but also a lot cheaper—a bag full goes for what you would normally pay for a few items elsewhere. Packages are coded to indicate seconds, market returns, and clearance (past or near freshness dates) and average 25%–50% off regular retails. Since the Campbell's Soup Company owns this famous snack foods company, it should come as no surprise to see soups stacked along the aisles drastically reduced. Look for grocery carts positioned around the store featuring buy-one-get-one-free bargains. Ask about the frequent buyer program, offering extra savings incentives.
Duffy Square, 10750 Montgomery Road; 513/489-8353. Mon–Fri 9:30am–6pm, Sat 9:30am–5:30pm, Sun 11am–4pm. Cash or check only.

TOTES OUTLET/LOVELAND—There's something captivating about Totes' products. The many different shapes and sizes of nylon carriers—rectangular to square lunch bags and coolers; cone-shaped and rounded bags; luggage and travel accessories; tote carryalls, gym, or beach bags; book bags and organizers—find you always needing another. Some fold up compactly to fit inside your purse or glove compartment. Others have removable shoulder straps. Most are available at savings of at least 35% off original retail prices at the Totes Outlet Store. The store, looking more like a summer home than a place of business, is located right next to the factory, within easy reach to be continuously refilled with all of Totes' famous products including umbrellas and rain gear. For the days when it's not raining, the store can also set you up with a pair of brand name sunglasses at a discounted price.
10078 E. Kemper Road; 513/583-2390. Mon–Fri 10am–6pm, Sat 9am–5pm, Sun noon–5pm. VS, MC, DS.

AMERICAN LUGGAGE OUTLET/BLUE ASH—While not a true manufacturer's outlet store, this discounter does have savings as if it was one—20%–50% below regular retail prices. For its small size it has a good selection of larger, brand name luggage, carry-ons, trunks, and tote bags. It also has the smaller organizers—personal leather goods, handbags, tote bags, and travel accessories. Here's a good source for briefcases, attaches, planners, agendas, and desk accessories, too. All are first-quality. Personalized with monogramming and volume discounts are available.
The Crossings of Blue Ash, 9525 Kenwood Road; 513/793-2996. Mon–Fri 10am–6pm, Sat 10am–4pm. VS, MC, DS.

AZZINI SHOE WAREHOUSE/BLUE ASH—Rows of brand name and upscale designer footwear in rich leathers and luxurious suedes look out of place within the barren warehouse facility, but it's a way to cut costs. Azzini passes savings onto customers by opening its doors to the public only on the weekends. Owner Lloyd Perlman (a

former U.S. Shoe executive) has a sixth sense for selecting beautifully crafted European and American-made footwear. All are women's styles, first quality, and made only with natural materials (no synthetics). Azzini's forte is to stock only the most current styles and most-wanted colors, so customers are assured of a fashionable selection. Over 8,000 pairs of shoes are available at any given time with new shipments arriving weekly. Some are fashion names more commonly found in New York or Chicago. Fine handbags to complement the shoes are available.
Blue Ash Industrial Park, 6811 Creek Road; 513/745-8900. Fri & Sat 10am–6pm, Sun noon–5pm. VS, MC. All sales final.

FECHHEIMER BROS. COMPANY OUTLET STORE/BLUE ASH—You don't have to be a postal worker to buy their uniforms. They're available at the Fechheimer distribution outlet store at low, factory-direct prices. Manufacturing uniforms for over 150 years, Fechheimer specializes in postal and public service uniforms, but also has some general styles. Although not everyone wants to dress like Cliff on *Cheers* and wear clothing adorned with postal emblems, some don't mind the subtle logos, especially since the prices on the apparel are so reasonable. Lightweight jackets go for $10 each. Pullover sweaters are $5 each. Trousers are under $8 a pair or 6 pair for $30. Those durable, comfortable walking shoes and boots (by Bates and New Balance), just like the postal workers wear, are up to 50% off. All the essentials—belts, gloves, hats, and winter wear—are here, too. There are heavyweight jackets and fatigues for weathering the rain, snow, and sleet when the mail, or anything else, must get through. Novelty items, miniature toy mail trucks, mailbox banks, and postage-stamp design tee shirts and sweatshirts are popular, as well as aprons (not for wearing behind the window) for the kitchen.
4545 Malsbary Road; 513/793-5400. Mon–Fri 9:30am–4:30pm. VS, MC.

AVOID SHOPPERS' PARALYSIS **Find out when new shipments arrive. Most stores have a certain day of the week set up to receive them. It's a good idea to find out this day and do your shopping soon after to take advantage of the best selection. Stores like Fashion Warehouse, Big Lots, and Value City Department Stores often announce when new shipments arrive, either through store signs or print advertisements.**

ORIENTAL WAREHOUSE/BLUE ASH—Shopping this warehouse will take you to over 25 different countries. Between the rafters and concrete floor are some of the most exquisite works of art and furniture you'll ever see in this small corner of the world. Many are one-of-a-kind pieces from the Far East and Asian countries like Thailand, Korea, the Philippines, Nepal, Myanmar (formerly Burma), and India. Others are from Central America, Spain, and Italy. The major emphasis is on furnishings from mainland China, like the beautiful lacquered and rosewood dining room sets, floor screens, batiks, Chinese roof tiles, and cabinets interspersed among the wall dividers. Accessories include statuary, vases, lamps, and

fish bowls. Pay attention to the fine intricate details of many of the pieces. Some of the floor screens were hand-carved and painted by up to seven different artists, from masters to apprentices. The process, known as *coromandel*, originated off the coast of India. Pigs blood is used as the adhesive. Yum. Others have a raised textured look formed from a buildup of glue and lacquering. This is known as *chinoiserie*. Some items are not what they appear to be. Crushed fish bones are used as imitation ivory and crushed egg shells are painted-on art works. Co-owner Scott Noel is, himself, a human work of art. He boasts having over 30 tattoos. (Check out his fingernails.) After living in Mexico for several years, Scott and his mother Jan started their importing business. First they sold sterling silver, clay figurines, and pottery from Mexico out of a small store on Beechmont Avenue. Later, they stumbled across a different source for importing larger items from the Orient and eventually moved to their current warehouse location. Now, after eight years in the business, they're going full thrust, largely because of the unusual selection, but also because the prices are kept down to an affordable level (some items claim to be at least 50% off) by employing a no-frills concept. Enjoy yourself. It's the most exotic warehouse around.
11297 Grooms Road; 513/530-0744. Mon–Sat 10am–6pm. VS, MC, DS, AE.

SNOOTY FOX/BLUE ASH—About as close to retail as consignment gets, the Snooty Fox has frequently been referred to as "the Cadillac of resale." It's the one so many others have tried to emulate, but have failed. With over 50,000 consignors, 55 employees, and five stores, it's the largest resale chain to offer quality apparel in the country. Started 15 years ago by one very enterprising woman, Donna Speigel, her stores stay attuned to the times. By positioning them in the city's nicest strip malls like the Shoppes at Harper's Point, they attract the best-dressed consignors. Fashion shows and workshops are also periodically arranged. The selection is carefully edited, must be in good condition, and is never more than two years old. Garments run the fashion gamut from ladies', men's, and children's apparel to bridal and maternity wear. A designer boutique is in every store and features status names like Escada, Anne Klein, and Donna Karan. The one name Donna singles out as racking in the most revenue over the years is Liz Claiborne. A line of all new accessories, handbags, jewelry, and scarves offers one of the better, discounted selections in the city. At her summer home in Jackson Hole, Wyoming, the locals convinced Donna to open another store. So there's now one more place where customers can get their "snooty" fix.
9500 Kenwood Road, Blue Ash; 513/791-6524. 7757 Five-Mile Road, Anderson Twp.; 513/231-1441. 7253 Wooster Pike, Mariemont; 513/271-5127. The Shoppes at Harper's Point, 11358 Montgomery Road, Symmes Twp.; 513/489-2434. 3190 Dixie Highway, Erlanger, Kentucky; 606/344-1635. Mon–Fri 10am–8pm, Sat 10am–5pm, Sun noon–5pm. VS, MC.

***ASIDE* Most consignment shops are operated by independent business owners, so you can expect to receive friendly, attentive service. They will only sell merchandise that is clean, well kept, or in good condition and clothing no older than a few years. Prices are usually set at 25%–50% off the original retail price with a first markdown after so many weeks. The merchandise is then marked down again and so on, until eventually it's sold as clearance.**

WHITING MANUFACTURING LINEN OUTLET STORES/BLUE ASH—Whiting has been manufacturing bedding in the Cincinnati area since 1949. Still owned and operated by the Whiting family, the Blue Ash factory cranks out thousands upon thousands of products each week. The company's state-of-the-art facility in Kentucky manufactures 30,000 comforters a week. With this high productivity level, new shipments, from comforters and comforter sets to bed pillows and draperies, are continuously arriving to replenish stock at its five area outlet stores. There, you'll find one of the broadest selections of bedding in the city. First-quality goods average a savings of 20%–50% off regular retail prices. Overruns and irregulars bring greater savings—over 50% off. The Blue Ash and Fairfield outlets have the largest selections. All occupy no-frills facilities where the merchandise is exposed among a mammoth interior. Handmade quilts hang like backdrops from the rafters. Hundreds of comforters in plastic, see-through wraps line the metal shelves. Draperies are displayed on window-like units. And, fabric scraps (the leftover cuts) are tossed in a big bin and sold by the roll. These are just $1.49 per yard. A roll of fabric ends is just $1 each. Large cardboard boxes feature truckload specials. To complement the bedding, bath linens are also sold at the outlets. But, these are not manufactured by Whiting. The main choices, also discounted, are first-quality Dundee linens and overruns from Fieldcrest and Cannon.
9999 Carver Road, Blue Ash; 513/791-8708. Mon–Sat 9am–6pm, Sun noon–5pm. 6975 Dixie Highway, Fairfield, 513/874-0550. Mon–Fri 10am–8pm, Sat 10am–6pm, Sun noon–5pm. 5716 Harrison Avenue, Dent, 513/574-5129. Mon–Fri 10am–9pm, Sat 10am–6pm, Sun noon–5pm. Delfair Shopping Center, Delhi Twp.; 513/922-6964. Mon–Fri 10am–9pm, Sat 10am–6pm, Sun noon–5pm Newport Shopping Center, 1709 Monmouth Street, Newport, Kentucky; 606/431-0650. Mon–Fri 10am–9pm, Sat 10am–6pm, Sun noon–5pm. VS, MC, DS.

BOONE FABRICS/DEERFIELD TWP.—This fabric discounter operates a bit differently than most. It makes use of a central buying core—the company's main headquarters located near the textile mills in Colfax, North Carolina. Fabrics are brought there from the mills in 200-yard bolts, then cut, divided into smaller portions, and shipped to each of the company's 10 stores. By offering goods in a no-frills environment and purchasing them in bulk, Boone keeps prices down and savings (averaging 20%–50% off regular retails) are passed onto the customers. With just one store in the Cincinnati area, Boone Fabrics offers only first-quality fabrics from over 114 different manufacturers. A complete line (several thousand) of in-stock fabrics for home decor is available in current

patterns and colors. Ask about volume discounts with the purchase of 50 or more yards.
9060 Kings Auto Mall; 513/683-5596. Tues, Wed, Fri, Sat 9:30am–6pm, Mon & Thurs 9:30am–8pm. VS, MC.

CINCINNATI MICROWAVE ESCORT STORE/DEERFIELD TWP.— The factory is state-of-the-art just like the products it manufactures. It is in a huge, white, modernistic building that reflects a high tech image. The factory is located towards the back. There, you'll enter a small room where one counter displays several models of radar/laser receivers and cordless telephones. You can buy them new, but the best way to save is to purchase a reconditioned model. It's suggested that you call first and ask which items are available at this special rate, especially since the inventory fluctuates. All models have a one-year warranty and can be ordered directly from the factory.
One Microwave Plaza; 513/489-3900. Mon–Fri 9am–5pm. VS, MC, DS.

KNOX SHOES/DEERFIELD TWP.—Unlike some of the bigger chains or warehouse stores, the selection at Knox Shoes isn't massive or overwhelming; it's well chosen. The store's main focus is on the top lines. Classics like Dexter, Rockport, Bostonian, Naturalizer, and Stride-Rite are featured. So are the fashion names—Eastland, Nine West, Easy Spirit, Calico, and Florsheim. As manufacturers update their product lines, Knox scoops them up. So the most current versions of the popular ongoing styles are always on hand. Owners Ed Dollin and father Lou began Knox shoes over three years ago. Coming from the manufacturing end, these guys literally know the footwear industry from the inside out. They know the quality grades. They know the styles that last. But most importantly, they know what customers prefer. While some may think they can get better deals at the discount chains, Ed warns them to watch out for brand names sold in cheaper grades. The idea at this store (and their other one in Mt. Vernon) is to offer good quality, name brand shoes (mainly leathers) for the family at reasonable off-prices. The owners also tout some of the old-fashioned customer services. They encourage each person, especially kids, to be correctly fitted using foot measuring devices.
9970 Kings Auto Mall Drive; 513/683-3555. Mon–Fri 10am–9pm, Sat 10am–8pm, Sun noon–5pm. VS, MC, DS.

ONCE UPON A CHILD/DEERFIELD TWP.—Recycling children's clothing is nothing new. Parents have been passing them down for years. Once Upon A Child has now expanded on this concept and made it into a thriving resale business. Part of a national resale chain with independently operated franchises, the stores are double the size of most resale shops and operate as efficiently as most regular retail chains. Seven of the eight area stores are locally operated through R and R Resale, Inc. under the direction of company president Becky Finger. A bit different than the old hand-me-down days, the company has formed stricter guidelines for accepting goods. Items must be in good condition and current with

no stains or flaws. They are then displayed systematically by size (newborn–14) and category—bedding, equipment, room decor, and furniture. Many are familiar brand names. Tiny hangers and clips keep clothing and smaller socks and slippers intact. Toys, youth sports equipment, and games fill the shelves. A built-in play area attracts the shortest shoppers.
9976 Kings Auto Mall Drive, Deerfield Twp.; 513/677-5700. 8315 Beechmont Avenue, Anderson Twp.; 513/474-5105. 9904 Colerain Avenue, Northgate; 513/385-3034. Glenway Crossing Center, 5138 Glencrossing Way, Western Hills; 513/451-7600. 7255 Dixie Highway, Fairfield, 513/860-0770. 2733 Madison Road, Hyde Park; 513/871-8700. Swallen's Center, 8087 Connector Drive, Florence, Kentucky; 606/282-8922. Tollgate Square, 9727 Montgomery Road, Montgomery; 513/791-1199. Mon–Sat 10am–8pm, Sun noon–5pm. VS, MC, DS.

Calico Corners

CALICO CORNERS/SYMMES TWP.—With over 1,500 bolts of fabric discounted everyday, the store is like a giant revolving door where customers continually shoot in and out. They may borrow an entire bolt or take home cut samples as part of the store's Fabric Approval Plan. Inside, the place spins. Fabric is carefully measured and cut. Custom workrooms are busy making draperies, slip covers, pillows, and servicing other requests (no upholstering). Signs read "Please touch the merchandise. You'll love it." Others direct you to a resource center with how-to-guides; a trims section featuring many choices; a line of Kirsch hardware; and a collection of M. Fay patterns. There are samples from the company's Brandywine Express fabrics from where over 2,000 choices can be made. Part of a larger chain, Calico Corners began in New York in 1948 by selling overruns and recycling fabric scraps from Bancroft Mills. Today, it's tough to get a franchise. Caryn Shaw has the only one in Cincinnati mainly because it was started by her aunt over 18 years ago. Though many first-quality decorator fabrics are sold here now, the company still buys seconds and overruns when possible. By purchasing items by the bolt directly from the mills and fabric houses the prices are kept down. For smaller needs consider the remnants—the ends of rolls (three yards or less).
Enyart Square, 11926 Montgomery Road; 513/693-5400. Mon & Thurs open 10am–8pm, Tues–Sat 10am–6pm. VS, MC, DS.

50% OFF SWEATS/SYMMES TWP.—The owners of the I Love Cinti Shoppes, Judy and Paul Hammond, also began 50% Off Sweats. At first, it was just an experiment. Situated in a strip mall, the building was initially used as a warehouse to stockpile sportswear and giftware for their area novelty stores. It was later that the couple decided to use the space more purposely. That's when they hired Todd Singer to manage their new idea and almost overnight transformed the warehouse into a discount store for activewear. It's been successful ever since. One of the reasons is because of the price. Most items in the store are at least 50% off department store prices, everyday. The other reason is the selection. Specializing in first-quality activewear by Jerzees from Russell Corporation, there is a wide variety of sweatshirts, hooded sweatshirts, tee shirts, sweatpants, and shorts in adult and youth sizes. With a license to print Cincinnati Bearcats merchandise, some of the best buys are on styles highlighting local sporting team themes. There are collegiate emblem hats and Cincinnati souvenir glassware, too.
Governor's Plaza Shopping Center, 9112 Union-Cemetery Road; 513/683-8351. Mon–Sat 10am-6pm (open later during summer months), Sun 11am–5pm. VS, MC, DS.

THE PAPER FACTORY/SYMMES TWP.—Great buys on paper, plastic, and Styrofoam tableware. The wide selection of designer patterns or solids are priced reasonably. A 25-pack of plastic coated, 8-3/4" plates comparatively priced at $4.40 is $2.64. The matching 6-7/8" plates compared at $3.22 is $1.94. A 24-pack of plastic cutlery, usually $2.50, is $1.50. Paper rolls of gift wrap go for 12¢–15¢ a foot in 24–30" lengths; foil wrap is 24¢ a foot. Customers can join the Rewinds Club for additional savings incentives. Flat wraps are priced well, but are not as good a deal as the rolls. The seconds, however, are priced even lower. There are gift bows, clusters of colorful helium balloons, pinatas, and party banners. Novelty items, party favors, balloons, and decorations fill in the bins. It's impractical to pay a lot for these short-lived trinkets so buy here.
Governor's Plaza Shopping Center, Union-Cemetery Road; 513/683-2288. Mon–Sat 10am–8pm,Sun noon–6pm. VS, MC, DS.

BUDGET BOUTIQUE SAMPLE OUTLET/LANDEN—You won't find out-of-style fashions or closeouts here, only the most current and hottest looks. Most are priced 40%–50% less than regular retail prices. The boutique, with over 60 lines including names like Leon Levin, Peter Popovitch, Northern Isle, and Foxcraft, sells nothing but manufacturers' clothing samples for women. These are first-quality fashions that are often a season or two ahead of what the department stores carry. With seven years in the business, owner Constance Gorman has everything well organized and neatly arranged, making the store comfortable to shop. The shop carries mostly sportswear, but there are some dresses and suits, too. The majority of fashions are in sizes 6–12. Larger sizes (14–16) are starting to be offered and petite sizes are available.
Landen Station, 3300 State Route 22; 513/683-4303. Mon–Sat 10am–6pm, Thurs 10am–8pm. VS, MC, DS.

SILK PLANT OUTLET/LANDEN—Lush greenery and tall, leafy trees look real enough to belong outdoors. Each tree is hand-constructed starting with a natural wood base. Almost any type of silk leaves can be attached to a trunk—over 50 different varieties from ficus to palm. Special orders are no problem. Owner Julie Jordan will personally create your order. An extensive collection of silk floor plants and fully assembled trees is on display. Individual florals and floral arrangements are here, too. But, besides the wide selection (one of the best in the city), the price—savings average 20%–50% off regular retails. Bring your own pot, if you like. Free, home consultation can be arranged.
Landen Station, 3304 Montgomery Road; 513/667-8880. Mon.–Fri 10am–6pm, Sat 10am–5pm, Sun noon–4pm. VS, MC, DS.

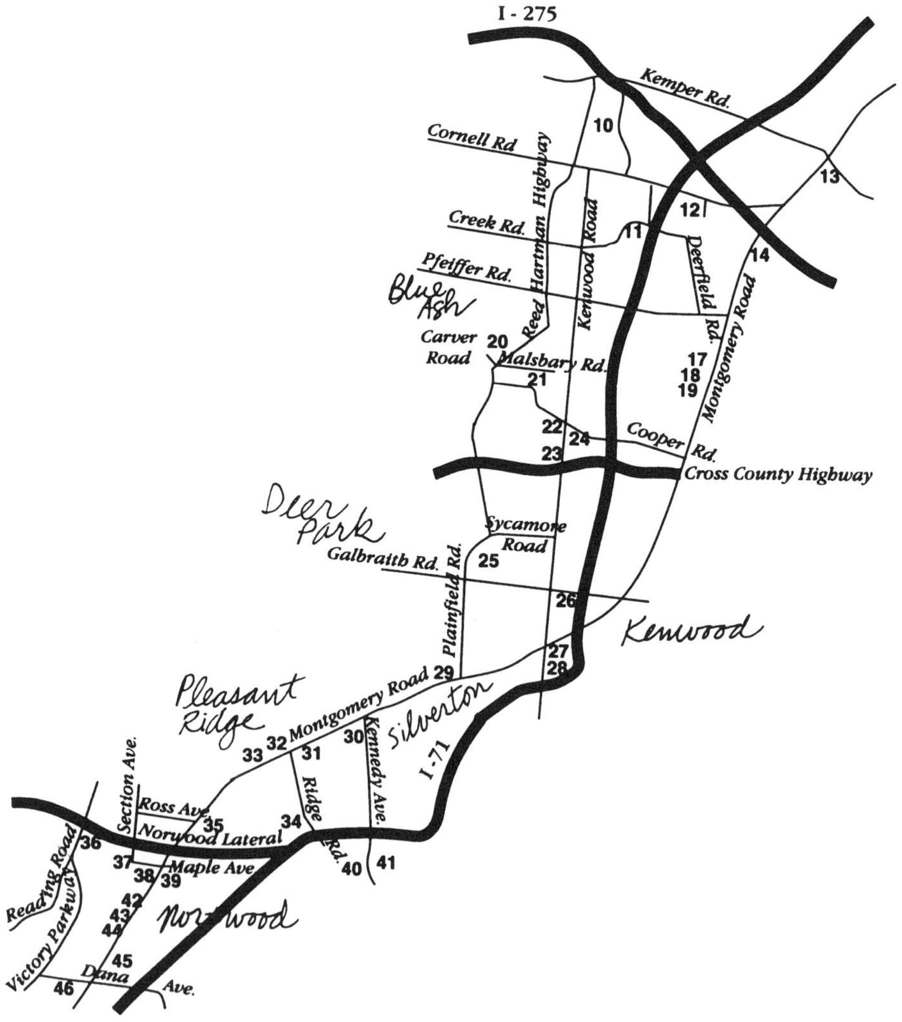

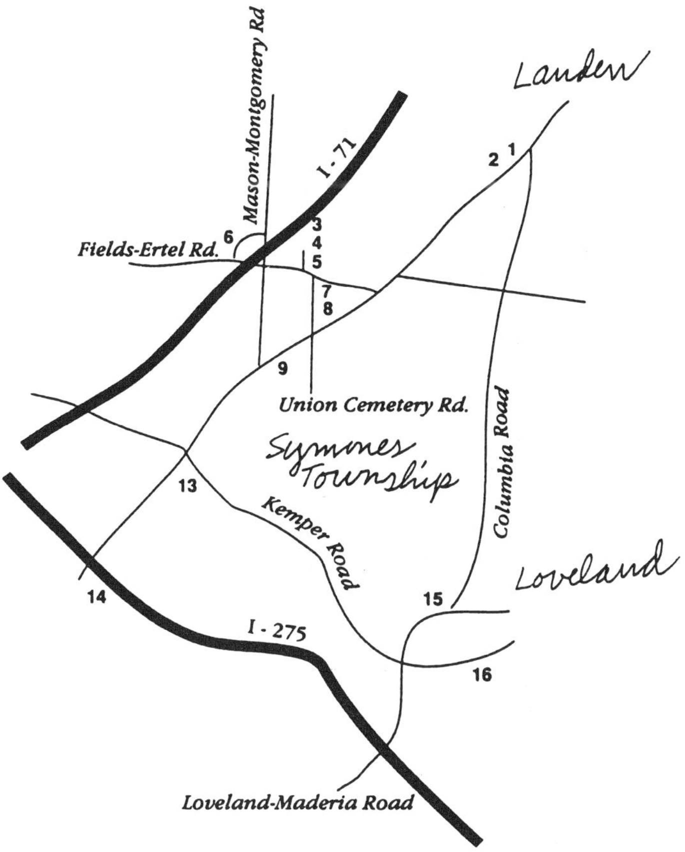

Admiral Window - 45
All My Children Maternity - 27
American Luggage Outlet - 22
Around the House - 19
Azzini Shoe Outlet - 11
Ben's Sportswear Outlet- 44
Boone Fabrics - 3
Budget Boutique - 1
Calico Corners - 9
Cappel's - 23
Cincinnati Microwave Escort Store - 6
Cotton Mill Factory Outlet - 15
Cover-Ups, Inc. - 30
Down Lite Int. - 12
Everybody's Records, Tapes & CD's - 31
Fechheimer Brothers - 21
50% Off Sweats - 7
Gentry Men's Clothier - 26
Hair Lucky Beauty Supply - 43
Hair Plus Beauty Supply - 33
Inch by Inch - 18
Jean-A-Faye - 25
Knox Shoes - 4
Lite-House Annex - 29
Loshins - 40
Mrs. Allison Wholesale Cookie Co. - 42
Office & Industrial Liquidators - 37
Office Furniture Outlet - 46
Once Upon a Child - 5 & 17
Oriental Warehouse - 10
The Paper Factory - 8
Pepperidge Farm Bakery Outlet - 14
Record Theatre Music & Video - 39
Regarding Books - 32
Saalfeld Paper Company - 36
Silk Plant Outlet - 2
Snooty Fox - 13 & 24
Sock Store - 35
The Surplus Work Clothes Co. - 38
Totes - 16
Velva Sheen Sportswear - 34
Wall Decor Outlet Store - 28
Warehouse Office Furniture Mart - 41
Whiting Manufacturing Linen Outlet - 20

Rookwood Pavilion

The East Side

The East Side has been a long-standing address for the well-heeled urbanite. It's an area where the confluence of old elegance and an upwardly mobile, middle class meet. Ironically, with its conservative, well-established neighborhoods—Hyde Park, Mt. Lookout, Oakley, and O'Bryonville—young professionals also find it the trendy place to live. Each community's identity is tied to a commercial focal point that attracts a city-wide clientele. It's nice to spend an afternoon on the East Side shopping its specialty stores and boutiques, sipping cappuccino in one of its quiet coffee shops or indulging in gourmet cuisine at fine eateries. But, toward evening, the local taverns become the preferred social scene. Until recently, neighborhood places were the only options in the area. Now, general shopping has shifted to Hyde Park

Plaza on Paxton Avenue. With its recent additions, the mall has been rejuvenated yielding new options. Encroaching on the East Side's borders, Rookwood Pavilion, the latest mall in the vicinity, has brought discounting up to social par by combining some of the architectural vestiges of the old LeBlond manufacturing plant with new construction. Though bargain hunting on the East Side attracts the hoi polloi, the ambiance still calls for dressing it up a notch even when scouting the deals. ¶ Further out, I-275 has defined the East Side's newest wave of shopping. Exits at Milford, Eastgate, and Beechmont show "Colerain-like" tendencies. Beechmont is going through its second childhood as old stores and malls have been recycled to appeal to a fickle clientele. Further to the north, Eastgate Mall led the way, but in the mid '80s Bigg's opened and quickly was surrounded by a maze of restaurants and discount wanna-bes, where it's hard to tell the roads from the parking lots. While Milford itself managed to preserve some of its old charm, I-275 and State Route 32 succumbed to gridlock. Recently, steps have been taken to alleviate the traffic problems around this exit, but the shopping remains a dead end.

OHIO PIKE SURPLUS BUILDING MATERIALS/AMELIA—What began as a garage full of odds and ends, five years later, needs an 11,000 sq. ft. building. Entry doors (some with leaded glass), interior moldings, windows, and cabinets are closeouts, clearance, and surplus inventory (some scratch 'n dent). By purchasing huge lots from major suppliers, often sight unseen, the owners, Eddie and Terry Hoskins, offer values averaging 30%–50% off retail. The selection varies every three months, so if you're looking for a specific item it's best to call first. There's carpeting, too. While Eddie runs one end of the business, his brother manages Terry's Carpeting Plus located in the same building. By going directly to the mills in Georgia or buying in lots, the company offers deals on carpeting, especially when buying in-stock merchandise.
2141 Ohio Pike (State Route 125); 513/797-4338. Mon–Fri 9:30am–5:30pm, Sat 9am–3pm. (Summer hours are longer.) VS, MC, DS.

BENJAMIN HEY MILL OUTLET/EAST END—From its Styrofoam cup lamp to its antique cash register Benjamin Hey demonstrates the true meaning of no frills. Inside the warehouse-like facility, 50-gallon drums topped with plywood are used to display bolt after bolt of first-quality fabrics for draperies, home decorating, and upholstery. There's even a picture of founder Ben Hey to keep a watchful eye over the colors of factory and Caron yarns available by the skein or hank. Owner Jim Barbara takes pride in exercising old fashioned business practices and is usually on hand to offer advice and opinions on anything from fabric to the state of the world. But even when he's not around, check the walls and posts. Jim keeps them covered with cartoons, articles, and clippings about things he thinks you should know. One piece of advice you should follow is to sign up on the store's mailing list to receive notice of special sales events.
4141 Airport Road; 513/321-3343. Mon–Sat 10am–6pm, Thurs 10am–8pm. VS, MC.

SWALLEN'S OUTLET STORE/FAIRFAX—Don't be put off by this drab, concrete warehouse facility. Inside, it offers bargain hunters the opportunity to save on Swallen's surplus items. Expect to find a wide selection of floor models, closeouts, and scratch 'n dent items. Some of your best buys will be on electronics, furniture, home accessories, and appliances. While it's hard to tell which items will end up at the outlet store, it's always worth checking out before paying full price somewhere else.
5700 Wooster Pike; 513/527-6505. Mon–Fri 10am–9pm, Sat 10am–6pm. VS. MC, DS, Swallen's.

AMERICAN BOOK DISPLAY/GLEN ESTE—Don't look for this company's publications at the local book store. This direct marketer sells them a different way—without retailers or vendors. The books are put on display for a limited period around an office or a school lounge, alongside an order sheet. They may be seen lying around your company watering hole one week or some other organization's office hangout the next. Potential customers can look them over leisurely and decide if they are interested in placing an order. If so, they simply sign up. Aimed toward the general interest reader with topics on sports, gardening, cooking, home improvement, and children's literature, these hard backs are all dressed up with deluxe covers. The company stands behind its products (even if a battery goes out on one of its electronic sound books). When 10 books are purchased, one is free. Started as a test three years ago by a Chicago publishing firm, the company now has 23 offices around the country. The one in the Cincinnati region is near Eastgate Mall in Glen Este. Customers can also shop here.
4440 Glen Este & Withamsville roads; 513/752-4199 or 800/854-2687. Mon–Fri 9am–5pm. Cash or check only.

AVOID SHOPPERS' PARALYSIS **Know the product market and pricing patterns of the stores you shop. Take some time to study prices not only at the stores you frequent but at others as well. Don't just stop at comparing price points in advertisements. If convenient, visit the store**

personally or call the store to check prices. Never be afraid to ask when an item will be placed on sale. Most everything (even in outlet stores) eventually goes on sale. Take your study a step further by learning how to predict when your favorite stores will mark down items the first time, the second time, and even for all-out clearance. Almost every store has a set policy on moving merchandise out for selling.

OLD NAVY CLOTHING COMPANY/HYDE PARK—Walking into Old Navy is like breathing fresh air—it's uncluttered, spacious, and bright. Just as the name says, casuals sold here are in cottons and denims that feel already broken in, not stiff and new. The latest division of the Gap's multitudinous network, it's the first store of its kind in the Tri-State. The store has clothing much like the Gap, only a bit downgraded in fabric weights and stitching. While the differences in quality are subtle, the differences in prices are noticeable. Inviting stacks of clothing and well-organized racks make it easy to find something for the whole family, even infants and toddlers. Plus-sizes are available.
Hyde Park Plaza, 3803 Paxton Avenue; 513/321-1683. Mon–Sat 9am–9pm, Sun 11am–6pm. Sycamore Plaza, Montgomery Road; 513/792-0032. Mon–Sat 10am–9pm, Sun noon–6pm. VS, MC, DS, AE.

SAVVY/HYDE PARK—For those in pursuit of designer labels, Savvy has them for less than regular retailers. The only difference is, the goods are gently worn. Sharon Menkhaus, the owner, selects only high-quality, current styles for women. One example of the bargains found here is a Jones New York blazer for $20. Neatly displayed around an old house typical of the neighborhood, the fashions include better handbags and ladies' shoes—many never worn.
3318 Erie Avenue; 513/533-1444. Mon–Fri 10am–7pm, Sat 10am–5pm. VS, MC.

THREAD SHED—CLOUD 9/HYDE PARK—With all the grace you would expect to find in a small boutique, Polly Haffner puts much of herself in the store—including her portrait which greets customers as they enter. Timeless classics, finely tailored suits, beautifully embellished apparel, and detailed fashion accessories are hand-picked towards the unusual by names like Bleyle, Ciao, Henry Lee, Leon Levin, Castleberry, Pendleton, and Herrera. Even though these fashions are not what you would call inexpensive, they're priced right for the quality. Look for the minute handwritten sign with an arrow pointing downward. This leads you down the steps to the Thread Shed. To make room for incoming stock, items collected from the upper level are transferred in regular intervals to the lower level. The same fashions that look so elegant upstairs among the rich surroundings look out of place when hanging from the rafters in the stark basement. However, the tradeoff is in the prices. These goods are marked 25%–50% (even 70%) off. It's always worth checking out since there might be something you can't live without.
Hyde Park Square, 2643 Erie Avenue; 513/321-9988. Mon–Sat 10am–5pm. VS, MC, DS.

Schmidt Paint & Wallpaper

FRED SCHMIDT/LINWOOD—It's small. It sells only paint and wallpaper, but customers keep coming back. Not because of the comfortable surroundings—the front of the store is a jumble of over 800 wallpaper sample books. Not because of the convenience—the road it sits on has long ago been bypassed by quicker more modern routes. It's partly because it offers quality—Porter Paints—and value—25% off all wallcoverings. Mostly, it's because of its owner, John "Fred" Schmidt. Continuing in the business his grandfather began over a century ago, John is described by his customers as a "walking computer full of advice." By purchasing paint in bulk and keeping overhead to a minimum he's able to compete with the big boys and offer something they don't have—Fred Schmidt.
5190 Old Wooster Pike; 513/871-3355. Mon–Fri 7:30am–5pm, Sat 8am–noon. Cash or check only.

THE WHOLESALE STONE COMPANY/MADISONVILLE—Not all of the big stones on the East Side are diamonds and gemstones. Some are just pure rock. With a large show area—a lot filled with decorative boulders and varying colors of quarried stone—this company has one of the rarest commodities in today's building and landscaping markets. By owning all of his own equipment and mining stone from his own quarries, as well as others, the owner, Jerry Crooks, pushes the prices down to wholesale level. According to Jerry, customers should keep in mind what pattern, what color (different shades are found in various parts of the country), and why they need the stone before making a trip. Veneer stone for covering standing objects; flagstone for any type of flat work such as patios, steps, and foyers; wall stone in different widths, and boulders for gardens are the most common types purchased.

Others, that go quickly, are the ones recovered from demolition sites such as the piers that once held the Central Bridge, or cobblestone from the streets.
6300 Warrick Street; 513/271-6300. Mon–Sat. 8am–5pm. VS, MC.

BANASCH'S FABRICS/NORWOOD—Fran Christensen and Alan Meis, owners of Banasch's, mix rich fabrics—fine wools, imported cottons, elegant French lace, luxurious silks, and beautiful linens—and showcase them at this long-established business that, up until recently, was a Downtown institution (since 1910). Its "Global Area" features African mud cloth, Guatemalan fabrics, Italian linens, Indian silks, and others from the far corners of the earth. Unique buttons made from antlers, bone, coconut, metal, and even odd substances found in remote rain forests are here, too. While the selection is upscale, values are passed on to the customer by purchasing the goods directly from the mills and buying fabric ends from designers such as Calvin Klein. Better-name patterns from McCall's, Vogue, Butterick, and Simplicity are half off the regular retail price.
Rookwood Pavilion, Edwards & Madison roads; 513/731-5757. Mon–Thurs 10am–8pm, Fri–Sat 10am–6pm, Sun noon–5pm. VS, MC, DS, AE.

ASTUTE FURNISHINGS/OAKLEY—From its store front location on Oakley Square, Astute has a limited but carefully chosen selection of previously owned furniture and home accessories sold on consignment. Some sets, but mostly occasionals and one-of-a-kind pieces, are spread throughout the first floor of the old building. Schooled buyers seeking antique furnishings and collectibles will find it worth canvassing. Out of his interest in the hardwoods and refinishing, Dick Schmeing began the store in 1993. It offers a good opportunity to pick up some bargains at 30%–40% off the price of comparable new items.
Oakley Square, 3052 Madison Road; 513/631-8886. Tues–Fri 10am–6pm, Wed 10am–8:30pm, Sat. 10am–5pm. VS, MC.

THE BOOK INN/OAKLEY—A block away from the mainstream, the Book Inn has a good selection of used books. It carries a good mix of hardbacks and paperbacks (even some current titles) among its pleasantly cluttered, well-organized interior. There's a noteworthy selection of collectible paperbacks, comic books, and signed editions. Owners Michelle and Chip Waddell display their most prized book—an autographed, first-edition copy of *Plowshare in Heaven* by Jesse Stuart (priced at $125) on the store's wall of literary relics. More collectibles are found below the counter. The average reader with varied tastes will easily uncover something to stimulate the mind.
4011 Allston Avenue; 513/351-1771. Mon–Sun 10am–8pm. Cash or check only.

PEACOCK CONSIGNMENT CLOTHING/OAKLEY—Sue Warm, the owner of the Peacock, has some advantages over her competition. Her well-known consignment shop is in a prime location to take in quality goods from the surrounding neighborhoods—most

prominently Hyde Park. Situated in the busy Oakley Square business district, it gets lots of traffic. But more importantly, it benefits from *her*. After 10 years, which in the consignment business is like light years, she has earned a reputation for being one of the best at her trade. There're not many places in the city you can go without consignment shoppers knowing about her store. Part of the reason is because she's very picky, not in a snobby sense, but rather in a caring way. Specializing in women's and men's clothing, along with fashion accessories, the store has an inviting selection of designer names that's carefully edited. Some of the more extravagant items are luxurious furs and fine jewelry. However, not everything has to be designer or upscale. The store stocks basic casuals, as well.
Oakley Square, 3048 Madison Road; 513/396-6464. Mon–Sat 10am–5pm, Wed 10am–8pm. VS, MC.

THE STORK COMPANY/OAKLEY—Tired of the hectic department store environment she once knew, Gail Scherz brings all of her years of experience to bear as owner of the Stork. Fitting into the narrow niche of consignment maternity wear, her modest store is not as crammed as many consignment shops, yet it still offers a sufficient selection to warrant a visit. With its full range of choices, the store, in the heart of Oakley, is a good source for the expectant mother. It also has children's wear and peddles an impressive collection of hand-sewn bibs, sweatsuits, bags, and pillows. By shedding some of the impersonal aspects of retailing, her store brings customers back even after her services are no longer needed.
Oakley Square, 2940 Markbreit Avenue; 513/841-0649. Tues–Sat 11am–6pm, Thurs 11am–7:30 pm. VS, MC.

ASIDE **Consignment and resale shops offer a variety of savings alternatives. You'll discover everything from children's, women's, men's, and vintage clothing to home furnishings and accessories, including cookware, kitchen appliances, baskets, and small decorative items. You'll also find recycled office furniture and office supplies as well as recycled sporting equipment. Stores will vary anywhere in size from a one-room strip mall store, or an old building, to an old house with over 15 rooms.**

TREASURES, INC./O'BRYONVILLE—While winding through 15 cozy rooms of this vintage house, you'll find previously owned furniture with remarkable details, framed prints by well-known artists, and special-edition collectibles. There are statuary, antiques, and hand-crafted items. One area is set aside as an Artist Room where each month a local talent highlights a series of current art works—oil paintings, watercolors, prints, or lithographs. Owner Barbara LeBlond began this unique consigning concept out of a love for collecting. Items vary from world travelers' mementos to objects that no longer fit the owner's home decor. Others are the precious belongings of a 99-year-old woman wanting a new home for her lifelong relics. "There's a history behind many of the items which makes me very sentimental," says LeBlond. Allow plenty of time to browse to fully appreciate its uncommon wealth. You may have to talk the owner into letting you buy.
1971 Madison Road; 513/871-8555. Tues–Sat 10am–5pm. VS, MC.

All My Children Maternity Outlet - **28**
American Book Display - **22**
Astute Furnishings - **3**
Banasch's Fabrics - **9**
Benjamin Hey Mill Outlet - **18**
Blinds Direct - **30**
The Book Inn - **7**
Cappel's - **5**
Coconuts Music & Movies - **8**
Cotton Mill Outlet Store - **29**
Discount Produce - **26**
Echo Furnishings - **20**

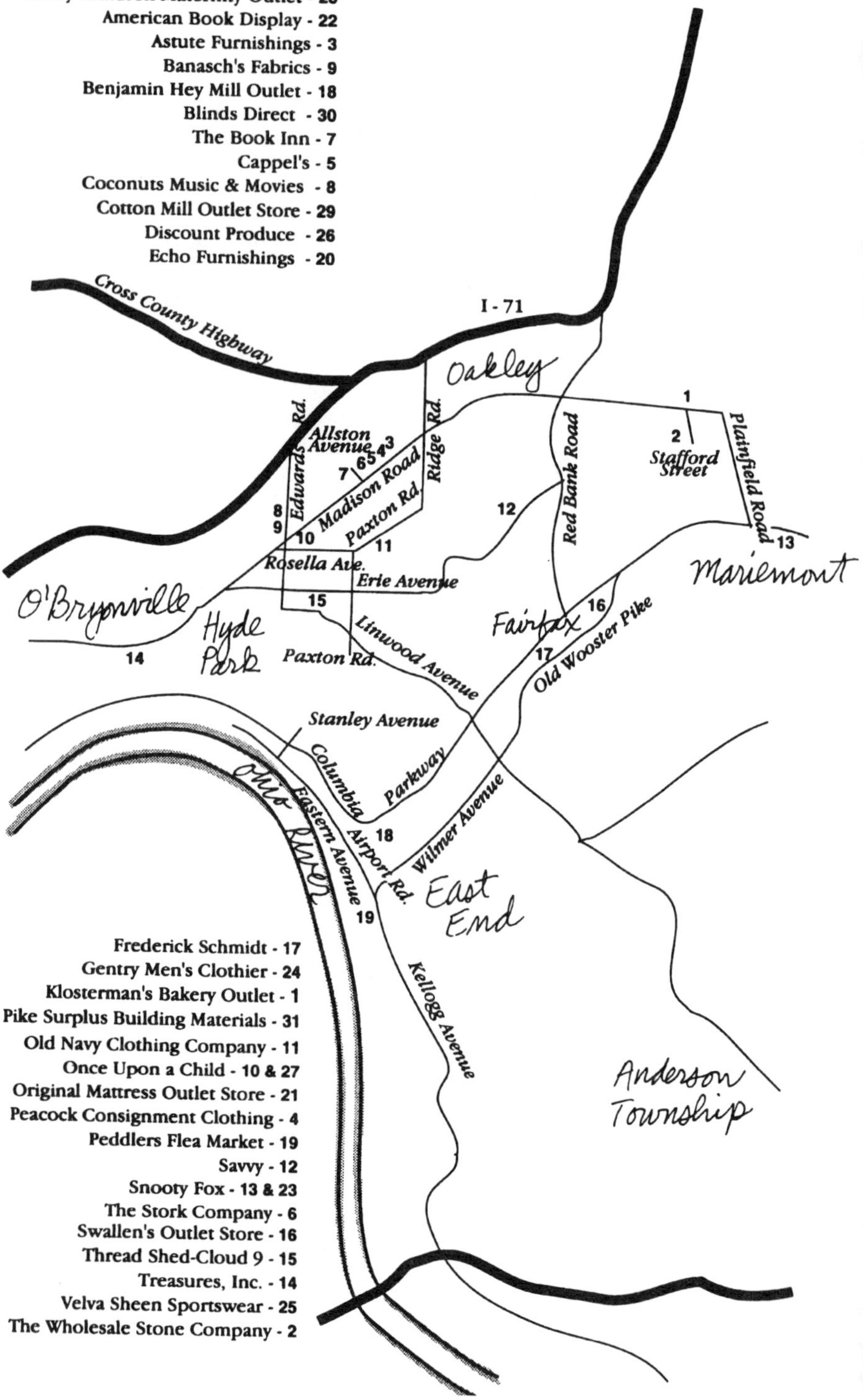

Frederick Schmidt - **17**
Gentry Men's Clothier - **24**
Klosterman's Bakery Outlet - **1**
Ohio Pike Surplus Building Materials - **31**
Old Navy Clothing Company - **11**
Once Upon a Child - **10 & 27**
Original Mattress Outlet Store - **21**
Peacock Consignment Clothing - **4**
Peddlers Flea Market - **19**
Savvy - **12**
Snooty Fox - **13 & 23**
The Stork Company - **6**
Swallen's Outlet Store - **16**
Thread Shed-Cloud 9 - **15**
Treasures, Inc. - **14**
Velva Sheen Sportswear - **25**
The Wholesale Stone Company - **2**

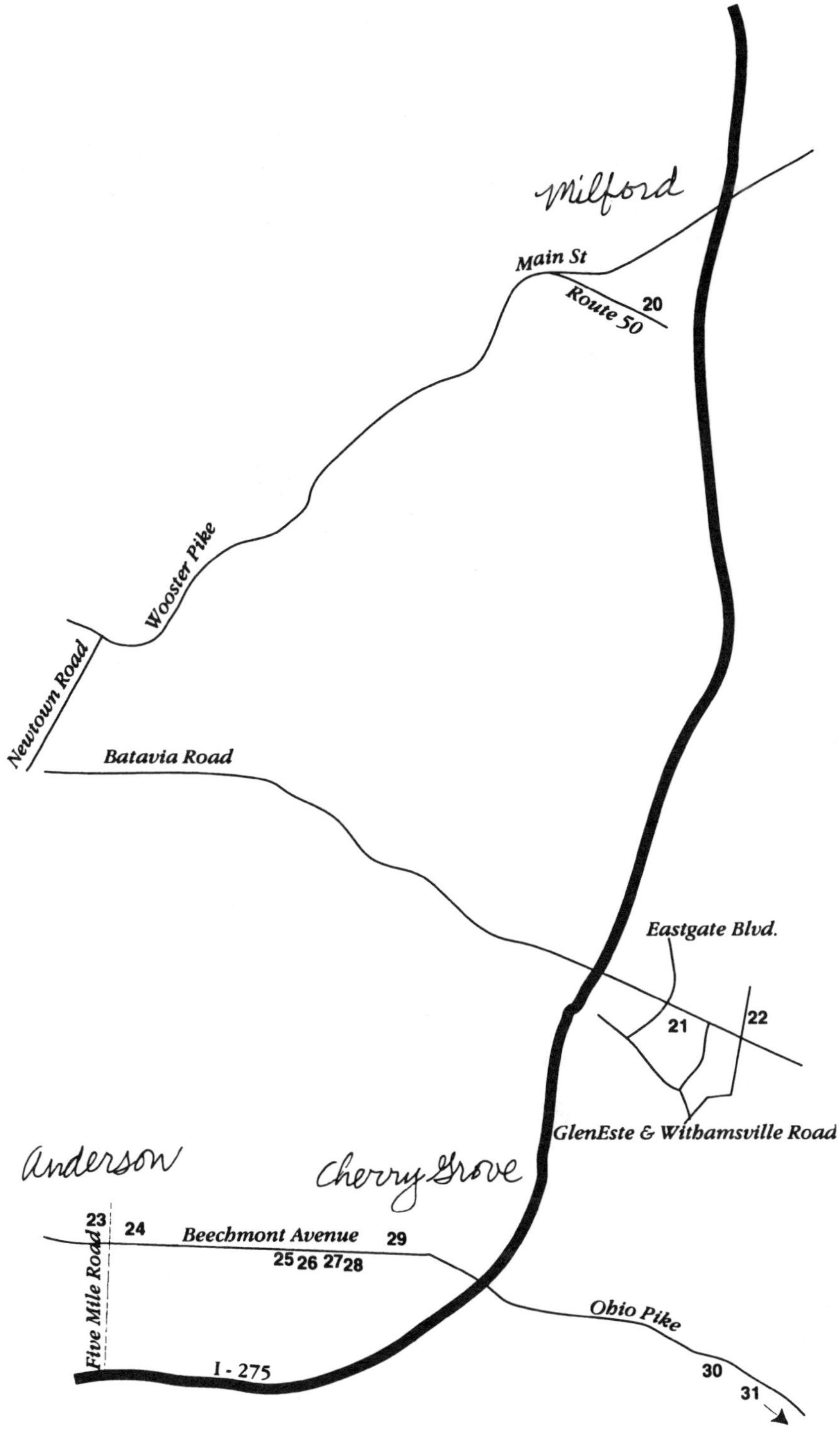
Milford
Main St
Route 50
20
Wooster Pike
Newtown Road
Batavia Road
Eastgate Blvd.
21
22
GlenEste & Withamsville Road
Anderson
Cherry Grove
23
24
Beechmont Avenue
29
25
26
27
28
Five Mile Road
Ohio Pike
I - 275
30
31

Ohio Factory Shops

The Outlet Malls

Outlet malls have been rising up out of the distant cornfields because of sensitive markets that have no relationship to corn, beans, and hogs. They're placed in the outback to avoid competing with department stores that offer goods by the same manufacturers at regular retail prices. In the last five to ten years Cincinnati's seen the arrival of five outlet malls within reasonable driving distances. They've become so popular that several expansions have been made. Now local shoppers can take advantage of savings on brand names without driving across the country. ¶ Today's outlet malls are different than those of yesteryear. They've come a long way to rival competition. The inventory they sell has changed from mostly irregulars and seconds to first quality and is generally a mix of closeouts and overstocks. Specializing in selling specific brands with an inventory that is current or just a season or two behind, outlet malls offer a savings of anywhere from 20%–75% off regular department store prices with everyday savings averaging 30%–40%. Developers have been careful to make sure that at least 80% of their tenants in the malls are true factory outlets, owned and operated by the manufacturers. The other 20% are usually "filler" stores or "captive brand" stores that sell brands that are not sold anywhere else.

DRY RIDGE OUTLET CENTER/DRY RIDGE, KENTUCKY
Small in size, the Dry Ridge Outlet Center is big in designer names. The powerhouse industry leaders—Liz Claiborne, Nike, and Mikasa—are its main anchors. Guess, Jones New York, JH Collectibles, Carter's, and Etienne Aigner are here, too. Opened in October of 1991, it's an earlier version of the Jeffersonville Outlet Center in Ohio. Owned and operated by the same corporation, McArthur/Glen Realty, it has some of the same characteristics but fewer, more compact stores. Conveniently located off of I-75 between Cincinnati and Lexington, much of its trade comes from travelers since this is the hot vacation route from Michigan to Florida. **Mall Layout:** Spread out around a parking lot, the mall is not designed for convenience. Patrons wanting to backtrack to their cars are forced to either retrace their steps or wind their way through the parking lot. Aesthetically, it's nothing more than functional with its generic-looking structure and minimal landscaping. A covered walkway with park benches positioned every so often as rest stops is the most elaborate attempt the mall makes in terms of design. Portable concession stands near the customer service center (in operation during summer months) are a poor alternative to a food court. **Location & Directions:** 1100 Fashion Ridge Road. From Cincinnati: Take I-75 South to Exit 159 in Dry Ridge; turn right off the exit and right again into the outlet center. It is approximately 25 miles from Cincinnati. The driving time is about 40 minutes. From Lexington: Take I-75 to Exit 159; turn left

off the exit and then right into the outlet center. It is approximately 42 miles from Lexington. The driving distance is about 50 minutes. **Services & Hours:** It's best to park at the southwest corner of the mall near the Customer Service Center. Maps of the mall and store listings are available as well as travel information on the area and Kentucky. Sign up for the mall's "Preferred Client" card at no charge for stores that offer special discounts on certain items. **Mall Hours:** Mon–Sat 10am–9pm; Sun noon–6pm. Holiday hours may vary. Customer information: Mon–Sat 10am–9pm; Sun noon–6pm. **Phone:** 606/824-9516 or 800/969-3767.

MAIN DRAWING CARDS—All the right names and a diverse product mix:

GUESS?—Guess devotees will find the huge selection of first-quality overstocks, irregulars, and discontinued items at prices substantially less than regular retails. A collection for kids is included in the back of the store. *606/824-9363.*

LIZ CLAIBORNE—Set off from the others in a larger, all-encompassing building, this famous designer's lines—Liz Claiborne, Lizsport, Elisabeth, and Claiborne for Men—are draped everywhere. This particular outlet is distinguished from the one in Jeffersonville, Ohio, by the goods it carries. It has more current merchandise with irregulars (most flaws are barely noticeable) intermittently mixed with first-quality items. *606/824-7554.*

MIKASA—It's hard to beat Mikasa's selection for the quality and value. Aisle after aisle of tabletop treasures such as dinnerware, stemware, and flatware are available. There is crystal giftware and photo frames, too. A shipping station is in the store for sending purchases anywhere in the country. *606/824-6800.*

NIKE—Shopping here is worth the trip to the mall. Nike's outlet boasts one of the widest selections around. Lots of workers run around with a helpful attitude and brag on the options for men, women, and children. They direct customers toward good deals on just about anything in the store. Embroidered logo sports caps, tee shirts, and a good selection of athletic shoes (in better grades than most discounters) are at notable savings. *606/824-4700.*

SPIEGEL OUTLET STORE—A smaller version of their Jeffersonville Outlet Center store, this one has only ladies' apparel along with a few domestic items—bath towels, home accessories, photo frames, and lamps. Some racks are topped by signs claiming items are straight from the catalog at discounted prices. *606/824-9250.*

OTHER STORES AT THE MALL—In alphabetical order:

ADOLFO II—The emphasis is on ready-to-wear knits by Adolfo II, Donna Toran, and other brand names. Neatly filed on the racks, these precisely cut styles bring about unimaginative looks that until accessorized seem a bit basic. Coordinated outfits displayed around the store offer some solutions. *606/824-9554.*

BASS SHOES—Bass, an old outlet mall standby, breeds familiarity with traditional sole. Like many of the company's outlets this one has a rustic, outdoors theme with a hint of cedar in the air. While other Bass stores are larger and highlight both casual wear and shoes, this one is limited to footwear for men and women with some tote bags and accessories. Reasonable factory-direct prices. *606/824-9637.*

BROWN SHOE COMPANY—A predictable format with the usual lineup of women's shoes by Naturalizer, Connie, Life Stride, and Naturalizer Sport. The savings potential ranges from 30%–50% off retail. However, it might do you just as well to check the discount stores in your own area for these popular lines. *606/824-3122.*

CAPE ISLE KNITTERS—Since 1881 Cape Isle Knitters has been one of the largest manufacturers of knits and sweaters in the industry. Well-known catalog companies and stores have sold its quality-made apparel for years under various labels. They've recently begun selling goods factory-direct with their own name at the outlet malls. Smaller than some of their other outlets, it has a full range of rich-looking, heavyweight knits in classic styles for men and women that net 25%–60% off regular retails. *606/824-9650.*

CARTER'S—The store is bright, uncluttered, and well organized, making it easy to look over the extensive selection for infants, toddlers, boys, and girls. The many racks offer savings on Carter's famous playwear, sleepwear, and layette sets (up to size 14). Toward the back of the store a few racks with irregulars or seconds have even greater savings. *606/824-7470.*

CLAIRE'S ACCESSORIES—The store is crammed with any type of small accessory that could complement a look—from jewelry and hair bows to mini bags and wallets. Expect to pay at least 25% less than what you normally would for non-sale items at Claire's regular mall stores. *606/824-9838.*

ASIDE **Plan ahead. Make shopping lists. Take time to evaluate your and your family's needs before venturing out to the outlet malls. This way you can take full advantage of your trip and not have to worry about running out of time and having to make a repeat visit.**

ETIENNE AIGNER—Aigner's traditionally styled shoes for women are everywhere. Handbags and small accessories are in the back of the store. While some of the items are manufactured specifically for the outlet store, much of the merchandise is from previous seasons. It's a trade-off for the lower prices. A narrow selection of raincoats and wool coats along with leather outerwear (not always in stock) is worth checking out. *606/824-3404.*

FAMOUS BRANDS HOUSEWARES—Metal racks are filled with cookware, bakeware, storage items, and small appliances. There are hundreds and hundreds of kitchen gadgets, some you never knew existed or wanted. Brand name products by Anchor Hocking, Durand, Intercraft, and Rubbermaid. *606/824-3510.*

GEOFFREY BEENE—As part of Philip-Van Heusen's formidable retail empire, Geoffrey Beene caters to the businessman who desires a little more style yet wants to remain within the confines of what's permissible in the work place. The line borders between the company's upscale Windsor collection and its own moderate namesake, Van Heusen. Although there is some sportswear among the selection, the store concentrates on dress shirts. Many are well displayed with matching ties making it easy for the "coordinating impaired" to pull together a becoming look. Prices are fair minded at 25%–50% off regular retails. *606/824-9652.*

GREETINGS 'N' MORE—The bulk of this store's inventory consists of greeting cards at everyday savings of 50% off retail. Of course, along with the cards that seem a bit generic are all the gift trimmings such as paper and ribbon. Large boxes filled with individual rolls of gift wrap are in back of the store and priced at 99¢ each, which seems appropriate considering the lesser grade of paper. Other choices include party favors, partyware, and seasonal items, all of which the store claims to be priced at 50%–75% below retail. *606/824-9477.*

JH COLLECTIBLES—This sizable store is a career woman's paradise. Its many classic choices of finely tailored suits, blazers, and sportswear bring gratification to those wanting a wardrobe uplift without paying a fortune. A "sample" rack of JH Collectibles' latest "trial runs" can't be ignored. Here, customers can save even more on selected styles merely because the manufacturer wants to try out new design elements (meaning an item may have an extra pocket or button). *606/824-5513.*

JONES NEW YORK—A breed apart from many other outlet stores, Jones New York merits special attention for its collection of current, first-quality merchandise. Not only are the prices less than retail (hovering at least 20%–30% below) but a greater selection is in store for misses' and petites' sizes. All of the merchandise is factory-direct, which makes you wonder why anyone would ever shop the department stores for these tailored classics—suits, blazers, and fashion separates. *606/824-7582.*

KITCHEN COLLECTION—Boatloads of kitchen accessories, appliances, cookware, bakeware, and storage things are stocked at Kitchen Collection. Many small kitchen gadgets are displayed around the store with some reserved near the front for impulse buying. Famous maker products—Hamilton Beach, Proctor-Silex, Kitchen Collection (the store's namesake), Wear Ever, and Anchor Hocking—are front liners. Most are priced moderately. *606/824-3310.*

LEATHER LOFT—For those with a leather obsession this is the place to find an excellent cross-mix of functional yet stylish pieces. The store carries the full spectrum of small leather goods, handbags, briefcases, organizers, and accessories. It also has a distinctive collection of all-leather and leather-trimmed luggage in individual pieces or sets. Multipurpose, leather garment bags are available for the overnight business traveler. Overall, the prices reflect excellent values. *606/824-3101.*

L'EGGS/HANES/BALI—This store makes it easy to pinpoint sizes and bargains with many accessible bins. The tiny ones divide the smaller items such as L'eggs and Hanes hosiery or men's and women's undergarments according to styles and sizes. The larger ones are heaped full of various buys marked as closeouts or irregulars. These bins are portable for easy positioning in high traffic areas, so look for them most anywhere on the selling floor. Hanes irregular sweatshirts and sweatpants are prime candidates for "bargain bin fillers." Other items such as Bali and Playtex bras and lingerie have their own sections. For everyday essentials, some of the best buys are on Hanes socks for men and women and men's slightly irregular underwear. *606/824-9570.*

MAIDENFORM—Maidenform's selection of first-quality merchandise merits attention. The sleepwear, as does the lingerie, ranges from elegant to practical and is notably less than regular retail. Unfortunately, the store's decor is not quite as impressive. The partial wooden, slightly raised floor and the track lighting are lame attempts at sprucing up what would otherwise be a satisfactory outlet decor. *606/824-9736.*

NINE WEST—Although its prices on items are reasonable with at least 30% off regular retails, the real draw in this outlet is the deep selection. Vast quantities of Nine West's casual and dress footwear, from flats to pumps, are conveniently arranged around the store. Fashionable boots also make a strong showing. The broad range of styles from this famous maker far exceeds what is found in department stores and other shoe retailers. *606/824-6620.*

SOCKS GALORE—This specialized store offers shoppers the convenience of purchasing socks for the entire family all in one place. Thousands of styles saturate its small selling space with names like Hanes, Isotoner, and L'eggs showing up everywhere. This should come as no surprise since Hanes owns and operates the store. The store has an exclusive line of the popular World's Softest Socks and Dri-Sox. Savings run at least 10%–15% off retail, and often more. Check out the store's frequent buyer program. *606/824-3040.*

THE SWEATSHIRT COMPANY—The Sweatshirt Company is a great source for stocking up on the basics. The standard selection consists of Discus and Tutlex sweatshirts, tee shirts, and sweatpants. The prices are anything but standard. They are notably less than what you would pay at the regular retail stores. *606/824-7008.*

VAN HEUSEN—Van Heusen's main stock has an eye-catching display along the back wall. Men's dress shirts are categorized according to fabric content, all-cotton or mostly cotton, and are moderately priced and perfect for the practical-minded. For more relaxed times, Van Heusen's casual sportswear for men or women is a good value at savings that net 20%–50% off regular prices. *606/824-9639.*

WELCOME HOME—This particular Welcome Home store doesn't seem quite as inviting as the name indicates. As part of a huge national chain, it pales in comparison to the ones at the outlet malls in Jeffersonville, Ohio. While the inventory includes many of the same type of goods—afghans, candles, table linens, picture frames, potpourri, brassware, and stationery—the store emphasizes the trivial and neglects the quality. *606/824-9648.*

WESTPORT LTD. /WESTPORT WOMAN—A good source for rounding out your wardrobe, Westport has casual and career wear at 20%–50% off regular retail everyday. A full range of misses' and women's plus sizes is available. *606/824-3805.*

Factory Stores of America Outlet Center

FACTORY STORES OF AMERICA/CARROLLTON, KENTUCKY

Occupying a functional "pole-barn-like" structure, this small outlet center looks more like a factory than a mall. If it were not for a bold band of exterior signs identifying the brand names contained inside—Lee, Wrangler, Barbizon, Jansport, Jantzen, Vanity Fair, and Health-tex—it would be difficult to make the distinction. Inside it's clear the mall centers around one focal point, the VF Factory Outlet Store. The store justifies the entire reason for shopping this otherwise undistinguished mall. Consuming at least one-third of the outlet center, it features excellent factory-direct buys for the entire family. It doesn't take long to realize that the other five stores largely depend upon the presence of VF to ensure their existence. **Mall Layout:** The six stores in this mall are all enclosed under one roof. A spacious aisleway in the center of the mall is often filled with additional vendors selling anything from crafts to jewelry. Periodic tent sales are held in the parking lot and serve as a temporary extension of the building. **Location & Directions:** Factory Stores of America, Hwy. 227. From Cincinnati: Take I-71 to Exit 44, Hwy. 227 North. From Madison: Take Hwy. 36 West to Hwy. 227 South. From Lexington/Frankfort: Take Hwy. 421 North to I-71 North to Exit 44, Hwy. 227 North. **Services & Hours:** The Customer Service Desk is in the VF Factory Outlet Store. There, information and brochures on the mall can be obtained. A centralized snack bar, "The Food Place," is located in the middle of the mall. **Mall Hours:** Jan–May 29: Mon–Thurs 9am–7pm, Fri–Sat 9am–9pm, Sun noon–6pm; May 30–Dec: Mon–Thurs 9am–8pm, Fri–Sat 9am–9pm, Sun noon–6pm. **Phone:** 502/732-6666 or 800/SHOP-USA.

VF FACTORY OUTLET—A gem of a store in the hills of Kentucky, VF Factory Outlet is loaded with great family casual wear. It features vast quantities of denim jeans, sweats, and tee shirts by Lee and Wrangler, along with Jantzen sportswear at half-off retail prices. Sleepwear and intimate apparel from Barbizon and Vanity Fair, and Health-tex playwear for kids, have half off savings. To save even more don't miss the store's "Warehouse Clearance Center." Overall, it's hard to beat VF's prices and selection on these famous brand name fashions. *502/732-6666.*

BANISTER SHOES—Even though this shoe store claims to feature over 40 brands, the selection is still hit or miss. It may have many different brands but that doesn't guarantee the size or style you want will be readily available. Don't expect exceptional choices; the prices and the merchandise are rather commonplace. *502/732-6913.*

BON WORTH—The factory for this brand is located in Hendersonville, North Carolina. With stores primarily in the south, outlets like this one are beginning to show up in the northern part of the country as well. This particular Bon Worth store has a big selection of mix and match separates for dress and casual wear at moderate prices. Available in misses', petites', and plus sizes, many of the fashions are slanted toward the conservative dresser with not much variance in style. *502/732-0716.*

ASIDE **Outlet Malls have special sales, too. Throughout the year outlet stores will have major sales. Often these are in conjunction with the holidays or seasonal changes. In January and February there are clearance sales. In August and September there are sidewalk sales.**

FAMOUS BRANDS HOUSEWARES—This store is filled with everything imaginable for the kitchen. Larger than some of the company's other housewares outlets, it has the same type of products by Anchor Hocking, Durand, Intercraft, Rubbermaid, and other brands—only more of them. *502/732-5883.*

PRESTIGE FRAGRANCE & COSMETICS—Featuring cosmetics and skin care products from Revlon, Almay, and Jean Nate, Prestige has good buys on some items from these lines, but don't expect to find a complete selection. This goes double for the store's offering of fragrances. Only a sampling of designer fragrances is showcased in the store. These items will be substantially reduced with legitimate factory-direct prices. *502/732-6948.*

VAN HEUSEN—One of the larger Van Heusen stores around, this one has a wider selection for both men and women. While the store still has its standard outlay of men's dress shirts, more emphasis is placed on its casual sportswear line. Of course, the prices are the usual 20%–50% off regular retails. *502/732-9255.*

FACTORY STORES OF AMERICA/GEORGETOWN, KENTUCKY

There's little that surprises shoppers at this outlet mall. If not for a few stores like Carolina Pottery and Stone Mountain Handbags, there are not many reasons to drive the extra distance to shop here. The routine standbys, most of which are found in outlet centers closer to home, are what dominate its retail space. However, if traveling through the area en route to the southern states, it may be worthwhile to check out the bargains. The mall is at a prime stopping off point by I-75 (just north of Lexington) in a commercial area that's surrounded by the usual herd of fast food restaurants, gas stations, and some retail stores. **Mall Layout:** In fragmented sections, the outlet mall lacks a certain flow. Angled in different directions, its two buildings are disconnected which makes for a disruption in shopping. The inclusion of partial awnings on the buildings is a flimsy attempt at adding design or protective covering during bad weather days. The long wooden benches on the walkways offer regular resting points. **Location & Directions:** From Cincinnati: Take I-75 to Exit 126. Turn right onto Route 62, then left onto Commercial Drive. **Services and Hours:** Park near the Carolina Pottery Outlet Store where the mall's customer service area is located. Maps and brochures about the mall, along with any special promotional offers or coupons, are available to patrons. The Main Street Eatery is the only food service in the mall. **Mall Hours:** Jan. 2–March 5 Mon–Sat 10am–7pm, Sun 1–6pm. March 6–Dec. 31 Mon–Sat 10am–9pm, Sun 1–6pm. **Phone:** 502/863-3660 or 800/SHOP-USA.

MAIN DRAWING CARDS—This mall doesn't have many of the big designer names. It does have a few names, though, that are not available closer to home. Listed below are the mall's main attractions.

CAROLINA POTTERY—The scent of potpourri signals customers this is not just a pottery store. In fact, little pottery is found between the concrete floors and fluorescent lighting of the huge warehouse-like interior. Customers will find a variety of merchandise from housewares to wicker; candles to silk flowers; and even a year-round "Christmas Shop." The helter-skelter approach to retailing is also reflective in its prices. Some glassware, which can be found in Cincinnati, is priced here 50% higher. There are good values here, but they are not on everything that meets the eye. *502/863-3660.*

CAROLINA CLOCK & RUG OUTLET—After passing though rows of Carolina Pottery's less than distinguished merchandise, there's a smaller, more noteworthy outlet (found inside the pottery store) featuring finely-crafted grandfather clocks by Howard Miller. Elegant mantel and table clocks, along with exquisite rugs (many hand-woven in Russia and China), are also found within the confines of this low-profile store. Note the collection of interesting art silks. It's hard to know whether or not the half-off prices on these items are good, but they appear to be a good values. *502/863-4481.*

STONE MOUNTAIN HANDBAG FACTORY—This store is a true manufacturer's outlet (There's even a certificate of authenticity hanging on the wall.). Since not many outlets like this are around, customers should feel fortunate to find these crafted, first-quality handbags and accessories at the store's exceptional value prices. The extensive collection (the largest in the area) of genuine leather goods, along with Stone Mountain's Saddle River and Ande lines, is another attraction. For the craft-minded, a stash of leather scraps can be found at the counter for next-to-nothing prices. *502/863-0519.*

OTHER STORES AT THE OUTLET MALL— In alphabetical order:

AILEEN—Aileen has first-quality, current-season merchandise with an emphasis on casual knits. In sizes for misses, petites, and plus-size women, the selection is ample with new shipments constantly arriving to replenish the moderately-priced stock. *502/868-0746.*

BASS COMPANY STORE—Founded in 1867, Bass is an established name in the footwear industry. Now owned by Van Heusen, it has expanded its lines to include casual wear. This particular Bass outlet features men's and women's footwear, with some tote and travel bags, but the store also has an entryway leading next door to the Van Heusen outlet for casual wear. *502/863-1117.*

BLACK & DECKER—Specializing in selling Black & Decker factory power tools and appliances, this store is an excellent savings source for the home workshop. Save up to 50% on a broad selection of reconditioned, discontinued, and excess products and those with blemished cartons and still receive the same factory warranties. Look for the generic boxes for reconditioned products, but don't overlook the clearance bins filled with small accessories, such as drill bits and circular saw blades. These items are coded with numbers to match prices ranging from 10¢–$9. *502/867-1302.*

BON WORTH—Bon Worth features comfortable sportswear for women in coordinating looks that are styled for the conservative dresser. A broad selection of misses', petites', and plus sizes is in the store at moderate prices. *502/863-0879.*

BOOT FACTORY—A giant, wooden cactus greets customers inside this true factory outlet store which features Laredo and Code West boots. The footwear, organized by size, is displayed on metal racks stretching to the ceiling. Each is packed with western-style boots intermingled with work and hiking styles. Most are discontinued and overstock items at 30%–60% off retail prices. There's also a good selection of Australian outback dusters and a wide variety of cowboy hats displayed throughout the store. *502/868-9426.*

BOOK WAREHOUSE—Well organized around broad categories, Book Warehouse has a wide selection of discounted books. The best bargains are on books first published several years ago, while more current titles are priced no less than at the local bookstore or Kroger. This is not a place to come searching for a specific title but rather to browse among the stacks for something that catches your eye. One of the better bargains is in the travel books. Even though many are a year or two old they are usually sufficient. In addition, there are some classical compact discs, audio cassette books, and calendars at discounted prices. *502/868-5487.*

ASIDE **Dress comfortably. Dress for the weather. The average outlet mall shopper will generally spend a good part of the day shopping the malls, since many have driven quite a distance to get there. It's a good idea to wear shoes that offer great walking support. Unlike most regular shopping centers, these malls often are not enclosed to cut back on costs. So dress warm in the winter, cool in the summer, and bring an umbrella for rainy shopping days.**

BUGLE BOY—Featuring Bugle Boy casual wear for men, women, and children, this store has a wide selection at factory-direct savings of at least 30% off regular retails. Children's fleece and denim wear are especially good buys. *502/868-0727.*

CASUAL CORNER & CO.—Don't expect to find bargains on closeouts and overruns from Casual Corner's regular mall stores here. Different fashions are bought specifically for the company's outlet stores. *502/863-1976*

CLAIRE'S ACCESSORIES—Loaded with small accessories from hair bows and jewelry to mini bags and wallets, the store has them for at least 25% less than Claire's non-sale items at regular retail malls. *502/863-5165.*

CORNING REVERE FACTORY STORE—This store, which is smaller than some of Corning's other outlets, still carries a good representation of the manufacturer's lines—Corning Ware, Pyrex, Corelle, Visions, Revereware, and Crown Corning Gift Glassware. A wide selection of open stocks and sets is priced reasonably with greater savings on seconds, discontinued patterns, and overstocks. *502/868-9212.*

DUCK HEAD—This store is worth visiting to take a spin on the barber's chair in the front of the store. Otherwise, the selection of merchandise is somewhat cliched, lacking in style and spirit. The store has the same style of striped shorts today as were on sale two years ago. The merchandise is surrounded by a decor that suggests outdoor ruggedness with a canoe; quality tailoring with an old-time sewing machine; and classic looks with a top hat. The prices are a little better than what would be expected at a department store sale, but the selection at this outlet is much greater. Several bargain bins in the store offer greater value, but watch out for damaged items. *502/868-9857.*

FACTORY LINENS—Since 1892, the Ritzenthaler Company has been manufacturing its quality lines of Ritz kitchen towels, cleaning cloths, and laundry aids. Several of its better known products such as the Tug O' War ironing board pad and cover set (regularly sold at other retailers for $20, found here for $11.99) and Wonder dish towels are at factory-direct prices. While items from other manufacturers are sold here (shower curtains and various linens), the best values are on the high-caliber Ritz products. *502/863-2266.*

FARBERWARE—The budget-minded cook will find good buys on Farberware cookware. The shelves are filled with items that may be reduced simply because they are overstocks or blemished. Second-quality items can be found in the store's bargain bins where most any of Farberware's products could end up. But, it's wise to check them over carefully for imperfections. *502/868-9075.*

L'EGGS/HANES/BALI FACTORY OUTLET—Since it's well organized, shoppers can find their favorite styles and sizes quickly in this store. Accessible bins divide smaller items such as L'eggs and Hanes hosiery or men's and women's undergarments according to size. The larger ones are filled with Hanes sweatshirts and sweatpants in closeouts and irregulars. Bali and Playtex bras and lingerie have their own sections. Hanes socks and slightly irregular underwear for men and women are the best buys. *502/868-9888.*

LEVI'S OUTLET BY DESIGNS—This huge, bi-level store is loaded with a big selection of Levi's casual wear. Arranged within definitive sections, it makes it easy for shoppers to locate Levi's most popular lines—Dockers, Levi's 500 jeans, silver or red tab denims, and Levi's Straus & Company casual wear. Don't expect to find prices much different than what the department stores offer during special sales. *502/868-0224.*

$9.99 STOCKROOM—The store's black decor highlighted by bold neon signs and purple carpeting, and annoying rock music blaring in the background, alerts the customer to whom this store caters. The racks of youthful clothing in juniors', misses', and plus sizes reflect trendsetting street fashions gone slumming. Some of the goods push the price envelope out to $12.99, but most hover around the $9.99 level. Of particular interest is the $9.99 rack of man-tailored, vintage-like blazers, thus making it possible for the trendy teenager to dress as her father did 15 years ago. *502/863-4629.*

THE PAPER FACTORY—For those special occasions, the Paper Factory has exceptional values on a better-than-average selection of partyware in current patterns and solid colors. Balloons, party favors, and decorations are another good reason to celebrate. The best values, though, are on the store's gift wrap that is available in large rolls referred to as "rewinds." Since this paper is bought in bulk and wound at the store without a core or fancy packaging, customers receive more for their money. The store's wall of bows has a huge selection of style and color choices for the finishing touches to packages. Stock up on greeting cards, stationery, and invitations. *502/868-0942.*

PRESTIGE FRAGRANCE & COSMETICS—Revlon, Almay, and Jean Nate cosmetics and skin care products are featured in this store along with some designer fragrances. While the prices on these items are lower than other retailers, the selection is much more limited. A "99¢ boutique" is worth checking out. *502/863-4117.*

RACK ROOM SHOES—Like all the other Rack Room Shoe stores, the prices are discounted. However, the same type of footwear is available closer to home at their regular retail mall stores. *502/863-5654.*

SOCKS GALORE & MORE—For as many socks that fill this one small store, it's well organized and easy to shop for the whole family all in one place. Many of the socks bear the Hanes label and are at everyday savings. A good color selection, along with bright colors kids love, is an added advantage of shopping here. The store's exclusive lines, Dri-Sox and the World's Softest Socks, are worth the stop. *502/863-2229.*

TOTES/SUNGLASS WORLD—This store doesn't carry quite the selection as some of the other Totes outlets, but stop in anyway. The usual basics—umbrellas, travel bags, rain coats, rain hats, luggage, and accessories—are in stock at savings of at least 35%. A selection of quality sunglasses from Ray-Ban, Serengeti, and Revo are showcased at the front of the store and average 25% off retail prices. *502/868-0132.*

TOY LIQUIDATORS—Shoppers won't find the most current toys on the market at this liquidation center. Instead, they will find exceptional savings on the ones from previous years by names like Mattel, Hasbro, Playskool, Tyco, and Nintendo. Bold signs identifying store specials on toys are everywhere. Be on guard for the bargain bins situated in front of the store that entice impromptu buying. *502/863-2282.*

VAN HEUSEN—A staple of most every outlet mall, this Van Heusen store differs very little from the rest. A good mix of this brand's casual wear for both men and women, along with the dress shirts for the career-minded man, are 20%–50% off regular retail prices. An entryway inside this store connects it with the Bass outlet next door. *502/868-5014.*

WESTPORT, LTD—Westport is Dress Barn's outlet mall equivalent. While the name is different, it has the same type of merchandise and the same lines—Westport, Princeton Club, and Atrium. The selection, in sizes that range from 4–14, is larger at the outlet mall store. However, the savings remain about the same with prices marked at 20%–50% off regular retails. *502/868-0818.*

WESTPORT WOMAN—This store is the plus-size version of Westport Ltd. It has the same lines—Westport Ltd., Atrium, Christopher, Melano, and Princeton Club—at 20%–50% off retail everyday. Sizes range from 14–24. *502/868-9075.*

OHIO FACTORY SHOPS, JEFFERSONVILLE, OHIO

In the middle of cornfields surrounded by fast food restaurants and truck stops, the Ohio Factory Shops Outlet Center is a midpoint oasis on the brain-numbing I-71 drive between Cincinnati and Columbus. Here, a melting pot of errant travelers, the curious, and the thrifty convene to share one common experience—the arduous search for bargains. Trucking traffic and byroads add confusion to getting into the mall, but once you're there, you're at Ohio's largest outlet center. Most shoppers have good intentions (to make their rounds to every single store), but unless you have several days, chances are you won't make it through all 75 stores. Well, you might, but it will hurt. **Mall Layout:** Many outlet malls are bland and generic with an almost antiseptic atmosphere. This one is different. Its sharp, contemporary village-like setting with covered walkways and landscaped courtyards has the stores conveniently arranged within sectional alcoves so that customers can easily jump back and forth from place to place. A park bench every so often offers a break in between store hopping. Since the wind is often a factor in this region, the staggered setup of the stores within this open-air mall makes it a little easier to tolerate the elements. An outdoor playground comes in handy when children become bored with the whole shopping ordeal. **Location & Directions:** I-71 at Exit 65 (Route 35, at Xenia Washington Court House Exit), *From Dayton*: Take Route 35 east, approximately 36 miles to I-71 intersection; the Ohio Factory Shops are located on the left. The driving time is about 35 minutes. *From Cincinnati*: Follow I-71 north to Route 35 exit; turn right onto Route 35 exit and left into the Ohio Factory Shops. The driving time is about 50 minutes. *From Columbus*: Follow I-71 south to Route 35 exit; turn left onto Route 35 and left into Ohio Factory Shops. The driving time is 35 minutes. **Services & Hours:** Park at the southeast end of the mall near the Food Court. There, maps of the mall and special store coupons can be picked up at the Customer Information Center. $5 coupon booklets (which are fully refundable if unused) and gift certificates can be purchased here. **Mall Hours:** Mon–Sat 10am–9pm; Sun noon–6pm. Holiday hours may vary. Customer Information: Mon–Sat 10am–9pm; Sun noon–6pm. **Phone:** 800/SHOP-OHIO (800/746-7644).

THE MAIN DRAWING CARDS—This mall seems to have a good mix of true manufacturers' outlets and factory-direct stores. A number of these stores are only available in certain regions. For instance, Designer Forum is only the second store of its kind to open in the country.

ANN TAYLOR—Sophisticated looks for women. Here, the well-heeled executive will give her wardrobe a stylistic uplift without dropping a fortune. Only first-quality merchandise in the most current styles is in inventory. Manufactured separately for the outlet store and sold for less, they're only slightly different from their full-price counterparts. However, the most appreciated deals are on Ann Taylor's own line of private label clothing. *614/948-2100.*

BALDWIN BRASS—Baldwin Brass has outgrown its selling space by at least a room's length. The outlet store is jam-packed with every inch devoted to displaying first-quality brass wares, home furnishings, and brass lamps. Getting around the store is a bit tight, but shopping for these brass goods is well worth the claustrophobic conditions. The savings average 35% off regular retail prices. Unlike the department stores, complete lines (not just a shelf or two) of Baldwin's products are represented. Because the manufacturer wants more of its product lines to be seen in one place, the store doubles as a showroom. There are only a few Baldwin outlet stores like this in the entire country. *614/948-2900.*

DONNA KARAN—Donna Karan has a regular following of women. In a relatively short time, this famous designer has made it to the higher ranks with her DKNY signature collection and sharp contemporary looks. Fresh provisions are brought in every other day in current styles for much less than department stores, 40%–60% off regular retails. *614/948-2188.*

EDDIE BAUER—Eddie Bauer's sporty looks are discounted here. Much of the apparel and footwear from this Seattle, Washington-based retailer is first quality. Overstocks and discontinued items from the company's inventory are sold for less than regular retail. Nylon carriers in various shapes and sizes, too. *614/948-2177.*

ESPRIT—The bold metal racks and spacious aisles that lead you in a circular direction around the store give Esprit a futuristic setting. Push carts (you'll need one) are ready to be heaped full of relaxed cotton looks that are designed for the younger set or adults who have "juvenile wanna-be's." A wide variety of Esprit shoes is at the center of the store. *614/948-9000.*

GUESS?—This big outlet store offers massive dosages of cotton denim jeans and casuals. Well arranged on convenient racks and wall shelves that are all over the place, shoppers must choose between endless supplies of first-quality overstocks, irregulars, and discontinued items. While you could find yourself caught up in all the Guess hype, try on your selections to make sure you are receiving the same fit on the styles you're accustomed to wearing. *614/948-9065.*

IZOD—This famous maker plays homage to the upscale, preppie dresser with cotton-rich sportswear for men and women. The varying fabric weights and textures of the apparel transfer into sporty knits that, for the status-conscious, are punctuated with the Izod emblem. First-quality overstocks and out-of-season goods are marked 50% off the lowest ticket price of every item in the store. Look for the "You Pay" signs for greater savings. The closest Izod outlet to this one is located in Monroe, Michigan. *614/948-9111.*

ASIDE **Acquaint yourself with the mall before shopping. Drive around to find out where the customer service office is located. It's usually close to the food court (if there is one) or near the center of the mall. Stop by and ask for a map of the mall and a listing of all the stores. By preparing ahead you can map out which stores you'd rather shop. Save your time and your feet.**

READING CHINA & GLASS—An all-inclusive home furnishings store, Reading China typifies the idea of one-stop shopping. The store is huge in outlet mall terms, and its sheer mass of goods can be overwhelming. (If you think this one is big you should see the one in Reading, Pennsylvania; it's three stories high.) Current, brand name accessories for every room in the house are stocked in full lines (a person could do their whole kitchen in an ivy pattern).

Relief is brought on by the well-defined sections that divide the fine china, crystal, housewares, gourmet foods, and linens. A handy shipping and bridal registry service is in the store since gift items are common purchases. *614/948-2035.*

SPRINGMAID-WAMSUTTA—Owned and operated by Spring Industries, one of the largest and oldest manufacturers of textiles for the home, the store offers the Springmaid and Wamsutta brands of bed and bath linens, curtains and draperies, kitchen and table linens, and pillows. Some were manufactured specifically for department stores but are now surplus merchandise. So don't be surprised if you see labels from names like Lazarus and J.C. Penney sewn on the products. The buys in this store are good with greater savings on selected irregulars. But only buy what you need. The store may have what you want one time, and not the next. But, where else could you get a 250-count percale comforter originally priced at $500 for $34.99? Bath accessories, such as soap dishes, cups, and dispensers, that normally sell for as much as $17 to $20 each in department stores are priced here at $1.99 to $3.99 each. *614/948-9100.*

OTHER STORES AT THE MALL—in alphabetical order:

AILEEN—Aileen's fashions for women run casual. No surprises are here among the inexpensive looks even though new shipments arrive at regular intervals from the factory. Generous savings of at least 35% off retail prices is normal on misses', petites', and plus sizes. *614/948-2989.*

ALLEN-EDMONDS COMPANY SHOE STORE—Allen-Edmonds merits high marks for its quality selection of fine leather footwear. Slight imperfections bring 25% savings on a well-defined collection of distinctive dress shoes, fashion casuals and stylish leather ankle boots. Styles with nothing more than a small scuff mark or a dab of shoe polish on the sole are considered irregulars. A wide size range (AAAA–EEE) makes it easier to find a great fit. Leather belts, ties, and aromatic cedar products such as shoe trees are also available. *614/948-9033.*

AMERICAN EAGLE OUTLET—Popular casual wear items you missed the first time around at American Eagle's regular mall stores may surface here for less. A good mix of off-season and surplus rugby shirts, outerwear, and relaxed looks is at moderate to low prices. *614/948-9605.*

AMERICAN TOURISTER/BUXTON—By combining two stores in one these famous makers fill any travel need. Buxton, a manufacturer of small leather goods since 1853, has only first-quality products at good prices. American Tourister has the big ticket luggage items at prices considerably less than most retailers. While some of their items are made exclusively for the outlet store, many are surplus or discontinued styles. Look for the yellow tags on irregular and clearance merchandise. *614/948-9306.*

APPLAUSE OUTLET—Lose yourself among the goofy items on the shelves at Applause. It will be hard to pull a kid out of this place let alone yourself without buying something. Every little nook and cranny in the store is filled with items for kids like rubbery cartoon figurines, plush toys, pop-up card sets, pencil sets, jewelry and those obnoxious crazy straws. The main attractions, of course, are the items with Disney themes (from previous years) as well as the prices. Everything across the board in the store is automatically reduced 50% off retail. *614/948-2028.*

BABY GUESS/GUESS KIDS—This small store just doesn't make full use of its selling space. The selection is sparse with not much effort put forth in displaying those tiny little Guess outfits for infants that seem to just blend into the stark atmosphere. Sizes on the items run from infants' 6 months to children's 14. Be sure to check over your selections carefully for flaws before making your purchases. *614/948-9222.*

BARBIZON—In between the casual wear and sportswear shops, it's nice to see a lingerie store to break up the monotony. A complete line of soft, feminine lingerie showcases names like Vanity Fair, Eileen West, Jantzen, and, of course, the Barbizon label. A well-chosen selection of first-quality merchandise is in nicely detailed styles. *614/948-9050.*

G.H. BASS COMPANY STORE—A longtime staple of outlet malls, Bass continues to deliver values with its quality line of footwear. In recent years, Bass has expanded its stores to include casual wear for men and women. This spacious outlet is big on both. Amid a rustic setting, it is filled with a good mixture of freestyle denims and relaxed cotton looks. Subdivided into two sections, the store offers casuals on one side and footwear on the other. The greatest values remain on Bass's own line of genuine leather shoes and suede-trimmed hiking boots. *614/948-9061.*

BOSTON TRADERS—This store, which really is not a true outlet, is for the ultimate prep. Classic lines of sportswear in thick natural fibers are here at lukewarm prices. The hottest buys on this men's and women's apparel are in the back of the store. You may have to sort through damaged goods and irregulars to find them, though. *614/948-9177.*

BROOKS BROTHERS—Brooks Brothers outlet store is made distinctive by its hardwood floors and rich-looking decor. It harbors finely tailored apparel for the traditional man in reservoirs of suits, sport coats, dress shirts, and slacks. A nice selection of women's apparel is also featured. All of the selection is first quality (no irregulars or seconds) with savings averaging 25%–30% off retail prices. Since the styling of Brooks Brothers' classic lines doesn't fluctuate drastically, buy the previous season items. *614/948-2030.*

BRUCE ALAN BAGS, ETC.—Almost every imaginable type of organizer is found here. The store has an excellent mix of first-quality leather handbags, small leather goods, and luggage at reasonable prices. Nylon accessories like backpacks, wallets, and tote bags are priced within reason. While the store carries mostly lesser names, it does have Eastpak organizers and Bruce Alan's own label products. Look for "knock-offs" of famous maker products available for much less than their more expensive counterparts. *614/948-9329.*

BUGLE BOY FACTORY STORE—Scads of denim jeans, fleecewear, and casuals are packed into the store, making it difficult to get around during busy times. The prices range from moderate to low on adults' styles with greater savings on irregulars. However, the best buys are on boys' cargo pocket pants and children's playwear found toward the back of the store. *614/948-9330.*

CASUAL CORNER & COMPANY—The main difference between this store and Casual Corner's regular retail counterparts is in the selection. A much broader range of style choices is in the larger outlet store with a higher concentration of casual wear and trendy junior fashions. Some famous maker labels that are not available at their regular stores are here. *614/948-9317.*

CHICAGO CUTLERY—The selection of cooking accessories in this store is as varied as the many types of cuisines. Chicago Cutlery's own highly rated brand of knives, sharpeners, and kitchen accessories is in ample supply with a well-defined collection of Magnalite cookware. Many of the Magnalite items have minor aesthetic flaws which are barely noticeable. These items not only have the same warranties as the new products, they are priced at least 30% less than regular retails. Savings averaging 50% off regular retails are on Chicago Cutlery's selected seconds as well. Excellent buys on solid wood cutting boards and pizza boards are in the front of the store. *614/948-2866.*

CLAIRE'S—This store is teeming with every type of small accessory item from jewelry and hair bows to mini bags and wallets. You can expect to pay at least 25% less for these items than what you normally would at Claire's regular mall stores. *614/948-2808.*

CLASS PERFUMES—Some of the more recognizable names are featured within the confines of this pint-size fragrance shop. The drawback is that only a few products from an entire line of your favorite scent may be represented. The prices are better than the ones you will find at most retailers. *614/948-2971.*

COLOURS & SCENTS—Cosmetics and fragrances in this small store are priced considerably less than regular retail. In fact, a sign in the store states it will not be undersold. Not a big variety of brand names but don't miss the miniature bottles of fragrances showcased around the counter. Many are highly sought by collectors. *614/948-9036.*

COLOURS BY ALEXANDER JULIAN—By eliminating the middleman to keep prices down, this outlet is for the man who has a craving for Alexander Julian's contemporary sportswear. Noted for a wide array of colorful shades (even mustard and olive) on nice fabrics, this famous maker adds spice to the usual casual looks. Everything in the store is up-to-date, first-quality merchandise that is priced with factory-direct savings. *614/948-9076.*

CORNING/REVERE—One of the broadest assortments of Corning manufactured products is in this store. All of Corning's lines—Corning Ware cookware, Pyrex ovenware, Corelle dinnerware, Visions cookware, Revereware cookware (first and second quality), and Crown Corning gift glassware—are here. If you can't find what you need in the way of Corning within the confines of this inventory you can place factory-direct orders. While the prices on Corning's first-quality items are economical, greater savings are on overstocks, discontinued, or cosmetic seconds. *614/948-9016.*

DANSKIN—Stretchy, form-fitting fabrics in vibrant shades are constructed into functional dance, aerobic, and active wear and sold here at 30%–50% off regular retail prices. There's an extensive selection, which includes plus and children's sizes, and generous supplies of Round-the-Clock hosiery and the Dance Frame lines. One of over 30 outlet stores across the country, this store will ship items anywhere in the United States. *614/948-9053.*

DESIGNER FORUM—J. Schoeman, the manufacturer of some of the biggest names in men's finer dress wear (Christian Dior, Palm Beach, Evan-Picone, Southbrook, Burberry's, and Halston) owns and operates this outlet store. By eliminating the middleman and lowering overhead, this store saves customers 30%–50% off retail prices. Only the second to open in the country, Designer Forum features current, first-quality styles with a wide selection of finely tailored suits, sport coats, and trousers. The store caters to all sizes with regular, short, and extra long fits (up to size 60). *614/948-9600.*

ASIDE **Look for bargains in the back of the store. Often stores will place a rack or two of merchandise priced below the normal sale items there. In many cases, these items will be priced at 50% off or more. It pays to check them out before searching through the other racks.**

DUCK HEAD OUTLET—We suppose those little embroidered duck emblems sewn on the manufacturer's clothing add to these otherwise nondescript casuals. The store has a fair selection of Duck Head's relaxed cotton looks in men's, women's, and youth sizes at reasonable prices. If you've got the patience you may try your luck searching through the bargain bins for the real deals. But, be careful: you may find rejects among the prize ducks—er, picks. *614/948-9047.*

DUCKS UNLIMITED SPORTSWEAR—Ducks and wildlife greet customers in this store. There's an appeal to the socially conscious outdoorsman who has a sense of obligation toward wildlife preservation. One-third of the manufacturer's profits goes toward the conservation of the country's wetlands. The store's decor centers around wildlife themes. Its back wall is lined with emblems highlighting various animals. There's a herd of thick heavyweight sweatshirts, sweaters, and tee shirts with hunting and wildlife logos. Even if you don't save a lot of money, why not help save an animal? *614/948-9229.*

EASY SPIRIT & CO. OUTLET—Those who appreciate the comfort of Easy Spirit shoes won't find the latest styles, but they will find excellent buys on the ones from previous seasons. With mostly first-quality choices, you'll find Bandolino, Joyce, Cobbie, and other famous brand shoes for women. The store has factory-direct prices that are considerably less than department stores. *614/948-9020.*

FARBERWARE—The Farberware Outlet doesn't put forth much effort in displaying its goods. Instead of aesthetics, it relies on pricing. The shelves are filled with cookware that may be reduced simply because it is overstocked or blemished. The budget-minded cook should head to the back of the store. There, items marked as second quality can be found in the large, cardboard boxes. Most any of Farberware's products, from frying pans to coffee pots, could be uncovered in these bargain bins. The catch is you'll have to sort through the items and look them over carefully for dents, scratches, unrounded alignments, or other imperfections. *614/948-9080.*

FACTORY BRAND SHOES—Unless you have plenty of time you might as well go right on by this store. The main emphasis of the store is selling up-to-date footwear for men and women. But since discounters similar to this one, which may also be owned and operated by Famous Footwear, are popping up everywhere why waste your time shopping here? Save it for the other stores in the mall where you won't find such a predictable lineup. *614/948-9023.*

FAMOUS BRANDS HOUSEWARES—The interior of this store reminds you of a mini warehouse. It is filled with every kind of kitchen gadget and cooking accessory imaginable, even those you won't find anywhere else. The plastic-coated bins and shelving units display brand name products by Anchor Hocking, Durand, Intercraft, Rubbermaid, and many others. Priced less than most retailers, check out the rack in the back of the store for even greater savings on clearance items. *614/948-9072.*

FILA—This store has a full range of athletic wear and sporty casual wear designed for both men and women. Many items are unisex. A limited selection of Fila's famous athletic shoes is available. One of the big selling points is that it sometimes receives certain shipments before the regular retailers. The manufacturer may also offer a select group of current goods only at the outlet. *614/948-9161.*

FLORSHEIM—You don't have to pay through the nose for Florsheim's fine quality shoes. They have them here for as much as $30 a pair less than regular retailers. Men's traditional dress styles, casual footwear, and boots are at exceptional values. A much broader size range and selection are other key factors that make shopping this store appealing. *614/948-9049.*

GALT SAND—Galt Sand is a cross-mix of all of the activewear shops at this mall. It has sweatshirts and tee shirts for most any taste from team or sporting motifs to environmental or wildlife themes. Some officially licensed products are reserved for diehard college and pro team fans. Overall savings average 30%–50% off regular retail prices. *614/948-9186.*

HARTMAN LUGGAGE—This outlet barely occupies enough space to call itself a store. It is tucked away in a small room within the Lenox store but it does have whopping savings of 40% off regular retail on Hartman's own handsome, quality-made luggage. Unfortunately, the buys are hit or miss since the styles vary constantly and are sold in individual pieces. Only irregulars are available but most have slightly noticeable flaws. The good news is the same warranties on Hartman's new products come with these items as well. *614/948-2120.*

JERZEES—In a mall that's heavy on sweatshirts and activewear, Jerzees offers something unique. Customers can choose from a number of colorful emblems and patterns and have them imprinted on their sweatshirt and tee shirt selections. The emblems, which are permanently affixed through a heat transfer process, cost from $2–$6 each. The store has a wide range of color choices that can be mixed or matched. Shirts with designs, fleece cardigans, and long nightshirts are available. This factory-direct apparel averages 30%–50% off regular retail prices. *614/948-2840.*

JOCKEY FACTORY STORE—Jockey has excellent values for men on its famous cotton-rich tee shirts, sport shirts, and sweatshirts. Socks and undergarments for men and women are first quality items in a variety of nice color choices and textures. Their year-round markdowns average 25%–33% lower that regular retails. *614/948-2650.*

JONATHAN LOGAN/VICTORIA CREATIONS—The Jonathan Logan label is the predominant name in this humdrum store. The prices may be reasonable but the fashions, for misses and petites, don't give you a sense of urgency to buy. The main emphasis of the store is on its dismal selection of career separates and casual wear. What little excitement there is comes in the way of accessory and jewelry items by Lisner, Givenchy, and Karl Lagerfeld. *614/948-2616.*

KITCHEN COLLECTION—A broad selection. It's bursting at the seams with every type of cookware, bakeware, kitchen appliance, and kitchen gadget known to man. A good representation of famous brands such as Kitchen Collection, Wear Ever, Anchor Hocking, and Proctor-Silex crowd the shelves. Not only is the selection full of helpful ideas for the cook, the prices seem reasonable. *614/948-9315.*

LAURA ASHLEY—This store doesn't give you the same Yorkshire feel as Laura Ashley's regular retail establishments. But, for an outlet it's about as cheery and cozy as it gets. In the front of the store, a nice selection of natural-fiber clothing in wholesome English country prints is generously reduced. While the merchandise may be from previous seasons, the styles really don't change that much. For those who want to add a simple uncomplicated look to their home decor the back of the store is awash with Laura Ashley's refreshing prints. Good buys on wallpaper, borders, printed lamp shades, bedding, and curtains may end up here in the form of irregulars or overstocks. *614/948-2015.*

LEATHER LOFT—A multitude of rich, supple leathers transformed into functional accessory pieces is at the Leather Loft. Hundreds are displayed on the shelves and racks along with handbags and belts. There's a well-chosen selection of briefcases, attache cases, and organizers. Leather-trimmed luggage and all-leather garment bags are handsome options. A clearance wall in the back of the store has greater savings on various items. *614/948-2133.*

LENOX—Long regarded as a premier manufacturer of fine china and crystal, Lenox even presents its selected seconds elegantly. Convenient arrangements that make use of shelves and table displays show off fine china dinnerware and hand-blown crystal stemware. A "Poppy Shop" highlights Lenox' casual dinnerware line. Beautiful figurines, candles, and table linens are cleverly displayed making it easy to pick up ideas for gifts and decorative table settings. *614/948-2120.*

LEVI'S STRAUS OUTLET BY DESIGNS—The open, spacious layout of this store makes it easy to locate Levi's denim jeans and casuals. However, once you find them it won't be as easy to see the savings. The prices don't give you that "bargain rush" feel. They are mediocre at best. The wide selection is the real selling point. A nice mixture of Levi's well-known lines, including Dockers, is in men's, women's, and children's sizes. But, be careful in making your selections. The items marked as irregulars could have flaws in the fit or stitching that can only be detected by trying them on. *614/948-2000.*

MARK CROSS—Mark Cross, now owned by Coach, is a sleek line of leather goods that shows a love for detail. This top-of-the-line manufacturer finely crafts its goods into handbags, organizers, planners, and small leather accessories. All of these items are first quality and at least 25% off regular retail prices. To uncover this broad of a selection anywhere else would be difficult—the next closest place to find a complete line of Mark Cross fine leathers is in New York. *614/948-2345.*

MATERNITY WORKS—A versatile mix of maternity fashions in career coordinates, casual wear, and lingerie is at factory-direct savings. Brand name styles by Mother Work, Mimi Maternity, Steena, and Maternity Works arrive in fresh helpings everyday. *614/948-2833.*

MOTHERHOOD MATERNITY—The same type of maternity wear you see in department stores is in this store. In fact, this company leases selling space from stores like Lazarus to sell their goods. By shopping the outlet you'll find "as is," irregular, and previous season merchandise for less. *614/948-2044.*

MUSIC FOR A SONG—While this store has a wide variety of music choices, don't assume you're getting the best price just because it's located at the outlet mall. It is on the same par pricewise as others in your own area. They rely on the impulse buyer. *614/948-9211.*

NATURALIZER, ETC.—Go ahead and make your rounds here but these could be purchased at the discount stores near your home. This store seems to carry the usual standbys—Naturalizer, Connie, and Life Style. *614/948-9030.*

THE NATURE COMPANY OUTLET—This outlet store is not on par with the Nature Company's regular retail stores. The merchandise, which consists of mostly surplus items, is sparse with "as is" and damaged items scattered throughout. The real deals are items that are still in their packages, such as those soothing cassette tapes and compact discs or interesting video tapes that are always played in the store. Educational books, toys, and activity kits for kids are also good buys. *614/948-2022.*

NORTY'S—For women who are partial to wearing Norton McNaughton, Norty's has a huge assemblage of inexpensive fashions that function well for business, social luncheons, or travel. Prices run from moderate to low on this first-quality apparel that is well arranged in misses', petites', and plus sizes. *614/948-2809.*

OLGA/WARNER'S—Here's an extensive selection of first-quality bras, panties, underwear, and sleepwear by Olga and Warner's. A good size range makes it easier to be fitted. Savings average 30%–40% off retail prices. *614/948-9039.*

PAPER FACTORY—Don't underestimate the savings and selection you can receive at Paper Factory. It is a great source for buying gift wrap and party supplies. The store's "rewinds" offer the best value on gift wrap. These large rolls of paper are sold for less since they are bought in bulk and wound at the store. The values on misprinted paper napkins and partyware run a close second (volume discounts are also available). Other items with savings worth mentioning are gift bows and ribbons, party favors and decorations, and greeting cards. *614/948-9068.*

PETITE SOPHISTICATE—The store's marketing strategy is hard to decipher. A separate buyer from the company's main line specialty stores purchases different goods for their outlet stores. The merchandise appears greatly similar, yet it's unrelated. Perhaps this is the justification behind the outlet prices, but why not just call it Petite Sophisticate Number Two? *614/948-2122.*

PRESTIGE FRAGRANCE & COSMETICS—Expect to suffer from olfactory overload as the meshing of scents infiltrates your senses. If you can withstand the close conditions, you may find your favorite fragrance or cosmetic at noteworthy factory-direct prices. But, keep in mind, the store only stocks a narrow range of choices within each product line so you may end up with the eau de toilette instead of the perfume atomizer you wanted. *614/948-9057.*

THE PRO IMAGE OUTLET—Sports enthusiasts will find Pro Image a good source for officially licensed products. The store can be sized up quickly with racks of sweatshirts, tee shirts, and jackets organized according to pro or college league: NCAA, NBA, NFL, NHL, etc. Sports caps from every team imaginable are displayed on wall shelves that almost reach to the ceiling. Team jerseys are also displayed on the walls. Heavyweight fabrics and embroidered emblems give many of the items more substance. Not only is the quality better, the prices are better than what you'll find in most regular shopping malls. *614/948-2050.*

PUBLISHER'S WAREHOUSE—You won't find the current best sellers at Publisher's Warehouse. But, if you're willing to search through the uninspired selection you might find a book you missed the first time around. Acquired primarily through closeouts and buyouts, the books are reduced for varying savings. Occasionally a hardback book can be found at the paperback price. The best buys, however, are on the Value Ware computer software (as low as $3.99 per diskette), out-of-date travel books, and hard cover picture books. *614/948-9122.*

RACK ROOM SHOES—Your sense of urgency to buy from Rack Room Shoes is nullified once you realize the store is just like all the other ones right in your own area. Because the prices in their normal retail stores are discounted every day, this one is no different than the rest except that it is located at an outlet mall. *614/948-9119.*

REED & BARTON—Silversmiths since 1824, Reed & Barton has a superb selection of first-quality sterling, silver-plated, and stainless steel flatware. Every three to four months the store features patterns of everyday and formal flatware on sale. So if you're in the market it's wise to check into which ones will be on sale next. Particularly impressive is the store's collection of 18-8 stainless steel flatware, which is one of the finest ever made. Check out the flatware boxes, jewelry boxes, and gift items. *614/948-2814.*

ROYAL DOULTON—Those who have a fondness for Royal Doulton's finely crafted china will find it at appreciable savings here. Many of the manufacturer's famous lines—Royal Doulton dinnerware, Minton bone china, Royal Albert bone china, and Royal Crown Derby—are arranged with an appealing lack of confusion. Only first-quality china is displayed on shelves surrounding the walls. Second-quality and discontinued patterns are well coordinated with table top complements such as crystal stemware and giftware. An excellent selection of Bunnykins, Beatrix Potter, and Brambly Hedge statuary is in the front of the store. *614/948-9200.*

S & K MENSWEAR—S & K is not an outlet in the true sense, but the store has a well-rounded selection of first-quality apparel for men. Everything from tailored clothing and fine sportswear to casual wear and outer wear is available at 20%–50% off regular retail prices. Names like Botany 500, Jones New York, Deansgate, Cricketeer, and Tailors Row are frequent choices. The prices in the store are reasonable due, in part, to the company's business philosophy. As part of a 160-store chain, S & K boasts having more buying power, yet pays for its goods up front. This, coupled with selling their merchandise in low-overhead stores, keeps prices down. *614/948-9323.*

SAS FACTORY SHOE STORE—This store peddles comfort in the form of footwear. Most styles are of handcrafted moccasin construction. Styles range from women's mocs and sandals to women's and men's walking and fitness shoes. A wide size range from women's 4–12 and men's 7–15 with widths of slim, narrow, medium, and wide (some in double widths) makes it easy to be fitted. A variety of SAS soft leather handbags is also here. All are first quality and at factory-direct prices. *614/948-2060.*

TOTES/SUNGLASS WORLD—A well-known source for essential accessories, the Totes outlet has a good mix of rainwear, luggage, and carryalls. Most of these items are priced 35%–70% off retail. Raincoats that are great for year-round wear and travel are exceptionally priced along with their popular umbrellas. Sunglass World, a recent addition to the Totes network, is tacked onto the selling space in front of the store. Famous maker sunglasses by Ray-Ban, Serengeti, and Revo are showcased in this area with 25% off retail prices everyday. *614/948-2112.*

TOY LIQUIDATORS—While you probably won't find the hottest toys on the market at this liquidation store, you will find good buys on past models. The selection of toys is in constant flux with new shipments continuously arriving in the form of buyouts and closeouts. For collectors, top-line baseball cards (like the Donrus Foil Series) in complete sets from previous years are at better than average prices. *614/948-9074.*

VAN HEUSEN DIRECT—Van Heusen caters to the traditional businessman. An eye-catching display lining the back wall makes a strong statement about the wide variety of dress shirts and ties in the store. Other men's apparel such as sportswear, jackets, and accessories is available. The store has also managed to make room for a woman's sportswear section. Everyday savings on first-quality merchandise average 20%–50% off regular retail prices. *614/948-9059.*

VAN HEUSEN FOR HER—It's unusual to see a Van Heusen store devoted solely to women. Prices average 20%–50% below regular retail prices. Styles range from casual to dressy casual and are slanted more toward the conservative dresser. The first-quality apparel (no seconds or irregulars) provides reliable resources for wardrobe additions. *614/948-2117.*

ASIDE **Ask about preferred shoppers' privileges. The savvy outlet mall shopper is always on the lookout for more ways to save. With the popularity of outlet stores on the rise, malls have been rapidly expanding and becoming more competitive. This increases your opportunity for finding even more bargains. Because new stores are always opening, it's important to include a visit to the customer service office in the mall as the first step of your bargain hunting ritual. You will not only find out which new stores have opened and where they're located, you can see if they have been added as participants in these special money-saving promotions. Take advantage of shoppers' privileges offered by the mall. It is always a good idea to inquire at the customer service center about these privileges and other special bonus offerings the mall may make available to customers. Some places, like the Jeffersonville Outlet Center in Ohio and the Dry Ridge Outlet Center in Kentucky, offer "Preferred Client" cards. Customers can sign up for the card (at no charge) and use it to receive additional savings on certain items available at participating stores. A list of these items is usually handed out with the card and is periodically updated. Other places, like the Ohio Factory Shops in Jeffersonville, Ohio, offer coupon booklets. The coupons in these books usually have an end-of-year or end-of-season expiration date and can be used toward extra savings on certain merchandise at participating stores.**

VILLEROY & BOCH—For those who don't mind buying seconds, Villeroy & Boch is the place for fine china, crystal stemware, and gifts. The manufacturer's second-quality merchandise is very similar to what is sold at fine department stores. The only difference (apparent to the inexperienced eye) is in the price. Even though this store primarily stocks seconds, the intricate details and finery of Villeroy & Boch's craftsmanship is still quite appreciable. Beatrix Potter collectibles are also available here but you are better off to buy them at the Royal Doulton outlet; the prices and selection are much better. *614/948-2985.*

WELCOME HOME—As the name implies, Welcome Home has a homey atmosphere amid stark outlet mall surroundings. Expect to spend time exploring. From cozy afghans and linens to framed art and potpourri, this store will tempt you into buying things you never knew you needed. New shipments arrive daily so it's easy to find something different every time. Reasonable prices. *614/948-9322.*

WESTPORT, LTD.—Westport is Dress Barn's outlet mall equivalent. While the name is different, it has the same type of merchandise and the same lines—Westport, Princeton Club, Atrium, and Melan. The distinguishing factor between the two stores is in the selection. The outlet store is larger and consequently offers a broader variety of styles. The quality remains the same as well as the prices of 20%–50% off retails everyday. *614/948-2827.*

WESTPORT WOMAN—This store is the plus-size version of Westport Ltd. It has the same lines—Westport Ltd., Atrium, Christopher, Melano, and Princeton Club—at 20%–50% off retail prices everyday. Sizes range from 14–24. *614/948-2827.*

WINDSOR SHIRT COMPANY—Windsor has many of the same styles of dress shirts and sportswear as Van Heusen, the manufacturer's affiliate. Under the PhilipVan Heusen umbrella, numerous menswear fashions like these are produced for major department stores. Even though the styles found at the outlet store may be from previous seasons, it's hard to resist the 25%–50% savings. *614/948-9190.*

YOUNG GENERATIONS—One of the better names for quality and value, Ruth of Carolina fashions for Young Generations are primarily sold in fine department stores and specialty shops. Quality-minded shoppers can buy these beautifully detailed dresses for girls here at 30% off regular retail prices (first-quality goods are at least $10–$20 cheaper). A savings of 50% off regular retail prices on slight irregulars. The company's other line, Pretty Me, is also sold here with the same savings and quality for preteens, early teens, and junior petites. While these lines have been around for over 40 years, this is the only outlet store in the Midwest to offer them. *614/948-9115.*

JEFFERSONVILLE OUTLET CENTER

In spite of its large size, Jeffersonville Outlet Center has not allowed its roster of brand name stores to become watered down with discount impostors. On the contrary, this sprawling megamall (over 70 stores) is a rich reservoir of authentic factory-operated outlets that feature the big industry leaders. The irony is that while this mall peddles a wealth of famous designer names, it's surrounded by open fields, grassy farmlands, and the commotion from the I-71 expressway. The area is in transit. With more mall expansions to come, fast food restaurants popping up almost overnight, and additional developmental plans, it's hard to know the scope of its potential. Who knows, maybe Jeffersonville will become the next Reading, Pennsylvania. **Mall Layout**: This rather functional "no frills" outlet mall is spread out in a circular format around a stadium-size parking lot. This design makes it easy for customers to drive up and park at any store (as long as a space is available). On foot, it's a different story. After shopping several stores the patrons are forced to either retrace their steps or wind their way back through the parking lot. **Location & Directions**: 1100 McArthur Road. Take I-71 to Exit 69 in Jeffersonville. **Services & Hours:** It's best to park at the southwest corner of the mall near the Customer Service Center. Maps of the mall and store listings are available. Patrons may sign up for the mall's "Preferred Client" card at no charge. Upon presenting the card when purchasing items, some stores offer special discounts on certain items. A list of these items and participating stores can also be obtained. Two concession areas that are small considering the size of the mall offer a limited menu and seating. **Mall Hours:** Jan–Feb Mon–Thurs 10am–6pm, Fri–Sat 10am–9pm, Sun noon–6pm; Mar–Dec Mon–Sat 10am–9pm, Sun noon–6pm. **Phone:** 614/426-6992.

MAIN DRAWING CARDS—Of all the outlet malls around this region, Jeffersonville Outlet Center has the largest choice of designer and famous brand names.

SAKS 5TH AVENUE CLEARING HOUSE—Altogether a breed apart from other outlet mall stores, Saks boasts having the most notable avant-garde designer names. An endless array of sought-after fashions—Donna Karan, Ellen Tracy, Dana Buchman, Kenar, E.D. Lee—is just dying to be tried on while promising to bring savings at clearing house prices. Although two-thirds of the store caters to the label-conscious woman, there's a men's section featuring names like Mondo and Perry Ellis. Distinctive items like Ceska's fine crystalware are showcased around the counter, along with a collection of Judith Leiber's exquisite leather handbags—one that normally sells for $3,200, found here for the bargain price of just $1,899. New shipments arrive three times a week so rest assured there will always be plenty of first-quality, high fashion finds from a mix of overstocks and items bought from vendors specifically for the clearing house. *614/426-8580.*

SPIEGEL—Organized much like a compact department store, Spiegel is subdivided into various clothing sections. Don't expect to find Spiegel's home furnishings here; much of the merchandise is clothing from catalog overruns and previous seasons with only a smaller section for bed and bath linens. The front of the store features high fashion names like Donna Karan and Dana Buchman. A DKNY barn jacket, which normally sells for $292 at other retailers and found here for $99, reflects the values at Spiegel. Another example is an Apart silk blouse, which normally sells for $48 in Spiegel's catalog, here for $21.99. While this store has its share of the high fashion names, it hasn't lost sight of the traditionalist. It has a big selection of classic looks. To get bargain hunters going, there's a fresh stock of first-quality merchandise constantly arriving. *614/426-8685.*

LIZ CLAIBORNE—Rack scanners will find this store easy to shop. A wealth of Liz Claiborne's fashions and accessories from previous seasons is conveniently arranged around the store, but some of it has obviously been out of the mainstream for a while. A good representation of this famous designer's most popular lines—Lizsport, Dana Buchman (her higher end fashions), Liz Claiborne, and Claiborne for Men—is attuned to devotees fashion needs, but in general prices are nothing to marvel over. *614/426-6466.*

MIKASA—Timeless Mikasa is a good value. This factory outlet offers exceptional buys on its treasures. Beautiful china dinnerware, crystal stemware, and flatware are attractively displayed throughout the store. A shipping station is handy for sending purchases anywhere in the country. *614/426-6688.*

REEBOK—The Reebok outlet has an energetic feel that jump starts customers into exploring its contents. The huge store, with its upbeat music playing in the background and clean uncluttered look, is loaded with athletic footwear and apparel for men, women, and children. Signs on the racks identify the specific use of the clothing and shoes according to sport—golf, tennis, cross-training, and so on. The selection of first-quality activewear runs deep with prices considerably less than regular retails. Reebok's quality footwear is available at better-than-average prices with greater savings on irregulars that are often only minor cosmetic flaws. *614/426-8524.*

OTHER STORES AT THE MALL—in alphabetical order:

ADOLFO II—For those in search of comfortable knit coordinates this store has an abundance by Adolfo II, Donna Toran, and Rafael. In misses' and women's plus sizes, the apparel is in current, first-quality styles at moderate prices. *614/426-9744.*

ANNE KLEIN—This outlet stays atop of the current trends with a fashion selection that runs only about six weeks behind department stores, yet has prices below regular retail. Everything in the store is first-quality merchandise from this famous designer's sophisticated career line (Anne Klein) or fine sportswear (Anne Klein II). The collection of Anne Klein accessories and jewelry can't be ignored. *614/426-9771.*

ASHLEIGH MORGAN—Shopping here is a mixed bag: a couple of Kasper suits; a few Tess & Nicola fashions; some Casablanca casuals; and who knows what else may end up among the selection. The store's wide variety of women's moderate career wear, sportswear, and accessories (at prices that bring values to the budget-minded) is the store's main attraction. *614/426-8668.*

AVIA—It's hard to beat the prices this outlet has on Avia's quality athletic footwear and apparel. Its closeouts remain fairly current (six months out at the most) with greater savings on irregulars that are only slight cosmetic flaws. The broad selection for men and women is another of the store's strong points. With not many of these factory outlet stores around (the next closest one is in Missouri) this one is greatly appreciated. *614/426-6335.*

B.D. BAGGIES/B & T BY DAMON—Specializing in comfort fits for men, B.D. Baggies cuts its goods generously. All of the styles in the store—jeans, slacks, casual and dress shirts, sportcoats, and jackets—are fuller cut with pants averaging 35-inch inseams. Several customers have become hooked on this brand after buying it while traveling out west. Most of B.D. Baggies' stores are located in the western states but are slowly beginning to show up in this region. *614/426-8474.*

BAGMAKERS—A large selection of handbags, backpacks, and small leather goods by famous makers like Stone Mountain, Brio, Perry Ellis, Mundi, Eastpak, and Bill Blass is fair-priced at below regular retails. Go to the room in the back of the store for larger luggage sets, duffel bags, and travel carriers. *614/426-6597.*

BASS—A major outfitter of routine "knock-around" casuals and genuine leather footwear, Bass has found its niche within the discount market. As with so many of its outlet stores, this one has a fresh outdoors feel with its rustic decor. Its spacious selling space is filled with a mixture of free-spirited denims and relaxed looks for men and women, as well as its famous footwear and hiking boots. Overall, for the quality, the items are good values. *614/426-6364.*

BIG DOGS SPORTSWEAR—Marge Schott, and others who have gone crazy over St. Bernards, will find this store appealing. The same unisex tee shirts and sweats found in the company's catalogs are at the outlet for 20%–50% off. All have canine motifs. The entry way leading to the changing rooms looks like a giant dog house. Stay away from the hydrant and watch your step. Sizes range from adult to youth. *614/426-6910.*

BOOK WAREHOUSE—Don't expect to receive good buys on current books at Book Warehouse, only the ones published several years ago. While the store has a wide selection, its better bargains are on picture and travel books that are less than recent but still useful. It's best to know going into this store that it's not a place to search for a specific title, but rather for something that may accidentally strike your fancy. *614/426-9210.*

BOTANY 500 & MORE—Botanty 500 executes a marvelous concept of selling men's suits "a la carte." Customers are encouraged to combine separates—plain or pleated slacks and single or double-breasted coats—to create the desired look and fit. These suits, along with sportcoats and other career apparel, are sold at prices more in line with the budget-minded. A Botany 500 suit that sells for $345 at other retailers is found here for $199. This same style was eventually reduced to $119. A first-quality selection in the most current looks is also the standard fare, as is a good representation of Bernhard Altmann dress shirts. *614/426-8448.*

BROWN SHOE COMPANY—The standard fare in this store runs short on the attention span. Its selection consists primarily of women's Naturalizer, Connie, Life Stride, and Naturalizer Sport shoes, several of which are found at discounters closer to home. *614/426-6890.*

BUBBLES & SCENTS—For those who find little fragrance soaps and bath and skin care products hard to resist, try Bubbles & Scents. At up to 50% off department store prices, names like Vitabath, Elizabeth Arden, Rigaud, Claire Burke, Pierre Cardin, and Royal Copenhagen line the shelves in this large store. There's a collection of children's bubble baths, shampoos, soaps, and comb and brush sets, featuring Disney and superhero themes. Perhaps another gimmick to make money, but it works. *614/426-8550.*

ASIDE **Be flexible and keep an open mind. You'll receive some of your best buys when purchasing irregulars. These items usually have unnoticeable flaws, and in some cases first-quality merchandise has been marked as irregular. This way the manufacturer doesn't have to answer to regular department stores as to why the product is sold for a cheaper rate at the outlet malls. Keep an eye out for good buys that are out of season. Just because you can't use a wool blazer in the middle of the summer doesn't mean you shouldn't go ahead and buy it, especially if you're getting a good deal on it.**

B.U.M. EQUIPMENT—Geared more toward the youthful set, B.U.M. casual wear is in vast quantities here at 20%–40% regular retail. Most of the merchandise consists of sweatshirts, tee shirts and sweatpants, with the ever-popular B.U.M. logo. When asked what these enigmatic initials stand for, the clerk in the store replied, "We're told they mean nothing." *614/426-9777.*

CAPE ISLE KNITTERS—One of the largest manufacturers of knits and sweaters in the industry, in recent years Cape Isle Knitters has begun to offer apparel under its own name at the outlet malls. Previously, its quality-made fashions could only be bought from other resources under different labels. Reflective of its latest marketing trend, this outlet is one of the largest in the area. It has an excellent selection of fresh, cotton apparel for men and women in quality heavyweight fabrics. Many of the items prove to be good values at prices substantially less than similar brands found at regular department stores. *614/426-6136.*

CAPEZIO—A promising selection of women's casual, dress, and athletic footwear is at this store. Names like Capezio, Bandolino, Pappagallo, and Easy Spirit are available here at factory-direct prices. *614/426-8809.*

CARTER'S—Synonymous with quality and value, Carter's does a good job of representing its line at this manufacturer's outlet. The store is bright, uncluttered, and well organized, making it easy to look over the extensive selection for infants, toddlers, boys, and girls. The many racks, well marked with sign toppers, offer numerous savings possibilities on Carter's famous playwear, sleepwear, and layette sets (up to size 14). Toward the back of the store a few racks with irregulars or seconds have greater savings. *614/426-6808.*

CHAMPION/HANES—A modern-day staple in today's casual and activewear market, Champion/Hanes has moved up the ranks as one of the top lines for the family. The basic "sweats" in heavy-weight fabrics are featured in first-quality or slightly imperfect grades and closeouts at substantial savings. Hanes sweatshirts and sweatpants in irregulars bring greater savings. A collection of officially licensed products highlighting collegiate, pro, Olympic, and nature conservancy themes is nice. *614/426-9788.*

CHAUS—A vast selection of current Chaus and Chaus Sport merchandise is sold here. Running about six weeks behind the department stores, there are advantages to buying it from the outlet. The selection is greater (with misses', petites', and plus sizes) and the prices are discounted 25% or more off regular retail. *614/426-6850.*

COLOURS & SCENTS—A mixture of cosmetics and fragrances sold in this small store is at prices considerably less than regular retail. The drawback is the store does't have as wide a variety of brand names as other retailers. Along with its regular sizes, don't miss the miniature bottles of fragrances showcased around the counter. Many of these are highly sought by collectors. *614/426-6885.*

COUNTY SEAT—Designed more for the youthful shopper, County Seat features denim and casual wear for young men and juniors. Some of the big names like Lee, Levi's, and Guess are uncovered here at prices worth checking out. *614/426-9291.*

CORNING-REVERE FACTORY STORE—Always a good source for Corning's and Revere's quality products, this outlet has a full range of the manufacturer's lines—Corning Ware, Pyrex, Corelle, Visions, Revereware (first and second quality), and Crown Gift Glassware. A wide selection of open stock items and sets is reasonably priced with greater savings on seconds, discontinued patterns, and overstocks. *614/426-8887.*

DAN RIVER—Many of the store's bed linens (including Colours by Alexander Julian, also manufactured by Dan River) are moderately priced. While the selection is large, it constantly varies so it's difficult to tell which styles will show up here next. Towels and bath accessories are found in the "Bath Shop" near the rear of the store. *614/426-9797.*

ELISABETH—Elisabeth has a full range of styles proportioned for women sizes 14–24 that are cut in regular or petite lengths. Conveniently arranged in an uncluttered setting, these fashions designed by Liz Claiborne include first-quality, odd-lots, overruns, and surplus merchandise from previous seasons. *614/426-8883.*

ETIENNE AIGNER—A extensive and versatile collection of Etienne Aigner shoes and accessories for women. Some of the items are manufactured specifically for the outlet store. All have Aigner's genuine leathers in the classic signature and traditional shades. An impressive selection of handbags by this famous maker is worth checking out, as is a rack of outerwear with mostly raincoats. *614/426-6009.*

EVAN-PICONE—Catering to the professional woman, this store primarily has sleek, classic lines by Evan-Picone. First-quality suits, separates, and dresses are in misses', petites', and women's plus sizes. For the budget-conscious woman, it's an excellent place to pick up career wear at factory-direct prices. *614/426-6186.*

JONES NY EXECUTIVE SUITE—This store is serious about business. There's a wonderful selection of classic suits from Jones New York. Finely tailored in distinctive men's and women's styles, these first-quality suits bring smart looks to the office place at prices below regular retails. Dress shirts, ties, and accessories are also available. *614/426-6685.*

G-III LEATHER—A sign proudly displaying G-III as America's largest leather apparel and outerwear company is prominently displayed in the store. After looking around, the claim seems quite valid. The selection of leather garments is vast with an especially good color selection and style range for men and women (some in larger sizes). Other leather and suede garments such as jackets, hats, vests, and skirts are good values. *614/426-8555.*

GEOFFREY BEENE—Owned by none other than Van Heusen, Geoffrey Beene has fashions slanted more toward the traditionalist desiring a little more style. Much of the selection consists of dress shirts for the office and fine sportswear for after hours, all of which are 25%–50% off regular retails. *614/426-6855.*

GEOFFREY BEENE LADIES—It's unusual to find a separate Geoffrey Beene store devoted solely to the woman. This outlet, one of only a few around, has an excellent selection of Geoffrey Beene's casual sportswear basics at savings of 25%–50% off regular retail prices. *614/426-9686.*

GENUINE KIDS—In vivid colors and prints, this quality fit clothing for girls and boys (sizes 12 months–16), has some of the same characteristics as OshKosh B'Gosh. In fact, it was recently acquired by this well-known name and is now one of its divisions. While the selection in the store runs deep, the prices are so-so. *614/426-8882.*

GREETINGS 'N' MORE—This store places emphasis on a selection of greeting cards for all occasions that are 50% off regular prices. Of course, all the trimmings and wraps for gifts are also sold around this central theme. Large bins filled with rolls of low-priced gift wrap are in the back of the store. Other choices include party favors, partyware, and seasonal items, all of which the store claims to be priced at 50%–75% below retail. *614/426-6491.*

ASIDE **Check into subsidized trips. Many outlet malls will help subsidize a bus trip to their facility for groups of 25 people or more. If you are planning a trip, you may want to call the outlet center ahead of time to learn more about the details. Often, the malls will give out shopping bags and coupon books when you arrive.**

HARVE BERNARD—This is where the classy business woman wardrobes herself with sophisticated, high-caliber fashions. Well-executed in choice natural fabrics such as pure wools, rich linens, and fine cottons (whatever the season calls for), the store's selection of Harve Bernard's traditionally styled suits and fine sportswear is impressive. The store, owned by the Bernard Holtzman Company, has only current looks in first-quality grades. Available in misses' and petites' sizes, these fashions, which are regularly sold to upscale department stores, are 30%–50% off normal retail prices. *614/426-8650.*

HOOVER—One of only two in the country (the other one is in Hillsboro, Texas), Hoover's outlet doubles as a showroom. The company's entire lines are represented in the store at prices that are equal to or better than regular retails. The best values are on the store's reconditioned models. These models have never been used and may be missing a box or have cosmetic flaws. The products in the store are fully warranteed by Hoover. Smaller items such as sweeper bags and belts are also available. *614/426-8711.*

JH COLLECTIBLES—This store is distinguished by its extensive selection of JH Collectible's sleek, classic lines for misses and petites. Heavy emphasis is placed on apparel for the career woman with some fine sportswear featured as well. A sample rack of JH Collectible's latest trial runs can't be ignored. Here customers can save even more on selected styles merely because the manufacturer wants to try out new design elements (an item may have an extra pocket or button). *614/426-8825.*

JOHN HENRY & FRIENDS—Catering to the label-conscious shopper with upscale tastes, John Henry has a variety of men's sportswear, dress shirts, and accessories at less than regular retail prices. Brands like Nino Gerruti, Thomson, Perry Ellis, and John Henry's own name are emphasized. Of particular interest are the store's collections of Liberty of London pure silk ties and casual wear with subtle "Peanuts" themes. A narrow collection of John Henry clothing for women is also available. *614/426-6951.*

JONATHAN MARTIN—Some of the same styles and designs found in this store by Jonathan Martin are also manufactured for the Limited. The selection of youthful looks, in mostly flowing printed dresses and trendy denim wear, caters to a junior clientele. *614/426-6875.*

JONES NEW YORK—A well-defined collection of Jones New York fashions for misses and petites is at this factory-direct outlet. It's worth checking here first before buying at the regular malls. There's a good chance the style desired will be at the outlet for at least 25% off regular retails, especially since it only stocks fairly current first-quality merchandise. A small line of JNY cosmetics is also available. *614/426-6681.*

JONES NEW YORK WOMAN—In proportioned fits especially designed for the plus size, Jones New York Woman has a better-than-average selection. These classic fashions are in fairly current looks that are marked at least 25% off regular retails. *614/426-6667.*

THE KITCHEN PLACE—Every outlet mall seems to have its kitchen gadget store. The Kitchen Place is this mall's entry. Filled with an almost overwhelming supply of little kitchen aids and appliances and bakeware and cookware, it fits the role very well. Proudly displaying the featured names—Rubbermaid, Mirro, Krups, Ecko, and others—the store has some good values. *614/426-8867.*

L'EGGS/HANES/BALI—The selection in this store for men and women is broad, yet well organized. Many of the items are categorized according to size which is appreciated in a store that sells a lot of small, everyday essentials. L'eggs and Hanes hosiery, socks, and undergarments are among some of its best buys with greater savings on irregulars. Bali and Playtex warrant their own sections with plenty of choices. Don't miss the bargain bins filled with Hanes' irregular and closeout sweatshirts and sweatpants, stationed around the store. *614/426-9791.*

L'CCESSORY—This store recently became part of Claire's network of accessories retailers. Within the confines of its small space, it has the same merchandise as many of Claire's other regular mall stores. The only difference is that this store has price reductions every day (not just during sales). *614/426-9269.*

LEATHER LOFT—The rich smell of genuine leather goods softens the willpower and the wide selection of wallets and checkbook covers toughens the choice. Big ticket merchandise gets your charge card in gear. Wonderfully supple leather garment bags, briefcases, and organizers, and luggage sets or individual pieces are nothing to shy away from. Fortunately, the prices seem fair-minded or one could really go for broke. *614/426-6870.*

LESLIE FAY—Leslie Fay features a vast selection for misses, petites, and plus sizes in this large store, but the ambiance doesn't breathe much life into them. Not much effort is put forth to spruce up the store with its tired-looking format. The store's main shopping advantage is in its selection. Kasper, Nipon Night (evening wear), Nipon Studio, Outlander, and other Leslie Fay brands are all found in vast quantities in this spacious store. A complete size range for misses, petites, and plus size women is another selling point. *614/426-6220.*

LILY OF FRANCE—This store has a wide selection of Lily of France, Christian Dior, and Carole Hochman sleepwear and lingerie in fine luxurious fabrics. At prices less than regular retail, it makes you want to turn in your old worn standbys for some of these refreshing new options. *614/426-6195.*

MAIDENFORM—Geared more toward the practical-minded shopper, this store's prices reflect that conservative mode. Well stocked with Maidenform's first-quality lingerie and sleepwear, the selection merits attention. *614/426-8877.*

MEMBERS ONLY—Known primarily for its moderate outerwear, Members Only licenses its products to department stores like Sears and Elder-Beerman. This outlet has a broad selection of lightweight and leather outerwear, as well as some sportswear, in current looks. While most of the items are in regular sizes for men, some big and tall and boys' sizes are available. At times, a slim selection for women is also found here. *614/426-6020.*

MUSIC 4 LESS—While this store has many choices of music on compact discs and cassette tapes, its prices are no better than the average record shop. It's an obvious "filler" store whose name is not fooling those who know good value. *614/426-8611.*

N.A.P.—The savvy shopper will be able to decipher which brand name sleepwear or lingerie is sold here even though some of the labels have been removed from the garments. It's not uncommon to see anonymous notables (like Victoria's Secrets, but who's telling?) show up among the selection. Other items that have labels intact are good buys here, too. In fact, the overall store has an excellent selection at reasonable prices. *614/426-8776.*

NEW YORK JEWELRY OUTLET—With price comparisons on its walls, this store claims to offer better savings on fine jewelry and watches. But, it's best to shop around to find out how much items normally sell for before being taken in by any jewelry store's claims, even at the outlet mall. While this store has a wide selection of gold jewelry, precious and semiprecious stones, and diamonds, its main attraction is its collection of watches. Distinctive styles by Pulsar, Citizen, Bulova, Movado, Seiko, Fendi, and Gucci are featured in the display cases. *614/426-6032.*

ASIDE **Check items carefully before buying. Most reputable outlet stores will mark all damaged, irregular, or second-quality merchandise so customers can easily distinguish these items from first quality. But it still pays to look items over carefully before making your selections.**

NINE WEST—This store's extensive selection makes it easy to uncover some real finds. Loaded with Nine West's casual and dress footwear, it has more variety and color choices than any department store would offer. Fashionable boots also make a strong showing. All of the merchandise is first quality and at least 30% off regular retails, making it even more enticing. *614/426-6757.*

OSHKOSH B' GOSH—Parents will find this store "user friendly." A circular path that winds around the store in bright blue and yellow colors makes it easy to shop without weaving through racks. This comes in handy with children in tow. The bright, attractive decor of the store also highlights the broad selection of Oshkosh B' Gosh playwear for children. *614/426-6294.*

PEPPERIDGE FARM—Not for the diet conscious, those tasty little Pepperidge Farm goldfish crackers, cookies, and snacks fill this store at 25%–50% off regular retails. Items are coded to indicate seconds, market returns, and clearance (past freshness dates). Several cases featuring frozen cakes and desserts are also in the store. There are free samples of Godiva chocolate, which is owned, along with Pepperidge Farm, by the Campbell's Soup Company. Just enjoy yourself. *614/426-6872.*

PERFUMANIA—While Perfumania may have a broad variety of designer fragrances for men and women, it doesn't carry complete lines like the department stores. Nor does it offer the free incentive gifts that go along with certain purchase quotas. It does, in fact, sell some of these bonus gift offerings separately, as well as testers and miniatures. However, the store does have good prices on the items it stocks with a color-coded system that helps the customer identify the best values. *614/426-6063.*

THE RIBBON OUTLET—Crafters need the variety of ribbons and trims found in this store. At factory-direct savings, they have several options on buying their goods. Customers can buy by the yard, pre-cut, or in entire spools. Look for the manager's specials on wearable art supplies, bows, novelty, and seasonal items and ribbon, of course. *614/426-8484.*

RUSS FACTORY STORE—Those popular plush and mechanical toys by Russ are 50% off regular retail prices across the board. The wide selection, along with ceramic items by other manufacturers, is scattered throughout its small selling space. There's also a broad collection of well-garbed trolls. *614/426-8511.*

SAMSONITE—A full range of Samsonite's hardside and softside luggage in discontinued, first-quality overstocks with slight cosmetic flaws are 30%–60% off. Of course, warranties apply on all of Samsonite's luggage products (even at its outlet stores). Other products made just for the outlet, along with a wide selection of carry-ons, tote bags, and garment bags, are available. *614/426-8850.*

SARA LEE—Don't miss this store. A leader in selling frozen baked goods, Sara Lee operates outlet stores to economically dispose of closeouts, overstocks, and slightly imperfect products economically. Its delicious varieties—pies, muffins, bagels, danish, cheese cakes, sweet rolls and gourmet desserts—are sold in individual, family, and party size packages. Savings of up to 40% off retails are realistic. Examples of the type of savings found at Sara Lee: a box of 15 croissants is $3.49; 24 bran muffinsfor $3.33. Other edibles are main dish entrees (like quiche and lasagna), Jimmy Dean sausage, and, of course, Sara Lee's famous All Butter Pound Cake. *614/426-6061.*

SOCKS GALORE—Probably one of the few places on earth without a missing sock, Socks Galore's advantage is in its selection and its convenience. Many of the styles bear the Hanes label, which shouldn't be surprising since the store is owned by Hanes. Of special note are the store's exclusive lines—Dri-Sox and the World's Softest Socks. *614/426-8835.*

SWANK—Swank, the manufacturer of various lines of small leather goods and accessories, has included many of them in this outlet. A large selection of handbags, ties, belts, wallets, and umbrellas is on hand. Featured brands include Pierre Cardin, L'aiglon, and Alexander Julian. A noteworthy collection of Anne Klein jewelry, made by Swank, is at exceptional savings. *614/426-8486.*

TRENCH SPORTSWEAR—For loyal fans, this store has team logo activewear with professional and collegiate emblems. Many, including tee shirts, sweatshirts, sports caps, and jackets, are officially licensed products. Pennants from every team imaginable also line the walls. *614/426-8601.*

VAN HEUSEN—For the practically minded, Van Heusen's dress shirts for men and sportswear for men and women bring good values at this outlet. Savings average 20%–50% off regular retails on this moderately priced line. *614/426-8884.*

WALLET WORKS—Primarily a factory outlet for Amity and Rolfs, Wallet Works has an extensive selection of personal leather goods, along with tote bags, luggage, and travel cases. A mixture of first-quality, second-quality, discontinued, and irregular items bring varying savings. Look for the noteworthy collection of Charles Hubert leather handbags. *614/426-6287.*

WELCOME HOME—One of the better organized Welcome Home stores around, it has an appealing lack of confusion. Toward the back of the store is an abundance of those cozy afghans. The rest of the store has an eclectic mix of candles, framed art, table linens, brassware, and gift items. Shipments arrive daily, so check out the store periodically. *614/426-9238.*

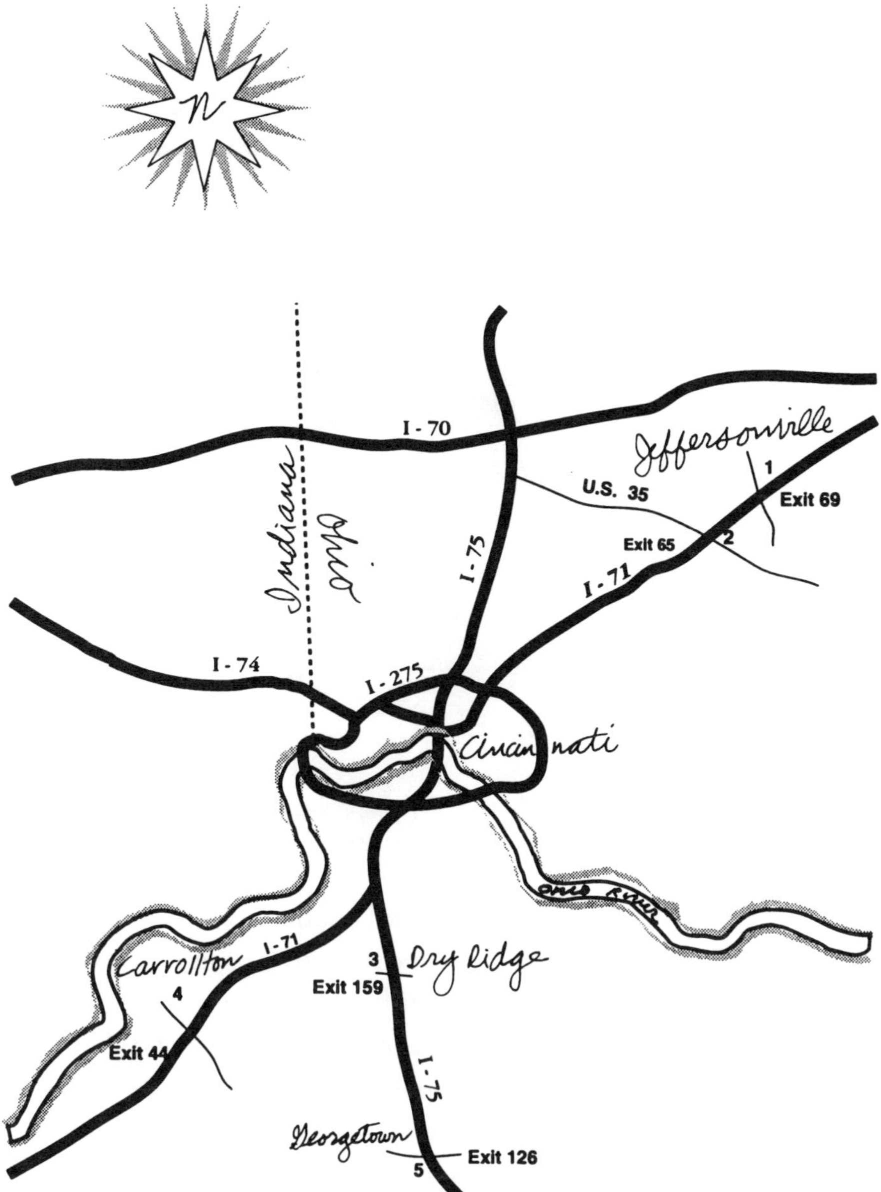

Dry Ridge Outlet Center - **3**
Factory Stores of America, Carrollton - **4**
Factory Stores of America, Georgetown - **5**
Jeffersonville Outlet Center - **1**
Ohio Factory Shops - **2**

Chains

Grocery stores and food chains were once the only ones cashing in on combining food and non-food related items, now the opposite is true. Discount department stores, like K-Mart and Target are building super centers featuring both groceries and their usual products. And competition means a buyer's market. The first Super K-Mart around Cincinnati opened in Hillsboro in February of 1995. The idea is to keep customers coming in for groceries every day. Bigg's, with its hypermarket stores, has taken one-stop shopping to a grand scale with various specialty departments and wide aisles lined with massive quantities of brand names. With Meijer entering the Cincinnati market, Bigg's and Kroger will have to face stiffer competition. One of the reasons Cincinnati was chosen as the place to build super food stores is that it boasts one of the highest consumptions, per person, of groceries over all the markets across the country. ¶ Another concept to hit the region is micromarketing where stores specialize in selling one category of products. Michaels primarily sells craft-related items. Staples specializes in office supplies. These "category killers" demolish competition by buying in volume and operating on low margins. They cater to destination shoppers wanting a big selection at low prices. The off-price chains, like T.J. Maxx and Marshall's, buy products in a number of ways. Much of their merchandise may be from previous seasons, but it can also be current. Some of the items arrive shortly after they hit the regular department stores. These stores offer lower prices by forgoing decor and service. ¶ Stores have taken the no-frills concept to the maximum. Discounters and mass-merchandisers are trying to cut their margins. Unfortunately, one of the first places to make cutbacks is in the service. Customers must contend with longer check-out lines and be willing to sacrifice time and personal attention to receive the best prices. And as old familiar retail names die out or change with the times, new ones arrive on the scene. It's hard to know which ones will be the survivors. Check this summary to find your way through the new and changing concepts in discount retailing—while they're around.

BIG LOTS/ODD LOTS—Low on aesthetics but big on inventory, this discounter sells surplus, closeout, and discontinued items at 30–70% below retail. Aimed at down-scale shoppers, it changes merchandise constantly. The turnover is designed to keep them coming back to discover what new products are available. Every store claims to be different as it attempts to sell shopping as an adventure.

BIGG'S & MEIJER—Out-of-towners drive to these places once a month and make it a family outing. It was overheard that one lady wanted a pair of horse-blinders to keep her focused while shopping. With over 100,000 items per store, the stores emphasize brand names and they buy "deep" so they don't run out of stock. But it's usually the customers who run out—of time. The "hypermarket" concept was introduced in 1984 by Bigg's. Combining grocery shopping with a variety store has mixed results. It's tough to get people to purchase food and non-food items on the same trip. The stores typically operate with a lower profit margin on food (about 12%) compared with its competitors' range of 20%–23%. Customers save 15% overall on groceries with true minimum prices—low overall prices on products not driven by weekly specials. Each week over 4,000 "Bigg Buys" are reduced lower than the usual prices on brand name products. Its tough competitor, Meijer, known for its produce department, aggressively advertises and pushes private label products as well as brand names. These are not the places to go when you just need milk. Bring a van.

THE BOOK RACK—Pay half price or trade two for one at this used paperback book company. From classics to romances, the store offers a nice alternative to paying full price. Be forewarned. Don't expect to find current bestsellers on the racks. They go quickly after trade-ins.

DAY OLD BREAD AND OTHER DELICACIES—If you're into counting grams of fat in every bite, you probably don't want to know that there are over twenty bakery thrift stores scattered around the area. Each one sells breads and baked goods that are too old to be sold at grocery stores but young enough to buy by the case, lock yourself in a room, and eat in their entirety before another freshness date goes by. Some foods are just surplus items or are in damaged packages. ***Dolly Madison Bakery Thrift Stores, Dolly Madison Cake/Saps Foods Thrift Stores, and Butternut Bread Thrift Stores*** sell many of the same products. Breads, snack cakes, and donuts dominate the shelves. In these shops, the closer to the freshness dates, the further the price break—up to 50% off regular retail. Look for ***Wonder/ Hostess Bakery Thrift Outlets. Klosterman Bakery Outlets.*** They offer a little wider (to match the thighs) selection than the others. Little Debbie and Husman's snacks are here, too. Not for the cholesterol-impaired.

DISCOUNT FLICKS—Subrun houses, the ones that show the movies after they've been at the major cinemas, offer low prices ($1.50–$2) on viewing not-so-old movies. Profit is made from all the snacks you eat. ***Regal Cinemas***, the fastest growing cinema chain in the world, begins daily matinees at 1:00pm, with the last feature at 9:30–10:00pm daily. With 10 or 11 auditoriums, it has lots of choices. Features change on Fridays. Two concessions specials are worth checking out. Wide screens and state-of-the-art stereo systems make these cinemas deluxe. ***Super Saver Cinemas*** operate the same way with multi-auditorium theatres, daily matinees, and nightly show times. Flashing neon in the lobby generate hype.

DISCOUNT DEPARTMENT STORES—No-frills, little service, and low prices characterize these mass-merchandisers. Their formula is simple—buy huge quantities direct from manufacturers, save on overhead, and sell in volume with low mark-ups. *K-Mart* has been around the city quite awhile. Attempts to upgrade its image by promoting merchandise like the Jaclyn Smith collection have yielded so-so results. Now, although K-Mart stores contain some good values, they appear tired and worn. The emergence of *Wal-Mart* has altered the discounting landscape. Founded in 1962 by American icon Sam Walton, it has perfected the art of mass-merchandising. The huge stores are so crammed that it is disconcerting to some shoppers. Expect to be sidetracked several times by sale items before you find what you came to buy. *Target* stores are a little more upscale. The stores are less cluttered and the merchandise is more appealing. The result is that customers feel the values are somewhat better.

DOTS—It sells some career wear, but specializes in sportswear and casual wear. Selling a mix of first-quality name brand overstocks, along with its own labels, this Cleveland-based retailer appeals to women from ages 14–49. Everything in the store is sold at $10 or less which leaves little room for sales. Clearance sales are twice a year.

ASIDE **What is a deep discount store? It usually offers customers a big spacious shopping facility, a wide selection, and deep discount prices. These stores are likely anchors for strip malls and discount shopping centers and are often known as superstores or category killers. They are usually national chains, buy in large volume, and specialize in selling one category of products such as health and beauty aids, toys, home improvement, or office supplies. The products these stores carry are usually quality name brands. Examples of deep discount stores in the Cincinnati area are Michaels for crafts; Staples for office supplies; Sally Beauty Supply for hair care; Drug Emporium for health and beauty aids; and Furrows for home improvement.**

DRUG EMPORIUM—Everything's here from health and beauty aids to first-aid items, often at good savings. Each store has over 30,000 items including a complete line of cosmetics, household cleaners, and snack foods. Every pre-priced item from the manufacturers is reduced (with very few exceptions). American Greeting Cards run about 40% off regular retail everyday and its pharmacy has hard-to-beat prescription prices.

THE ELECTRONICS GAME—In the rough and tumble world of electronics and appliances it is often the customer who gets hurt. Picking your way through the low price claims of stores implying they will not be undersold, it's hard to decipher the real truth. Manufacturers often sell the same products to retailers with only cosmetic differences. However, the products have different model numbers making comparison shopping difficult. ***Swallen's*** is a longtime Cincinnati discounter and it's more than an electronics store. It has major appliances and furniture as well as housewares. Each of its stores often caters to the area's needs. One of its units has a separate marine center with boat supplies. For years, ***Steinberg's*** was Swallen's main rival. While both try to maintain their profit margins, aggressive customers who are willing to walk can nudge the price down. Two recent players on the Cincinnati scene are ***Sun*** and ***Circuit City*** and are highly competitive in the market. However, Sun with its combination of famous name and off-brand products, and its powerful marketing strategy, is the place to shop before buying. One way Sun attracts shoppers is by selling the Top Ten, best-selling compact discs at $9.97 each. While not strictly an appliance and electronics store, *Wal-Mart's* willingness to sell below the normal profit margins enables it to offer good values on a limited selection of electronics.

FACTORY CARD OUTLET—Don't waste money on expensive greeting cards. Ones that normally sell for $1.25–$1.75 are here for 39¢. In addition, it carries discounted party goods and plush animals. Remember it's the thought that counts. Better yet, make your own card.

FOOTWEAR PACESETTERS—Over half of million pairs of shoes are discounted in and around the city—everyday,—more than there are feet to fill them. Most are first-quality styles by brand names at up to 50% off that you will try on with no help from the discounters. Scattered around the shops are benches, shoe horns, and mirrors so customers can fit themselves. ***El-Bee Shoe Outlets***, one of the oldest and largest chains in the area, places its shoes on racks that reach eye level. They are arranged by size and displayed in open shoe boxes. This makes it more difficult to pick out a style, but cuts costs on expensive displays. Like this early discounter, ***Rack Room Shoes*** and ***Famous Footwear*** push moderately-priced, name brand shoes. These stores organize footwear according to style and display items along the counter tops and shelves. Venturing a little more toward the upscale market is ***Designer Shoe Warehouse***. Its bright, white walls and fluorescently lit interior give it an antiseptic, impersonal feel. The stores close midweek for restocking. On the other end, ***Shoe World*** and ***Payless Shoe*** Stores offer inexpensive off-brand shoes and name brand knock-offs. One shoe giant that makes use of an uncanny approach to retailers is ***Shoe Carnival***. (see entry)

THE FRAME SHOPS—***Frame & Save*** has a modest selection of prints and photos. Many are the usual frame store fare—city scenes, animals dressed-up, and the latest in poster art wisdom. If you're into prints of dogs playing poker, these stores have quite a few. With over 100 selected custom frames at 50% off per store, prices fair well with competition. You can save an extra 20% off your total ticket by framing your own items (with in-store assistance) at most Frame & Save stores. Some stores have floral centers with silk flowers. From the large selection of fakes, you can make your own arrangements or take advantage of the in-house floral designer. One of its rivals, ***Frametastic*** leaves all pretenses behind. These stores are more like workshops. Employees piecing together frames are in plain view. The selection of framing materials is good and their prices easily beat the competition. Though the in-stock selection of prints is limited, each store offers thousands from catalogs. Many are unusual designs not found in stores.

HALF PRICE BOOKS—Now the largest used book dealer in the country, Half Price Books has more than just previously owned books. About one-third of its books, bought from publishers' warehouses, are ones which never sold. The stores, staffed by employees encouraged to dress down in tee shirts and jeans, are crammed with discounted books and calendars (look for Ian Adams' Ohio calendars), but the most interesting sections remain their used books—an eclectic library of titles that once taken home never have to be returned.

HOME IMPROVEMENT—Competition makes home improvement a buyer's market. Even the small guys like ***Ace*** and ***True Value***, can put up some competitive numbers. But it's tough competing with the superstores on selection. ***Home Quarters Warehouse (HQ), Lowe's Home Improvement Warehouse, Furrow's Building Materials, Contractor's Warehouse and Western Home Center*** all have similar set-ups—huge areas shelving building supplies that stretch to the ceiling. Some, like Contractor's Warehouse and Western Home Center, are favored by professionals. HQ and Furrow's try to be more user-friendly to do-it-yourselfers, while Lowe's has more things like televisions and other home electronics.

LINENS & LOTS MORE—***Linens 'n Things*** has taken an aggressive approach to retailing by replacing many of its smaller stores with 30,000 sq. ft. superstores. That's four times as big. It now offers more housewares and more shopping ease. Price comparisons are posted on many items. ***Linens, Etc.*** sells on a similar premise with bed and bath linens as the main draw and home furnishings and gift items at everyday low prices. *Homegoods* has huge stores that carry more than 300,000 items. Specializing primarily in home furnishings, it does carry some fashions. Claiming to have merchandise at 25%–60% off department and specialty store prices, you'll find some real bargains.

THE LINENS OUTLETS—***Whiting Manufacturer Linen Outlet Store***s are locally based with the main factory site on Carver Road. Manufacturing bedding and linens, Whiting's outlets also have other brands in first-quality, seconds, irregulars, overruns, even thirds at up to 50% off. ***Cotton Mill Factory Outlets***, owned by

Leshner, has bed and bath linens from first-quality items, seconds, and irregulars at substantial savings. Both companies sell quilts, pillows, and draperies.

MICHAELS CRAFTS—This "category killer" pursues market dominance by offering a broad mix of crafts, picture framing materials, and hobby and art supplies at up to 50% off regular retail everyday. To generate ideas, experienced crafters often demonstrate their talents in the store. Craft supplies for all ages. If you join the no fee Kids Club, each child receives a bimonthly newsletter, membership card, name badge, and craft items (supplied by vendors) .

OFF-BRAND FOOD STORES—Customers that frequent these stores don't buy into the idea that choosing brand names products is always better. ***Aldi***, short for "all discount", is strictly a no-frills grocery chain which typically sells about 500 items per store. Most of its off-brand packaged foods, at 20%–30% below supermarket prices, are displayed by cutting the tops and sides off cartons and stacking them along the aisles. It doesn't sell fresh meats, only frozen. And, customers must pay for the use of bags and shopping carts. Its competitor, ***Save-a-Lot*** has off-brand foods (and some non-related food items) at savings of up to 40% everyday when compared to brand name equivalents. Some of the items are under different labels in regular grocery stores. Offering canned, frozen, and packaged foods, these stores carry only the product's best-selling size rather than a wider selection like most supermarkets. You might find a few brand names at either of these stores. Don't expect service. You bag your own groceries.

ASIDE **Some food discounters specialize in generic or off-brands. For consumers who aren't concerned with brand names, this type of store can offer some real savings. Packaged or canned foods (and other non-related food items) can be purchased under private, generic or off-brand labels and consumers can save as much as 40% - 60%. Most of the goods are packaged by manufacturers and bought at one central location. Some of the items are actually the same as more well-known brands just packaged under different names. Stores that sell these types of products usually can't offer as great a variety on specific items as the regular grocery stores. However, the products they do offer usually span a wide category range—anywhere from breakfast and snacks foods to cleaning and paper supplies. Some familiar brand name items may also show up at these stores. Off-brand grocers around Cincinnati include: Save-A-Lot and Aldi Food Stores.**

OFF-PRICE DEPARTMENT STORES—Like their retail department store counterparts, these off-price merchants offer a variety of apparel, home furnishings, and giftwares. They do it with lower prices, lower service, and lower ambiance. ***Marshall's*** touts itself as the nation's largest off-price retailer. Its stores are typically located near big-name department stores. It banks on the idea that shoppers will look there first before searching for cheaper prices. Overruns and special purchases dominate its inventory. It carries first-quality apparel for the entire family although some clearly marked irregulars may show up. *T.J. Maxx* buys factory overruns and items department stores can't sell. The clothes are often wedged tightly into the racks that endlessly stretch across the floor. If you manage to pry out something you like, it likely will be from a previous season. With more of an upscale department store atmosphere, ***Stein Mart*** has merchandise conveniently arranged by lifestyle. The selection runs deeper and is more current than its rivals. It shies away from buying last season's merchandise. ***Value City***, with its famous big-name department store buyouts, is normally 90,000 sq. ft. (about three times as large as most off-price stores) and has a broad cross-section of goods. All typically claim around 20%–60% off retail prices.

OFFICE WARS—The future of the office supply stores will be determined on the retail battlefield where only a few large suppliers will be left standing. The concept began with ***Staples*** operating from the premise of selling huge volumes and cutting out the middleman. After it, other deep discount superstores, like ***Office Max*** and ***Office Depot***, followed in the Cincinnati market. These companies are virtually indistinguishable from one another. Each uses warehouse-like displays, stack merchandise to the ceiling, and price identically. One alternative to shopping the superstores is to order by phone from ***Viking***, a mail-order supply company offering general office and computer supplies at 30%–50% off manufacturers' list prices

---

ASIDE **What is an off-price or discount store? They offer lower prices than regular retail stores on brand name items...everyday. Merchandise is usually sold at least 20% off regular retail prices at off-price stores and can be current or leftover from the last season. These stores often purchase their inventory from a number of manufacturers in large volumes. They also often purchase factory overruns and items departments stores have a hard time selling. They buy opportunistically. Therefore, the selection they offer is usually varied and not as complete as regular retail stores. Examples of off-price stores around Cincinnati are Linens, Etc. for household products, T.J. Maxx for fashions, and Marshall's for fashions and home furnishings.**

PLAY IT AGAIN SPORTS—New and used sporting goods, there aren't many great bargains among the new stuff and not much is worth having among the heavily used and abused. (A lot of golf clubs show up here, but after close inspection it's easy to see why.) The exercise equipment is sufficient, but the best buys are on the equipment that can take the abuse like baseball bats and heavy duty weights.

PLUS SIZE, PLUS SAVINGS—With more than one-fifth of women's apparel sold in size 16 or larger, this merchandiser has found a niche in the crowded field of fashion retail. As more manufacturers get into supplying plus-size fashions, a discounter for this size range became quite feasible. The market really opened up recently when the ***home-shopping networks*** revealed that about half of their sales were in sizes 14 and above. While not really a true discount store, it offers reasonable prices on a wide selection—career and casual wear, lingerie, accessories, hosiery, and coats—from brand names like Leslie Fay, Sharon Anthony, and Kathy White.

SALLY BEAUTY SUPPLY—Why pay higher salon prices or regular retails when Sally Beauty Supply has comparable beauty products at 20%–40% off salon-quality hair and nail care products, as well as some cosmetics and hair accessories. Nail art kits, even some with rhinestones, are priced well within reason. With over 500 stores nationwide, this Alberto-Culver unit is growing with plans for rapid expansion.

SAM'S CLUB WAREHOUSE STORES—Wheeling oversized shopping carts in and out of aisles flanked with industrial shelving two stories high, warehouse members stuff bulk goods picked from among the thousands of items offered at big discounts. Restaurant-size portions from the giant freezers and multiple packages of dry foods are tossed in. Some space is left for anything from auto supplies to clothing, but there is no dressing room or sales person to help you. Checking out is no problem if you can find a Volkswagon-sized carton to carry the stuff home. Where do people put all these things? Memberships are $25 a year.

SHOE CARNIVAL—It's madcap retailing at its finest, which is a nice way of saying, "Bring aspirin." Footwear sales at Shoe Carnival is more of a Michael Jackson Moonwalk than an Arthur Murray Waltz. Customers periodically grab for discounts in "money machines" (glassed-in booths where coupons and cash blow around) or they may try their luck at winning hula hoop contests for additional savings. Set in an environment of loud music, bold color, and flashing neon lights with a carnival-style barker spouting off in-store promotions, an open stock of shoes is moderately priced. It's a little weird, no, it's real wierd, but worth the time, since there are many name brand shoes for men, women, and children.

TUESDAY MORNING—Filled with merchandise ranging from seasonal items to luggage and crystal, most of the stock is high-end gift merchandise priced at 50%–80% below suggested retail. Buyers purchase canceled goods, overruns, and at off times of the year to keep prices down. All merchandise is new and not replaced when sold. The stores are only open at various times of the year.

VIDEO GAME EXCHANGE—This store found its niche in exploiting the short attention span of video game players. The company specializes in buying, selling, and trading used video game cartridges. Old games can be traded in by customers for credit ($25 a shot) toward the purchase of new or used games. With over 3,000 games, customers can find something to feed their addiction.

WOMEN'S OFF-PRICE APPAREL—A store desperately in need of a new name, *Dress Barn* targets women between the ages of 18 and 40. This national chain carries current, first-quality merchandise in juniors' and misses' sizes. *Hit Or Miss* is another aimed at the working woman with fashions for after hours. Both chains claim to have 20%–50% off regular retail prices on famous designer names.

Special Sales Events

The true bargain hunter knows that some of the best savings are found at warehouse sales and special semi-annual and annual sales events. These growing, popular affairs are becoming regularly scheduled, though it's difficult to pinpoint the exact day of the sale in advance since most retailers establish the actual dates closer to the event. The calendar in this section, is based on sales held during the previous year (and prices or discounts offered). Watch the local newspaper for advertised promotions. In some instances, you may need to sign up on mailing lists to be notified of sales. Remember, too, that these sales don't necessarily occur at a regular store. Many are held in warehouses or tents so you can anticipate minimal amenities—like dressing rooms. ¶ Battling it out for the bargains at these free-for-alls can be quite profitable. However, reaping the rewards only comes after doing a lot of work and being quick on your feet. Be prepared to rummage through piles and heaps of goods, while swiftly looking them over for flaws. If you set something down don't expect it to be there later. To go for the kill, arm yourself with these guerrilla shopping tactics: ¶ Do a preliminary sweep by quickly browsing through the place. Try not to become overwhelmed by the choices. Pinpoint where the items' location. Don't spend too long on the things that aren't your preferences. ¶ Eyeball the racks and bins to decipher how items are arranged. Are they organized by size, style or brand name? Are the goods marked as firsts, seconds or irregulars? This will allow you to quickly find the level of quality or sizes you are seeking. ¶ When shopping for clothes examine labels and make sure you check the size on the tag against what the garment looks like held up to yourself. Sometimes fashions are mismarked or aren't in standard fitted proportions. If there *is* a dressing room don't take more than four garments in at a time. Taking more only creates indecision. If there's not a dressing room, head for a mirror. ¶ You may want to bring your own shopping bags since some places don't offer them. Remember, once you buy something you're stuck with it, since most of these events offer goods as final sales only.

January

ANNUAL CONVENTION CENTER FUR SALE/DOWNTOWN CINCINNATI—You can save more here than at any other sale, but it may cost you, say, $20,000 to do so. A $25,000 mink fur coat could go for over 20% off—saving you $5000. Other furs may be less than $1000. The finer furs—full-skin sable, mink, and lynx—sell for big bucks, but beaver, lamb, rabbit, fox, coyote, and raccoon are popular, and less expensive. Many are 50%–75% off their original prices. The average price for one of these high-class hides is around $2500. This esteemed sale, held at the Cincinnati Convention Center, is for all kinds of extravagant tastes. Held annually, starting on New Year's Day, over a thousand furs (an inventory above $5 million) are featured by Evans Furrier. Based in Chicago, it's the largest furrier in the world. Evans leases retail space all year at several area Lazarus Department Stores. Free monogramming and alterations are available by appointment.
Cincinnati Convention Center, Fifth & Elm streets. For more information call the Fur Salon at Lazarus - 513/369-6253.

HICKORY FARMS ANNUAL 50% WAREHOUSE SALE/WEST CHESTER—For over 35 years Hickory Farms has been a big part of the holiday-giving tradition. But after the festive season, the leftovers have to go *somewhere*. The company's local warehouse showroom is packed full of them at 50% off savings. Cheeses in logs, crocks, party shapes, and slabs, along with beef sticks and other sausage-like meats, are the most popular foods. Gift sets and baskets, as well as nuts, cookies, and fruit cakes in collectible tins, run a close second. Mustards, sauces, chocolates, and jellies round out this holiday appetizer's groundwork. The items are all well-preserved with a "seems-like-forever" shelf-life.
5142 Duff Drive, (off 747 - just north of Tri-County); 513/874-2332. Mon–Fri 9:30am–5:30pm. Sale continues through January. VS, MC, DS, AE.

February

ANNUAL SUN & SKI SPORTS DOT SALE/KENWOOD—At this winter clearance event the sale prices drop with the tick of the clock. So hold out and you can nab some exceptional buys on quality, high performance ski equipment and ski apparel. Look for the color-coded dots. Each one represents certain discounts off the lowest ticketed price. Items go on sale at the end of January all the way through March until they are cleared away. It's a gamble. If you wait too long the items you want or the sizes you need may be gone later. But, it's worth taking a chance if you're into the savings scene.
Joseph Banks Building, 7565 Kenwood Road; 513/745-0099. Mon–Fri 10am–9pm, Sat 10am–7pm, Sun 11am–5pm.

MERTACK'S ANNUAL FLOOR SAMPLE SALE/COVINGTON, KENTUCKY—This is the time to add a piece of furniture or a few accessories to your home decor at greater savings than Mertack's usual everyday discounted price. Everything on the floor (no special orders) is an extra 10% off the ticketed price making it hard to pass up the savings if you see something you like.
440 Scott Street; 606-431-3311. Mon–Sat 10am–5pm, Thurs & Fri 10am–8pm. VS, MC, DS.

STERLING CUT GLASS SEMI-ANNUAL CLEARANCE SALE—Loaded with all the fine breakables, Sterling Cut Glass has been making its mark by doing hand-cut monogramming since the turn of the century. Getting its start in Cincinnati, the company's stores are giant showcases filled with quality hand-engraved crystal and fine glassware. Stemware, serving pieces, giftware, picture frames, mugs, and champagne flutes (the kind you throw in the fireplace after a romantic dinner) are displayed like museum pieces around the stores. Lucky for those with an appreciation for finer quality, an extensive collection is priced from 20%–50% off at these semi-annual sales. The reduced prices include monogramming. Selected items, some with minor flaws, are up to 75% off.
One W. Fourth Street, Downtown Cincinnati; 513/381-4646. Mon–Fri 10am–6pm, Sat 10am–5pm. 2107 Grandin Road, Hyde Park; 513/ 321-6151. Mon–Thurs 10am–8pm, Fri 10am–6pm, Sat 10am–5pm. 7727 Kenwood Road, Kenwood (no phone listing & hours yet). VS, MC, AE.

VALERIE MAKSTELL INTERIORS FAMOUS CLEARANCE SALE/ DOWNTOWN—For those with discriminating tastes, this sale is becoming a prestigious, fine furniture, sales event. These dramatic designs jazz up almost any interior at good prices. Valerie Makstell normally offers high-quality furniture discounted at 35% off retail, but twice a year the store bumps up the savings at least 5% more on in-stock furniture and custom orders. On big ticket items this can amount to a lot. Extra savings on floor samples and discontinued merchandise may reach 70% or more. The store has many unusual and one-of-a-kind pieces not found anywhere else in the city. Displayed in an old, renovated warehouse the sale generally lasts several weeks, but it's best to hit it early for a shot at the best buys. Remember, though, all sales are final and merchandise is sold as-is with no holds or returns.
1050 Mehring Way (Take Pete Rose Way to Mehring Way at Freeman); 513/241-1050. Mon–Sat 10am–5pm, Sun noon–4pm. VS, MC, DS.

March

CHAPEAU CREATIONS HAT LOVERS SALE/ROSELAWN—Her creations can be seen topping off outfits in the grandstand at Ascot, on a park bench along des-Champs-Elysees in Paris or on a moonlight walk at a beach in Acapulco. Closer to home they are seen in the clubhouse at the Kentucky Derby. One would never suspect these distinctive, ornate hats were designed in a small

Chapeau Creations

Roselawn shop. The humble woman behind the operation, Ruth Kropveld, is a third-generation milliner from Germany. She learned her craft in Europe and has been applying her trade since coming to Cincinnati in 1947. Many of the one-of-a-kind styles top $100, but are sold as salesman's samples in the workshop showroom. Hat lovers can buy them here at wholesale prices during certain times of the year. The hand-adorned hats and berets have earned Ruth prestigious awards such as the one that distinguished her as 1992 Hat Designer of the Year by *W. Magazine.*
Roselawn Center, 7385 Brookcrest Drive, (corner of Brookcrest & Section Road off of Reading); 513/631-6055. Sales run from March–June and September–December. Mon–Fri 9am–5:30pm. VS, MC. All sales are final.

GENTRY MEN'S CLOTHIER WAREHOUSE SALE/SHARONVILLE— Gentry's big semi-annual warehouse sale offers a huge savings opportunity that's unparalleled to others. For those wanting to capitalize on noteworthy fashion buys for men, Gentry is a repository of designer names in sportcoats, topcoats, dress slacks, dress shirts, ties, and fine sportswear. The selection consolidates merchandise from 20 Gentry stores. The man serious about upgrading his professional image will find over 8,000 finely-tailored suits drastically reduced. Held at the company warehouse, it's easy to spot. Just look for Gentry's huge "SOS" (Sale of Sales) balloon.
2851 E. Kemper Road, (I-275 to south on Mosteller Road then left on Kemper); 513/771-1199. Daily 9am–9pm, Sun 11am–6pm. VS, MC, DS, AE.

MORGAN'S ANNUAL CANOE RENTAL CLEARANCE SALE/ OREGONIA—Gary Morgan gives a firm handshake, a warm smile, and a plug about the quality canoes found scattered around the grounds when you arrive at their annual canoe sale. He's the general manager and one of the five brothers (they're all hardy outdoorsmen) brought up with river water running in his blood. His parents, Bob and June, began shuttling Gary and the boys upstream via canoe at any early age, just as they did their first customers over three decades ago. The family now operates three facilities in the Tri-State area—the Fort Ancient Canoe Livery in Oregonia, Ohio; Brookville Canoe Center in Indiana; and Mad River Outpost in Springfield, Ohio. Every year, to kick-off the season and help thin out their canoe inventory, they have a sale. For two weekends (the last weekend in March and the first weekend in April), previously-rented canoes from all of Morgan's locations are brought to the Fort Ancient Livery where aluminum models go for as little as $160. With several brands to choose from (like Grumman and Michi-Craft), a new canoe would normally cost between $500 and $600. For a little better product try the 17-foot, Old Town Discovery model which runs from $475-$550. These Polyethylene canoes, sold after a season or two of use, hold up well. The canoes, all lined up outside the livery, are in good shape, guaranteed not to leak and backed by a one-year warranty. Customers are encouraged to take one out for a trial run on the Little Miami River (a convenience you wouldn't have if you bought one elsewhere). New canoes are also on sale, as well as paddles, jackets, and accessories. River enthusiasts can buy these anytime, but the best prices are during this special sale.
5701 State Route 350, (I-71 to Exit 32 or State Route 123 Morrow Exit, south on Rt. 123 1 block to State Route 350 or Interstate Mart, left on Rt. 350 then two miles to the river); 513/932-7658 or 1-800-WE-CANOE. Sale at Fort Ancient location only. VS, MC.

April

CINCINNATI POLICE SPRING AUCTION/DOWNTOWN CINCINNATI—Most anything that anyone could steal or lose is likely to turn up at these twice-a-year police auctions. For one day in the spring and the fall confiscated and unclaimed items are auctioned off. As the auctioneer conducts the bidding you find yourself wondering how all of these items could have been lifted from their owners, especially the larger ones like bicycles, furniture and electronics. Smaller items, ranging from knives and tools to sporting goods and cellular phones, commonly show up here as well. Although good buys can be had here, it's hard to tell whether you'll find something you need or, perhaps, something you never knew was *missing*.
Cincinnati Convention Center, Fifth & Elm streets. For more information call 513/352-6480.

TEE SHIRTS & SWEATS, ETC. SEMI-ANNUAL DOCK SALE/ SHARONVILLE—Some of the same sportswear you see in the department stores are sold at wholesale prices at this sales event. Sweatshirts go for $10–$20; tee shirts are $1–$7; and sports caps are priced next to nothing. **Originells**, a local design company specializing in silkscreening and embroidering, sells to the public, its surplus goods, irregulars, and misprints twice a year. Mostly adult sizes. Some youth.
11255 Reading Road; 513/733-0071. VS, MC.

June

DECOR LIGHTING WAREHOUSE SALE/BLUE ASH—The store sells high-quality lighting fixtures. However, at this semi-annual sale, it's your chance to buy many of them at below cost. Lights to supply almost any kind of need—fluorescent, incandescent, indoor, and outdoor—are among the selection of surplus, overstock, scratch 'n dent, and closeout items. One-of-a-kind models and ceiling fans are also at hefty price reductions. There's plenty to choose from.
6909 Cornell Road, (Convenient to I-71 & I-275, 1-1/2 miles west of Montgomery Road); 513/530-0085. Mon–Fri 9am–5:30pm, Thurs 'til 8pm, Sat 9am–5pm. VS, MC, DS.

July

SUPREME GOLF WAREHOUSE TENT SALE/WEST CHESTER—Once a year Supreme Golf clears out its warehouse. Up goes the tent and down comes the prices on clubs, bags, shoes, apparel, and accessories. Overflowing with an exceptional selection, all merchandise in the tent is sold at or below cost. If you can find what you need among the scrambled items it will be hard to resist the prices. For the serious golfer who wants to replenish supplies or pick up a few extra performance clubs, or for the novice wanting a good start on equipping oneself for the links, this is a sale you won't want to miss.
10025 Princeton-Glendale Road (State Route 747 - 1 mile north or Tri-County Mall); 513/874-1880. VS, MC.

August

THE BEACH WATERPARK/MASON—Just before you're ready to turn in the towel and call it quits for the summer, The Beach Waterpark has its end-of-the-season promotion (usually the first week of August). This is where the waterlogged can look ahead and for a limited time (only a week) receive special rates for the next season. Individual passes are sold at a special two-for-one rate, but you must sign up at the park office in person. The other requirement is that you bring in a canned good from any area IGA store.
2590 Waterpark Drive, (I-71 to Kings Mill Road); 513/398- SWIM or 7946.

VALERIE MAKSTELL INTERIORS FAMOUS CLEARANCE SALE/ DOWNTOWN—For those with discriminating tastes, this sale is becoming a prestigious, fine furniture, sales event. These dramatic designs jazz up almost any interior at good prices. Valerie Makstell normally offers high-quality furniture discounted at 35% off retail, but twice a year the store bumps up the savings at least 5% more on in-stock furniture and custom orders. On big ticket items this can amount to a lot. Extra savings on floor samples and discontinued merchandise may reach 70% or more. The store has many unusual and one-of-a-kind pieces not found anywhere else in the city. Displayed in an old, renovated warehouse the sale generally lasts several weeks, but it's best to hit it early for a shot at the best buys. Remember, though, all sales are final and merchandise is sold as-is with no holds or returns.
1050 Mehring Way (Take Pete Rose Way to Mehring Way at Freeman); 513/241-1050. Mon–Sat 10am–5pm, Sun noon–4pm. VS, MC, DS.

U.S. SHOE ANNUAL SALE/MADISONVILLE—Anyone with an uncontrollable urge to buy shoes should leave town. With over 30,000 pairs of shoes drastically reduced, this infamous manufacturer's sale could put a serious shoe buyer over the edge. Held at the factory, this one-day event brings in the crowds as styles by Cobbie, Joyce & Selby, Easy Spirit, Bandolino, Evan-Picone and Pappagallo sell *fast*. Supplies are constantly replenished, so the stock is always good. All proceeds from the sale benefit the United Way, so if you do have a shoe "thing" at least you know the profits are going to a good cause.
One Eastwood Drive, (I-71 right into Duck Creek Road and right into U.S. Shoe facility). Call 527-7000 and ask to hear the recorded message about the details of the sale.

September

CHAPEAU CREATIONS HAT LOVERS SALE/ROSELAWN—Her creations can be seen topping off outfits in the grandstand at Ascot, on a park bench along des-Champs-Elysees in Paris or on a moonlight walk at a beach in Acapulco. Closer to home they are seen in the clubhouse at the Kentucky Derby. One would never suspect these distinctive, ornate hats were designed in a small Roselawn shop. The humble woman behind the operation, Ruth Kropveld, is a third-generation milliner from Germany. She learned her craft in Europe and has been applying her trade since coming to Cincinnati in 1947. Many of the one-of-a-kind styles top $100, but are sold as salesman's samples in the workshop showroom. Hat lovers can buy them here at wholesale prices during certain times of the year. The hand-adorned hats and berets have earned Ruth prestigious awards such as the one that distinguished her as 1992 Hat Designer of the Year by *W. Magazine*.
Roselawn Center, 7385 Brookcrest Drive, (corner of Brookcrest & Section Road off of Reading); 513/631-6055. Sales run from March–June and September–December. Mon–Fri 9am–5:30pm. VS, MC. All sales are final.

GENTRY MEN'S CLOTHIER WAREHOUSE SALE/SHARONVILLE— Gentry's big semi-annual warehouse sale offers an incredible savings opportunity that's unparalleled to others. For those wanting to capitalize on noteworthy fashion buys for men, Gentry is a repository of designer names in sportcoats, topcoats, dress slacks, dress shirts, ties and fine sportswear. The selection is incredible with merchandise consolidated from 20 Gentry stores. The man serious about upgrading his professional image will find over 8,000 finely-tailored suits drastically reduced. Held at the company warehouse, it's easy to spot. Just look for Gentry's huge "SOS" (Sale of Sales) balloon.
2851 E. Kemper Road, (I-275 to south on Mosteller Road then left on Kemper); 513/771-1199. Daily 9am–9pm, Sun 11am–6pm. VS, MC, DS, AE. 

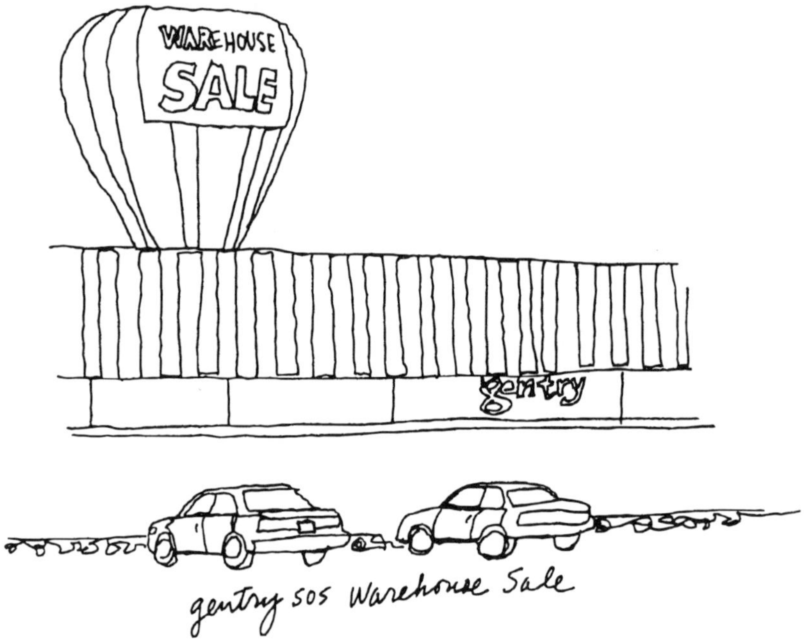

NATORP'S NURSERY OUTLET INVENTORY REDUCTION SALE/ MASON—For one week in the fall you can shop with the professional landscapers when Natorp's opens its wholesale nursery to the public. With over 25,000 pre-dug and container-grown trees, shrubs, evergreens and perennials at or below wholesale prices, you can afford to grow your own forest. All plants are ready for immediate pickup.
8601 Snider Road, (I-71 to Fields-Ertel Road (exit 19) then right on Snider); 513/242-1375. Mon–Fri 11am–7pm, Sat 8am–5pm, Sun 11am–5pm. VS, MC.

PARAMOUNT'S KINGS ISLAND AMUSEMENT PARK/KINGS MILLS—As the season comes to a close and you haven't quite come down from your roller coaster high, Kings Island offers its special membership rates for the next year. Savings can run as much as $90 for a family pass (consists of a family of four). Add other members in the household for another low fee. Special rates on individual passes (ages 7–59) are reduced, but they are even lower for seniors (age 60 and over) and children (ages 3–6). The passes are good toward the rest of the current season at the park and all of Paramount's parks across North America. The offer is available for a limited time only (usually the last week in September into October).
Kings Island Season Pass, Department 953; 513/573-5700. Call to order your season pass or come by Paramount's Kings Island any time the park is open to the public.

SKEFFINGTON'S FABULOUS FALL SALE/NORWOOD—Catering to those with busy social calendars who want to make standout entrances, Skeffington's Fabulous Fall Sale has the proper attire to outfit you for any black-tie extravaganza. New and used formal wear—tuxedos that call for bravos; Swashbuckling shirts and fancy ties; gut-hiding cummerbunds; Sunday-go-to-meetin' shoes and waiter-like dinner jackets—are at prices that would wake up Count Dracula. The sale is only available at the Grande Central Station facility and runs from September into October.
Central Park Plaza, 4600 Smith Road; 513/631-2223. Mon–Fri noon–8:30pm, Sat 10am–5pm. MC, VS.

STERLING CUT GLASS SEMI-ANNUAL CLEARANCE SALE—Loaded with all the fine breakables, Sterling Cut Glass has been making its mark by doing hand-cut monogramming since the turn of the century. Getting its start in Cincinnati, the company's stores are giant showcases filled with quality hand-engraved crystal and fine glassware. Stemware, serving pieces, giftware, picture frames, mugs, and champagne flutes (the kind you throw in the fireplace after a romantic dinner) are displayed like museum pieces around the stores. Lucky for those with an appreciation for finer quality, an extensive collection is priced from 20%–50% off at these semi-annual sales. The reduced prices include monogramming. Selected items, some with minor flaws, are up to 75% off.
One W. Fourth Street, Downtown Cincinnati; 513/381-4646. Mon–Fri 10am–6pm, Sat 10am–5pm. 2107 Grandin Road, Hyde Park; 513/321-6151. Mon–Thurs 10am–8pm, Fri 10am–6pm, Sat 10am–5pm. 7727 Kenwood Road, Kenwood (no phone listing & hours yet). VS, MC, AE.

October

CINCINNATI POLICE FALL AUCTION/DOWNTOWN CINCINNATI—Most anything that anyone could steal or lose is likely to turn up at these twice-a-year police auctions. For one day in the fall and the

spring confiscated and unclaimed items are auctioned off. As the auctioneer conducts the bidding you find yourself wondering how all of these items could have been lifted from their owners, especially the larger ones like bicycles, furniture and electronics. Smaller items, ranging from knives and tools to sporting goods and cellular phones, commonly show up here as well. Although good buys can be had here, it's hard to tell whether you'll find something you need, but you may get lucky. That is, if someone doesn't out bid you first.
Cincinnati Convention Center, Fifth & Elm streets. For more information call 513/352-6480.

DECOR LIGHTING WAREHOUSE SALE/BLUE ASH—The store sells high-quality lighting fixtures. However, at this semi-annual sale, it's your chance to buy many of them at below cost. Lights to supply almost any kind of need—fluorescent, incandescent, indoor and outdoor—are here. Among the selection are surplus, overstock, scratch 'n dent and closeout items. One-of-a-kind models and ceiling fans are also at hefty price reductions. There's plenty to choose from at this sale so your chances of finding something you want are greater.
6909 Cornell Road, (Convenient to I-71 & I-275, 1-1/2 miles west of Montgomery Road); 513/530-0085. Mon–Fri 9am–5:30pm, Thurs 'til 8pm, Sat 9am–5pm. VS, MC, DS.

MEES DISTRIBUTORS WAREHOUSE CLEARANCE SALE/ NORTHSIDE—Though the official time for this event is in the fall, there's an ongoing sale at the company's warehouse. Customers can save from 25%–80% off original prices on ceramic tile, marble and accessories that are discontinued, closeout or sample items. A few irregulars and seconds bring greater savings. A huge 100,000 sq. ft. building is filled with these types of goods, so it's well worth checking out before paying more for regular stock.
1541 W. Fork Road, (at Colerain); 513/541-2311. Usually held on a specific weekend in October - Sat & Sun noon-6pm. VS, MC.

November

EDDIE BAUER ANNUAL CLEARANCE SALE/COLUMBUS—Even though this sale is held in Columbus, it's well worth the drive. Held at Veteran's Memorial Hall near downtown, it features merchandise collected from Eddie Bauer stores nationwide. Large see-through bags are handed out when you walk in the door. Customers wander around dragging the bags across the floor as they toss in bargain after bargain. Everything is initially marked down at 50% off retail with deeper discounts as the sale progresses into December. Items sold here include first-quality fashions from previous season inventory, surplus merchandise, and discontinued styles and colors. The last day of the sale offers the deepest discounts with continuous markdowns taken on items all day long.
Veteran's Memorial Hall. Call your local Eddie Bauer store for more information. VS, MC, DS.

December

GIFT & HOUSEWARES WHOLESALER WAREHOUSE SALE/BLUE ASH—Held early in December, this once-a-year sale couldn't come at a better time. It's a great opportunity to pick up Christmas and other seasonal decorations, as well as unique gift items at hefty price reductions. A large room of a warehouse is filled with wind chimes, windsocks and flags (mostly seconds and irregulars) priced anywhere from $3–$25. Colorful ornaments, nutcrackers, oil candles, bells and holiday jewelry are stacked on long rows of tables. These surplus, discontinued and slightly defective items go for 50%–75% off original prices. Many are only a few bucks. Some are less than a buck. Hundreds of other items including bird feeders, bird houses and one-of-a-kind samples go for a bit more. If not for the concrete floors and the rafters you would think you were in a giant gift store, but the prices reflect the no-frills environment. The sale is usually held over a long weekend Thursday-Sunday at New Creative Enterprises.
5345 Creek Road, (I-275 to Reed Hartman Highway to Creek Road); 513/891-1172. VS, MC, DS.

T-SHIRTS & SWEATS, ETC. SEMI-ANNUAL DOCK SALE/ SHARONVILLE, OHIO—Some of the same sportswear you see in the department stores is sold at wholesale prices at this sales event. Sweatshirts go for $10–$20; tee shirts are $1–$7; and sports caps are priced next to nothing. Originells, a local design company specializing in silkscreening and embroidering, sells its surplus goods, irregulars and misprints twice a year to the public. Most items are in adult sizes with some youth.
11255 Reading Road; 513/733-0071. VS, MC.

UNIVERSITY OF CINCINNATI BOOK STORES HOLIDAY SALE/ CLIFTON—Starting the first Saturday in December, this two-week sales event peddles more than the usual college book store items. And many are 10%–30% off. Trade, reference and children's books are part of the offerings, of course. Gift items such as toys, binders and back packs are also on sale. But so are several hard-to-find items. A wider selection of art supplies—from all sorts of brushes and markers to different stocks of paper and cards—are in abundance here. School and office supplies, along with a large variety of electronics including portable radios and Walkmans, toasters and irons and every kind of calculator imaginable, align the shelves. It should come as no surprise that one of the best places in the city to find Cincinnati Bearcats insignia apparel and novelty items is right here, as well. A computer shop pushes a huge selection of IBM and Macintosh compatible software, from complex spread sheets to kids' games, averaging lower prices than most suppliers. Though the sale is held on the campus, it doesn't necessarily mean it's geared toward the student body. Take a look around; you may be amazed at what you'll find. Remember, too, that the other four campus book stores at the local college branches also participate in the sale. However, the selection is limited at these locations, so it's

best to shop the main store if you want the wider scope.
University of Cincinnati, Campus location; 513/556-1700. Mon–Fri 7:30am–9pm, Sat 9am–5pm, Sun noon–5pm. VS, MC, DS.

Periodic & Continuous Sales

CS CRABLE SPORTSWEAR TENT SALES/BLUE ASH—It's a real free-for-all. Stacks of embroidered and screen-printed tee shirts, sweatshirts and activewear are quickly strewn about as customers root around to find the proper style and size. Much of the merchandise never hits the table and is just tossed in cardboard boxes around the tent. The merchandise primarily consists of overruns, but some seconds are mixed in so it's best to check items carefully before purchasing. Many styles are adorned with colorful college team emblems. These periodic events are unadvertised yet always drawl a crowd, so it pays to call and get on the mailing list for advance notices of sales.
7741 E. Kemper Road (between Montgomery Road & Reed Hartman Highway); 513/753-3400. VS, MC.

FRONTGATE WAREHOUSE SALES/LEBANON—The quality-minded, the value-conscious, and those just wanting to marvel at ingenious products come here during Frontgate's seasonal warehouse sales where Land Rovers, Mercedes Benz, and BMW's fill the parking lot. They come in search of the extraordinary, and they find it at reduced prices (up to 60% off) on overstocks, closeouts, and scratch 'n dent items. The items, loosely displayed on long tables, around the floor, and against the walls of the warehouse, are designed for the home—an indestructible mailbox (made in Cincinnati), a solid brass fireplace fixture set, a woodchuck firewood cart, a compact foldaway bed, heated pet pads, cat or dog teepees, etc. Hard-to-pass-up bargains include a Health Mate cedar home sauna for four (slightly damaged) marked down from $4,595 to $1,995 and a large gong handmade from industrial materials, reduced from $450 to $395. For those claiming to be professional home chefs, an impressive selection of commercial grade cooking equipment is available. The sales clerks and stock personnel, all wearing Frontgate tee shirts, dart around helping customers. Seasonal sales are usually held in the spring, late summer, and midwinter. Watch for sale ads in local newspapers or call the main office for more details.
2800 Henkle Drive, (Take I-71 to Exit 28, just north of Kings Island, Route 48 north to Fujitec Drive, then right on Henkle); 513/933-8050 ext. 382. VS, MC, DS, AE.

LOVELAND CANOE RENTAL INVENTORY SALES/LOVELAND — Rental canoes can be purchased at this Little Miami River Outfitter. Battered and well used after hundreds of trips down river, they usually run about half off the price of a new model. The selection comes from well-known brands like Grumman. And even after several seasons of use they may not look like much, but they still hold up well.
200 Anshutz Avenue; 513/683-4611.

Library Book Sales

FRIENDS OF THE PUBLIC LIBRARY OF CINCINNATI AND HAMILTON COUNTY USED BOOK SALES—As the library weeds out its collection, it has periodic used book sales. Ranging from fiction to nonfiction and children's to some reference, these books can be purchased at a fraction of their original cost (some as low as 50¢). Records, compact discs, video tapes, audio cassettes, magazines and a limited supply of encyclopedias are also available. Proceeds go to reading programs and to purchasing other books for the Library's collection. One of the Library's most popular events is the Annual Used Book Sale on Fountain Square. Held every June, a series of long tables, stacked from end-to-end with books, form a labyrinth around much of the square and the Tyler Davidson Fountain. The books, mercifully categorized by topic, number in the thousands. Some readers snatch up the classics, others look for the odd or the unusual. One man even found his old high school year book. Listed below are the Library's upcoming, regularly-scheduled sales. Check your local branch fordetails.
First Weekend after Labor Day in September (Fri–Sun)–Main Library Parking Lot Tent Sale (A Collectible Auction is held the Thursday before, inside the Main Library), 800 Vine Street; Last Weekend in October–Green Township Regional Branch Library, 6525 Bridgetown Road; November–Madiera, Indian Hills & Kenwood Regional Library, 7200 Miami Avenue; Last weekend in January–Main Library Mini Sale of Fiction, Mysteries and Records, 800 Vine Street; Third Weekend in March–North Central Regional Branch Library, 11109 Hamilton Avenue; First Weekend in June (Fri–Tues)–Annual Used Book Sale on Fountain Square, Fifth & Vine streets; Third Weekend in July–Symmes Township Regional Branch Library, 11850 Enyart Road. The Anderson Library Committee has an annual used book sale the first weekend in March. Held at the Beechmont Mall during regular mall hours, the sale benefits the Anderson Regional and Mt. Washington Branch Libraries.
For current sale dates and more information call 513/369-6960. Cash or check only.

UNIVERSITY OF CINCINNATI LANGSAM LIBRARY BOOK SALES/ CLIFTON—These sales offer some good opportunities to pick up used books to add to your home library at prices way below their original cost. Most of them are donated, but don't fit the needs of the library collection. The wide variety includes fiction, poetry, arts and humanities, social science, and history books. Sometimes magazines are available. The sales, held the first Wednesday of every other month of the academic year, are from 9am–4pm at the Langsam Library in the fourth floor lobby. Sales take place in October, December, February, April and June. The funds are used to buy books better suited for the library.
Langsam Library, Fourth Floor Lobby (main walk-in level), Martin Luther King Boulevard. For more information call 513/556-1990. Cash or check only.

Terms of the Trade

FIRST-QUALITY—merchandise that has no flaws

IRREGULARS—goods with minor defects or flaws that do not affect their use or wearability such as miss-sized items, faded dye lot groups or items with crooked stitching

OVERSTOCKS OR OVERRUNS—the surplus goods that are leftover after manufacturers sell to regular retailers. Sometimes items are over produced on purpose and often marked as irregulars so that full price retailers will not be aggravated at manufacturers for selling it cheaper somewhere else

SECONDS—goods with flaws, sometimes that are very noticeable. These flaws are more serious than irregulars and may be stained or mismatched

DISCONTINUED OR CLOSEOUTS—items that are no longer being manufactured or the last stock produced of a particular line. Sometimes models or styles have been changed, therefore, last season's merchandise is closed out or discontinued

CURRENT OR IN-SEASON GOODS—this season's merchandise in the styles that are most timely or fashionable

PRIVATE LABEL—products that are sold under a store's label. Full-price retailers offer these items to compete with brand-name outlets. It is difficult to compare prices on these items so customers have a hard time figuring out whether they are actually saving money when buying them

DESIGNER LABEL—an item that carries a particular designer name as a mark of quality, high fashion or status

WHOLESALE—items that are sold directly from the company that sells to regular retailers. Since there is no middleman to sell the goods, savings are passed onto the customers

FLOOR SAMPLES—items used as displays in retail stores. These items are sometimes sold at discounted prices and should be checked over carefully for signs of wear before buying

BUYOUTS—items sold by one retailer to another at discounted prices. These items are usually end-of-season or leftover merchandise

EVERYDAY LOW PRICES—prices that are low year-around

MILL ENDS, REMNANTS—ends of the rolls of carpet or fabric gathered from textile manufacturers, mills and cut houses

OFF-PRICE—merchandise sold at least 20% off regular retail price everyday

Alphabetical Index

Product Index

APPAREL

Accessories

Activewear/Sportswear

Bridal/Formal Wear

Children's Wear

Footwear

Ladies' Wear

Lingerie/Foundations

Maternity Wear

Men's Wear

Outerwear

Resale/Consignment Clothing

Uniforms/Army Surplus